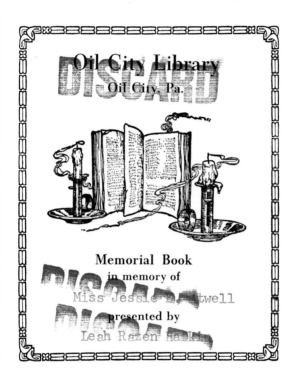

NEW
COLLECTED
POEMS

Robert Graves

NEW
COLLECTED
POEMS

Introduction by
JAMES McKINLEY

1977
Doubleday & Company, Inc.
Garden City, New York

Library of Congress Cataloging in Publication Data

Graves, Robert, 1895–
New collected poems.

I. Title.
PR6013.R35A17   1976   821'.9'12
ISBN: 0-385-11507-5
Library of Congress Catalog Card Number 76–14051

FOREWORD

These *Collected Poems*—due to appear after my eightieth birthday
—will probably be my last. My first collection was published in
1926 and later collections in 1938, 1947, 1959, and 1965, and until
this present publication the volumes have not greatly increased in
size. During each of the last ten years I have written more poems
and discarded fewer than at any other time, with the exception of
1974 when I wrote only five. I notice, however, that the annual sur-
vival rate of new poems, prior to 1965, was in fact five, and now in
my eightieth year it is unlikely to rise significantly again.

Most of the new poems included in this volume have been read to
audiences in Budapest and some to those in Warsaw and Crakow.

R.G.

Deyá
Majorca
Spain

CONTENTS

I

II

III

IV

V

VI

VII

VIII

IX

X

XI

XV

XVI

XVII

XVIII

XIX

XX

XXI

OCCASIONALIA

XXVI

XXVII

XXVIII

XXIX

XXX

INTRODUCTION

Two of Robert Graves's many American acquaintances—Allen Tate and John Crowe Ransom (whose work Graves promoted first in England)—sponsored as much as anyone the literary dictum that an author's work should be considered separate from his life. 'Tis a useful rule. Critics doubtless *can* focus better if not distracted by the convoluted, contradictory, ofttimes befuddling phenomena of lives, however more complex, even more interesting, than any poem might be those life patterns.

Happily for such textual analysts, this volume of Graves's collected verse, spanning more than fifty years of poetic production, provides ample material. I believe the consensus again will be that Robert Graves's poetry is unique in this century, that in expressing with classic lucidity the joys and terrors of romantic love—the major theme—he makes the reader feel keenly the uneasy balances of existence—between the absolute and the ephemeral, between ego and id, between man and woman. Graves, we can say, is the best love poet writing in English.

Splendid and deserved. Yet seeing only his poetry, we are blinded to much of Robert Graves. Not only to the other work: his vivid historical novels, his iconoclastic criticism and translations, his clear-eyed social commentaries, above all his myth making, his vision of the supremacy of Primal Woman, the White Goddess. But, more importantly, to the life which, despite Tate and Ransom's axiom, is the source, the indispensable reciprocal of all Graves's ideas and art (at last count over 130 books, countless articles, essays, lectures, and oddments).

That life surpassed eighty-one years last July. Graves has reached from Queen Victoria past Sarajevo and flappers and Bloomsbury and literary leftness and Adolf Hitler and Hiroshima and the Cold War and flower children to seize on our own days as his, too. In his passage, alternately serene and tumultuous, Robert Graves has encountered most of the ideas and many of the people whose lives we all share as part of modern literature. He's also touched events, places, persons important only to him. Both circumstances urge us to some knowledge of his life, for if art is alchemical mutation, compression, sanitizing of experience, it can't but be better understood if we know something of the primal pulp out of which the writer refines the smooth surface of his pages. What sort of man, then, is Robert Graves? What life has brought him his peculiar literary visions?

Certainly one quite different from what his parents might have expected. Graves was born on July 24, 1895, in Wimbledon, outside London, into a High Victorian family whose rectitude can be surmised from the verse the children's nanny recited on arrival in their house: "Emily Dykes is my name, England is my nation; Netheravon is my dwelling place, and Christ is my salvation." When Robert arrived, there were seven children—of an eventual ten—already extant, five older children by his father's first marriage (ended by his wife's death) and two toddler daughters by his second wife, Amalie von Ranke Graves. This gemütlich German mother was very glad of her new son (the girls had been fine, of course, "to practice on") and she taught him pride, piety, and the pre-eminence of hard work as the way to a productive life. Robert's elfin Irish father, Alfred Perceval Graves, instilled his new son with the Graves family's long and distinguished tradition of achievement (in fields as disparate as science, theology, diplomacy, the arts), with a disconcerting habit of absent-mindedness, a love of songs and poems and games, and an irrepressible literary bent. The Graves home—large, suitably staffed and ruled by women—was host to poets, scholars, musicians. A. P. Graves himself, though he earned his living as a superintendent of schools, was a promoter of Gaelic culture, a translator of Irish and Welsh verse, an incorrigible raconteur, and a poet-songwriter whose sweet and light lyrics his more gifted son would repudiate along with much else. Graves's childhood passed swiftly among the doomed pleasures of Victoria's twilight. There was genteel schooling, folk-song collecting, afternoon tea and evening prayer, parlor games, meetings with luminaries like Swinburne (who tousled the small Robert's hair) and John Yeats (who told A. P. Graves that his son "Willie" had found "a profitable little byway in poetry"). Amy and Alfred's German-Irish alliance—which may account for Robert's lifelong amalgam of Teutonic discipline and Celtic wit—occasioned a few trips to the grandparents in Bavaria and every summer at the house in Wales provided by his mother's inheritance. (Wales in particular stamped Robert with a sense of nature's analogues to man.) The Graves alliance endured in good humor and propriety, but on the large scale, World War I ended English affection for Germany.

Robert Graves, like most of his generation, served in the war. Like many, he was severely wounded. He went to war from Charterhouse, the English preparatory school he detested but which had brought him his first mature friendship, with the famous and ill-starred mountaineer George Mallory (later to die on Everest, at the top, Graves said). There, too, Robert Graves wrote his first serious poems. Mallory showed them to Edward Marsh, patron of poetry and then secretary to Winston Churchill. Marsh encouraged the eighteen-year-old officer in the Royal Welch Fusiliers, but told him to modernize his diction, that the sugary poems derived from his upbringing and his youth were in an outmoded fashion. Such advice, and the wartime friendship with the older, more laconic Siegfried Sassoon, confirmed Graves as a poet, which then in England meant "Georgian." Indeed, the war confirmed Robert Graves in many things. It shocked him out of smug gentility and into a psychological funk which only literary creation could relieve. The shell which tore open his chest in July 1916 seemed to open him to the world. He was reported dead, and the sense of posthumous reprieve filled him. He absorbed Sassoon's self-deprecating bitterness (in recompense, Graves prevented what he thought was a ruinous antiwar stance by Sassoon). He experienced life as the senseless line of bodies on the wire, and when the armistice came, like his friends quick and dead —Sassoon, Edmund Blunden, Wilfred Owen—he retreated to peace. He had published books, was an established "war poet," a scornful visitor at Lady Ottoline Morrell's at Garsington, a Georgian. He was also neurasthenic, given to nightmares, motiveless fears, recurring visions of horror.

Graves married in 1918. Nancy Nicholson was the daughter of Sir William Nicholson, noted dandy and painter (her brother, Ben Nicholson, is today a leading British artist), and a friend of Max Beerbohm, Oscar Wilde, many of the celebrities. The union gave Graves entrée to a chic, decidedly un-Victorian society, but he and Nancy refused it, mostly. They rusticated themselves at Oxford, where Robert fitfully pursued a degree. They lived and worked in a cottage in John Masefield's garden. Nancy was herself a painter and a vehement feminist who kept her name and gave it to her daughters as they came (two) while the boys (also two, just as Nancy wanted it) took their father's surname. Graves wrote, helped keep house, cared for the children, tended a shop they'd opened (and quickly bankrupted), all attempting to become solvent. They moved to a more remote village. Graves's work, reflecting his domestic and psychological lives, became either pretty "escape" poems or fearful psychic investigations. To shrug the latter he played village football, took interest in the "folk." His father introduced him to T. E. Lawrence of Arabian fame, and Lawrence liked the brooding, handsome young poet. Lawrence introduced Robert to Ezra Pound, saying, "Graves . . . Pound. Pound . . . Graves. You'll dislike each other." And they did. Thirty-five years later, Graves ridiculed Pound, and the Eliotan school Ez had helped along. Other people came in and out of Graves's life, as his poetry won fewer popular readers but more serious attention: the Sitwells, Thomas Hardy, the Woolfs, Edmund Gosse, many others. But being known didn't insure survival as a writer. Graves scrambled for money, sometimes borrowing from his parents, sometimes from Nancy's, sometimes some of what Sassoon called his "Jew money." He got money from Rupert Brooke's "memorial," a fund Marsh established and then distributed to needy poets. T. E. Lawrence helped him by giving Graves some draft chapters of what would be *Seven Pillars of Wisdom* to sell. Robert wrote reviews, songs, poems, essays, anything which could simultaneously make a little and save his sanity. But by 1925 he was worn thin with a sort of desperate domesticity—at a point as critical as his chest wound. A change was needed, and his discovery of Ransom and the Fugitives—particularly the work of a young woman named Laura Riding Gottschalk—precipitated it. Nancy admired her poetry, too, and they wrote that she should come be with them.

Come she did, bearing ideas about what poetry should be (not exactly what Robert Graves was doing) and how lives should be lived now, in this time *après la guerre* when history had stopped and mankind's sole obligation was to seek the truth of existence. Poetry was a way, as she'd told Tate and Ransom and Hart Crane. She told Graves that, too, and he was taken by it, particularly since he'd come to similar conclusions during his psychological struggles. Laura Gottschalk's vital mind and dark Semitic beauty made her the most impressive female he'd ever met, the incarnation—though he didn't grasp it that way yet—of the Muse Goddess, whose service, Graves later wrote, was perfect freedom, whose cruelty and capriciousness were the poet's price for his inspiration. Laura, Robert, Nancy, and family went in late 1925 to Egypt, where Graves held the only salaried job of his life, as professor of English literature at Egyptian University (a job secured partly through his friends Arnold Bennett and T. E. Lawrence). They returned the spring of 1926. Graves issued his *Collected Poems,* as though ending a phase. By 1927, Graves, Riding, and Nicholson were in London. For the next two years they attracted the admiration of young men from the universities like Peter Quennell, William Empson, and W. H. Auden (who imitated Laura's poems), along with the disdain of writers like T. S. Eliot and Wyndham Lewis. Riding (for she now no longer used Gottschalk, being divorced) and Graves turned out quantities of significant work. Laura did criticism, essays, stories, and startling, influential poems. Robert wrote more poems, in a changing style, and an authorized biography of T. E. Lawrence which sold well enough to keep them all going. The literary twosome founded the Seizin Press, printed their books by hand, including one by Gertrude Stein—a subject of special interest to Laura. They traveled together. They wrote books together. With all this, Graves gradually severed his old friendships, estranged himself bit by bit from his family, from Nancy. Laura's assertive personality left no room for them, any more than could her poetic ideas leave his writing ways unchanged. He began to purify his diction, to try to think more clearly, to arrive at truth-in-words—not mere emotional effect in his work.

In 1929 his estrangement from Nancy was completed by the thud of Laura Riding's body hitting the ground behind 35A St. Peter's Square in London. Her attempted suicide from three floors up that spring broke not only her spine but also the fragile connection between Graves and Nancy. Laura leaped, it seems, for love—she'd been rejected by an Irish poet who'd joined their group (and who came to favor Nancy over Laura—clearly, not to be tolerated without a dramatic gesture). Seeing Laura in agony, appreciating the intensity of her feelings, Robert chose to stay with Laura, perhaps as she had expected. His marriage was ended (though not officially for several years) and his devotion to Laura Riding was solemnized. Graves helped her recover from the surgery, reported to his outraged family how well she was doing, how she could by July walk around a table. In the proverbial white heat Graves wrote his famous autobiography, *Good-bye to All That,* bidding his whole past, the England of schools and war and a familiar literary establishment, farewell. When Laura was well enough to travel in October, they left England (there had been some talk of deporting Laura, attempted suicide then being a criminal act for aliens) and went to Europe. By November they were in Majorca, in the mountain village of Deyá. The island then was remote and primitive, and the exiles supposedly had gone there on the advice of Gertrude Stein who'd visited Majorca years before. "It's paradise, if you can stand it," she's reported to have told them.

Robert Graves had changed utterly, for the second time. He was thirty-four years old, tall, black-haired, with a dramatically crooked nose and imprisoning gray eyes (see his poem *Face in the Mirror* for a better description). He was, if reluctantly, free of all he had been in thrall to. He lived now in what would be his permanent home except for the upset of two wars yet to come. Indeed, today we always think of Robert Graves in Deyá, there among the stark, dramatic beauty of that rocky place, surrounded by orange and lemon trees. We see him, as in photos, trudging up and down hill, past the silver-green olive trees whose trunks are as gnarled as the affairs he left in England. He looks both fulfilled and defiant. And so he was.

Riding and Graves stayed in Deyá until the Spanish Civil War in 1936 forced their evacuation. Robert's immense success with his honest autobiography mostly financed them. They built a lovely house—which is still Graves's home. Laura's propensity for queenly rule found a perfect site in the village. While Robert wrote increasingly powerful poems and then the successful *Claudius* historical novels (once more the main source of their income), Laura Riding created a literary society. Since they were by choice divorced from the larger literary world, she assembled another one. Poets, novelists, even scientists like Jacob Bronowski, usually young and terribly impressed by her astute criticism, her fine poems, visited and corresponded with her. She dreamed of establishing a "university" in Deyá. Young men and women came to serve as secretaries or good listeners and disciples. The Seizin Press produced a number of remarkable books. Laura took up historical novels and analytic essays on the large questions of aesthetics, ethics, history. Laura, with Robert's help, began a magazine, *Epilogue,* along lines she described, notably that poetry could be "truth," especially in the modern world where history had "stopped," leaving a value vacuum. They worked, swam, walked, talked, bought jewelry for all and sundry, dressed extravagantly, were very much their own fiefdom, King and Queen of Deyá. Laura's personality stamped Robert's, all their guests', and followers' with high seriousness. Low bedroom farce provided relief as the visitors and adopted natives entangled. Midway in this period, Laura and Robert became friends and partners only, lovers no more.

With Franco's invasion in July 1936, the British ordered all their subjects out of Spain. Taking only a few belongings, Laura and Robert, their secretary, Karl Gay, and Alan Hodge (then a visiting undergraduate, now coeditor of *History Today*) became refugees. They fled by ship to France, by train and boat to England. The next four years saw Robert and Laura moving from one friend's accommodation to another—to Switzerland, back to England, to a chateau in Brittany, and finally to America.

As always, they had projects besides their individual work. Robert was involved in another *Collected Poems*, in more historical novels, in movie schemes for *I, Claudius*. Laura was obsessed with what she called a *Protocol*—an ethical document signed by their intelligentsia which through moral suasion might impede the gathering world war. In addition, she employed Robert and their constant stream of visitors (among them the poets Norman Cameron and James Reeves, Hodge and his wife, Beryl, the older Graves children on odd visits) in compiling true word meanings, for a projected dictionary of poetic truth so constructed that its user could find *precisely* what a poem meant. In the spring of 1939 Robert and Laura were in America, in Pennsylvania, near, appropriately enough, New Hope. There perhaps they could work without fear of another war or personal crisis displacing them.

It was not to be. Laura soon became infatuated with Schuyler Jackson, the poet-friend of their mutual friend T. S. Matthews (soon to be managing editor of *Time*), who had urged them to come to America, who had even built a house for them called Nimrod's Rise. After harrowing, embarrassing scenes which included the nervous collapse of Jackson's wife, Laura and Schuyler announced they were together forever. A shattered Graves returned to England. Laura in 1941 married Schuyler Jackson. They lived happily in Florida, raising fruit and compiling the dictionary, until Jackson's death more than a quarter century later. For much of that time

Laura Riding Jackson was silent as a poet and essayist. Over the past few years, however, she has reasserted herself, in a literary renaissance remarkable for its effectiveness and for the virulent dislike of Robert Graves displayed.

Unquestionably, the scarifying break with Laura marked another watershed for Graves. Another way of life was ended. Traumatized, although safely sheltered by friends in Essex, he watched Hitler overwhelm Poland in September 1939. It seemed analogous to his condition. Yet within a few weeks his existence again took new direction and vitality. Beryl Hodge (soon to be divorced) joined him. They are together to this day as man and wife. Robert and Beryl moved to Devon for the war's duration. An astounding range of literary works proceeded. More novels, books of poems, essays, collaborative works on war, on the craft of writing, the first draft of *The White Goddess*, that startling book tracing the mythic nature of Woman of which its publisher, T. S. Eliot (now reconciled to Graves's uniqueness), said in 1948, "I don't know what it means, but it should be published." Graves knew what it meant. It was his fiction for creating fiction, a conception of the primacy of woman which would fuel his future love poems and his life and prove the anodyne for the rigorous, sexless rationalism of the later Riding years. The idea also went well with his domestic life. Robert, now in his forties, and Beryl began his second family, and as with Nancy, the children—eventually four in all—did fine, mostly, in a household disrupted by his ceaseless work and the war's upheavals. Misfortune struck his first family, though, when Graves's son David was killed in action in Burma, suffering the fate his father had escaped in 1916. For the rest, it was writing, child rearing, and planning for the return to Majorca.

That came in 1946, via a memorable flight from England, hopscotching down to Deyá, visiting friends as they went. The children, Robert and Beryl, manuscripts, and some belongings, flew down to reclaim a difficult paradise. Robert found the house he and Laura built undisturbed. The natives were glad to see him; he'd lost some land, but not their affection. He has never since left Deyá except on lecture tours or visits to England, America, Hungary, Russia, the rest of Europe. Today he is an honorary citizen of Deyá, an honor which pleases him more than any other—even his election as Professor of Poetry at Oxford in 1961. It's not difficult to understand why he's stayed in Deyá. From 1946 until today it has been the beautiful base for his ascendance to world stature as an original and influential literary figure. To be sure, that ascendance has been marked by personal troubles, by sorrows and disappointments great and small (considered frequently for the Nobel Prize, it seems he will not win it— and the nation for which he fought has not seen fit to knight him, obviously preferring Americanized film comedians). Nonetheless, Graves's rise since 1946 has been steady, an accretion so glacial it may have motivated him to say "nothing of biographical interest has happened since 1929." We know better.

Much has, especially since his return to Deyá, but it is commonly enough known to allow only the briefest summary.

During the 1950s Graves lived quietly. Like an English country gentleman, he alternated gardening, walking, and marmalade making with the monumental daily writing (impossible without the help of his secretary, Karl Gay) which produced a stunning array of poems, novels, essays, historical confections, and demythologizing speculations (new accounts of the Greek and Hebrew myths, for example, and a rewriting of certain Gospels). Graves continued the solitary ways of the 1930s, shunning well-marked literary paths and fashions as he cut his own way. He kept up his old acquaintances, as with Max Beerbohm and Winston Churchill, and a few young poets came around betimes, notably Alastair Reid and W. S. Merwin. Mostly, though, Beryl raised the children and Robert wrote— alone except for work, family, a coterie of friends.

Graves's critical essays, his perverse readings of the greats of past and present now attracted the attention of critics who might not agree but who could not gainsay his insistence on the correct meanings of words, his interpretations of mythic elements, of the textures and rhythms of poems. His own poems, hard-edged and insightful, won him the admiration, then the imitation of the young "Movement" poets in England, Thom Gunn and others. He traveled to Israel, Hungary, mainland Spain for honors and medals. Universities in England and America invited him to speak. The United States embraced Robert Graves permanently in 1957 after a series of lectures. We found his rebellious nature refreshing, his matriarchal notions fetching. His explorations with hallucinatory drugs, magic mushrooms served with ancient history, were *à la mode*. We wondered at a man who could construct an operative code for living out of the belief that man's role is to be alternately inspired and dejected by his love for women—operative, I say, because Graves, then and since, has lived, sometimes uneasily, between the domesticity of woman-as-wife/mother and the enchantment of woman-as-lover/beguiler. In odd affirmation of this insight, White Goddess cults sprang up in California and even in Missouri. And once Graves's reputation was spread through his many books, through the best magazines, English undergraduates not yet born when he first achieved notice honored him by election to the poetry chair at Oxford, a post he held from 1961 to 1966. With that, Robert Graves could say he had persevered and won, on his terms and as a poet.

To conclude this skimpy history, a personal note may be tolerable. I have known Robert Graves since 1964, certainly not long as one measures Graves's life. Yet long enough to have seen him in the later phases of his renown and to understand something of them. I have seen some of his many visitors. Family members seeking aid and shelter, young poets seeking advice, the usual self-seeking sycophants and parasites endemic in "colonies" of artists, the contemporaries and friends, the cabinet ministers, movie stars, thinkers, musicians, Sufis, writers, artists, whose partial roster indicates the breadth of Graves's interests and Deyá's appeal: Ava Gardner, Alec Guinness, Peter Ustinov, Idris Shah, Kingsley Amis, Julian Huxley, Alan Sillitoe, Colin Wilson, Anthony Burgess, Julian Bream, Joan Miró (also a Majorca resident), Brett Whitely, and on to myriad Americans, Frenchmen, Hungarians, Persians, Israelis, the many nationalities whose acquaintance Graves has had. Of course, one may say that's not surprising, since he had been with the well-known almost from birth.

But Graves has suffered, too, in this later period. The untimely death of his daughter Jenny Nicholson, a talented writer, pained him deeply. There have been financial struggles to educate his second family, calls on his purse from far-flung relatives, an agonizing breakdown of one of his younger sons, the theft by an agent of substantial money, some critical backlash against his work, the usual pains, medications, surgeries of growing old. He has, frankly, inflicted suffering, too. His belief that the Goddess comes to him has led him to emotional involvements with young women which have distressed his wife and children, though their patience has soothed him to serenity in these, his declining days. Ironically, he who most believes in women is, at eighty-one, the patriarch of Deyá. Grandchildren come to visit, along with the streams of other people. His honors, including a 1968 Olympic gold medal to go with the bronze one gained forty-four years before, have continued. Indeed, the most recent decade—from his seventieth to his eightieth years—embraced what may be his greatest poetry, full of love tempered by wisdom and the sense of history, both personal and universal.

Graves sometimes stands these days on a terrace far above his home, near a sheep shed where he in past days often came to write (and which he has named variously for his incarnate Goddesses). From that height he can see his gardens, his village, the trees sweeping down to the Mediterranean where he often swims. He cannot, presumably, see across it to the many books and monographs being written about him. Nor does he care, not having read the dozen or so already in print. But I think that he can see and feel the glories and agonies of our century, can feel the pessimism rising about mankind's future, can resolve again to struggle against it with his conception of the fundamental nature of man and woman. I think that because all these concerns, indeed his whole long life, are in these poems, in this volume which stands as his latest collected judgment on himself and on us all.

James McKinley

NEW
COLLECTED
POEMS

IN THE WILDERNESS

He, of his gentleness,
Thirsting and hungering
Walked in the wilderness;
Soft words of grace he spoke
Unto lost desert-folk
That listened wondering.
He heard the bittern call
From ruined palace-wall,
Answered him brotherly;
He held communion
With the she-pelican
Of lonely piety.
Basilisk, cockatrice,
Flocked to his homilies,
With mail of dread device,
With monstrous barbèd stings,
With eager dragon-eyes;
Great bats on leathern wings
And old, blind, broken things
Mean in their miseries.
Then ever with him went,
Of all his wanderings
Comrade, with ragged coat,
Gaunt ribs—poor innocent—
Bleeding foot, burning throat,
The guileless young scapegoat:
For forty nights and days
Followed in Jesus' ways,
Sure guard behind him kept,
Tears like a lover wept.

THE HAUNTED HOUSE

'Come, surly fellow, come: a song!'
    What, fools? Sing to you?
Choose from the clouded tales of wrong
    And terror I bring to you:

Of a night so torn with cries,
    Honest men sleeping
Start awake with rabid eyes,
    Bone-chilled, flesh creeping,

Of spirits in the web-hung room
    Up above the stable,
Groans, knockings in the gloom,
    The dancing table,

Of demons in the dry well
    That cheep and mutter,
Clanging of an unseen bell,
    Blood choking the gutter,

Of lust frightful, past belief,
    Lurking unforgotten,
Unrestrainable endless grief
    In breasts long rotten.

A song? What laughter or what song
    Can this house remember?
Do flowers and butterflies belong
    To a blind December?

REPROACH

Your grieving moonlight face looks down
  Through the forest of my fears,
Crowned with a spiny bramble-crown,
  Bedewed with evening tears.

Why do you say 'untrue, unkind',
  Reproachful eyes that vex my sleep?
Straining in memory, I can find
  No cause why you should weep.

Untrue? But when, what broken oath?
  Unkind? I know not even your name.
Unkind, untrue, you brand me both,
  Scalding my heart with shame.

The black trees shudder, dropping snow,
  The stars tumble and spin.
Speak, speak, or how may a child know
  His ancestral sin?

THE FINDING OF LOVE

Pale at first and cold,
Like wizard's lily-bloom
Conjured from the gloom,
Like torch of glow-worm seen
Through grasses shining green
By children half in fright,
Or Christmas candlelight
Flung on the outer snow,
Or tinsel stars that show
Their evening glory
With sheen of fairy story—

3

Now with his blaze
Love dries the cobweb maze
Dew-sagged upon the corn,
He brings the flowering thorn,
Mayfly and butterfly,
And pigeons in the sky,
Robin and thrush,
And the long bulrush,
Bird-cherry under the leaf,
Earth in a silken dress,
With end to grief,
With joy in steadfastness.

ROCKY ACRES

This is a wild land, country of my choice,
With harsh craggy mountain, moor ample and bare.
Seldom in these acres is heard any voice
But voice of cold water that runs here and there
Through rocks and lank heather growing without care.
No mice in the heath run, no song-birds fly
For fear of the buzzard that floats in the sky.

He soars and he hovers, rocking on his wings,
He scans his wide parish with a sharp eye,
He catches the trembling of small hidden things,
He tears them in pieces, dropping them from the sky;
Tenderness and pity the heart will deny,
Where life is but nourished by water and rock—
A hardy adventure, full of fear and shock.

Time has never journeyed to this lost land,
Crakeberry and heather bloom out of date,
The rocks jut, the streams flow singing on either hand,
Careless if the season be early or late,
The skies wander overhead, now blue, now slate;
Winter would be known by his cutting snow
If June did not borrow his armour also.

4

Yet this is my country, beloved by me best,
The first land that rose from Chaos and the Flood,
Nursing no valleys for comfort or rest,
Trampled by no shod hooves, bought with no blood.
Sempiternal country whose barrows have stood
Stronghold for demigods when on earth they go,
Terror for fat burghers on far plains below.

OUTLAWS

Owls—they whinny down the night;
   Bats go zigzag by.
Ambushed in shadow beyond sight
   The outlaws lie.

Old gods, tamed to silence, there
   In the wet woods they lurk,
Greedy of human stuff to snare
   In nets of murk.

Look up, else your eye will drown
   In a moving sea of black;
Between the tree-tops, upside down,
   Goes the sky-track.

Look up, else your feet will stray
   Into that ambuscade
Where spider-like they trap their prey
   With webs of shade.

For though creeds whirl away in dust,
   Faith dies and men forget,
These agèd gods of power and lust
   Cling to life yet—

Old gods almost dead, malign,
    Starving for unpaid dues:
Incense and fire, salt, blood and wine
    And a drumming muse,

Banished to woods and a sickly moon,
    Shrunk to mere bogey things,
Who spoke with thunder once at noon
    To prostrate kings:

With thunder from an open sky
    To warrior, virgin, priest,
Bowing in fear with a dazzled eye
    Toward the dread East—

Proud gods, humbled, sunk so low,
    Living with ghosts and ghouls,
And ghosts of ghosts and last year's snow
    And dead toadstools.

ONE HARD LOOK

Small gnats that fly
In hot July
And lodge in sleeping ears,
Can rouse therein
A trumpet's din
With Day of Judgement fears.

Small mice at night
Can wake more fright
Than lions at midday;
A straw will crack
The camel's back—
There is no easier way.

One smile relieves
A heart that grieves
Though deadly sad it be,
And one hard look
Can close the book
That lovers love to see.

A FROSTY NIGHT

'Alice, dear, what ails you,
    Dazed and lost and shaken?
Has the chill night numbed you?
    Is it fright you have taken?'

'Mother, I am very well,
    I was never better.
Mother, do not hold me so,
    Let me write my letter.'

'Sweet, my dear, what ails you?'
    'No, but I am well.
The night was cold and frosty—
    There's no more to tell.'

'Ay, the night was frosty,
    Coldly gaped the moon,
Yet the birds seemed twittering
    Through green boughs of June.

'Soft and thick the snow lay,
    Stars danced in the sky—
Not all the lambs of May-day
    Skip so bold and high.

'Your feet were dancing, Alice,
    Seemed to dance on air,
You looked a ghost or angel
    In the star-light there.

'Your eyes were frosted star-light;
    Your heart, fire and snow.
Who was it said, "I love you"?'
    'Mother, let me go!'

ALLIE

Allie, call the birds in,
    The birds from the sky!
Allie calls, Allie sings,
    Down they all fly:
First there came
Two white doves,
    Then a sparrow from his nest,
Then a clucking bantam hen,
    Then a robin red-breast.

Allie, call the beasts in,
    The beasts, every one!
Allie calls, Allie sings,
    In they all run:
First there came
Two black lambs,
    Then a grunting Berkshire sow,
Then a dog without a tail,
    Then a red and white cow.

Allie, call the fish up,
    The fish from the stream!
Allie calls, Allie sings,
    Up they all swim:
First there came
Two gold fish,
    A minnow and a miller's thumb,
Then a school of little trout,
    Then the twisting eels come.

Allie, call the children,
    Call them from the green!
Allie calls, Allie sings,
    Soon they run in:
First there came
Tom and Madge,
    Kate and I who'll not forget
How we played by the water's edge
    Till the April sun set.

HENRY AND MARY

Henry was a young king,
    Mary was his queen;
He gave her a snowdrop
    On a stalk of green.

Then all for his kindness
    And all for his care
She gave him a new-laid egg
    In the garden there.

'Love, can you sing?'
                    'I cannot sing.'
    'Or tell a tale?'
                    'Not one I know.'
'Then let us play at queen and king
    As down the garden walks we go.'

LOVE WITHOUT HOPE

Love without hope, as when the young bird-catcher
Swept off his tall hat to the Squire's own daughter,
So let the imprisoned larks escape and fly
Singing about her head, as she rode by.

9

WHAT DID I DREAM?

What did I dream? I do not know—
    The fragments fly like chaff.
Yet, strange, my mind was tickled so
    I cannot help but laugh.

Pull the curtains close again,
    Tuck me grandly in;
Must a world of humour wane
    Because birds begin

Complaining in a fretful tone,
    Rousing me from sleep—
The finest entertainment known,
    And given rag-cheap?

THE TROLL'S NOSEGAY

A simple nosegay! was that much to ask?
(Winter still nagged, with scarce a bud yet showing.)
He loved her ill, if he resigned the task.
'Somewhere,' she cried, 'there must be blossom blowing.'
It seems my lady wept and the troll swore
By Heaven he hated tears: he'd cure her spleen—
Where she had begged one flower he'd shower fourscore,
A bunch fit to amaze a China Queen.

Cold fog-drawn Lily, pale mist-magic Rose
He conjured, and in a glassy cauldron set
With elvish unsubstantial Mignonette
And such vague bloom as wandering dreams enclose.
But she?
      Awed,
          Charmed to tears,
               Distracted,
                    Yet—
Even yet, perhaps, a trifle piqued—who knows?

THE HILLS OF MAY

Walking with a virgin heart
   The green hills of May,
Me, the Wind, she took as lover
   By her side to play,

Let me toss her untied hair,
   Let me shake her gown,
Careless though the daisies redden,
   Though the sun frown,

Scorning in her gay habit
   Lesser love than this,
My cool spiritual embracing,
   My secret kiss.

So she walked, the proud lady,
   So danced or ran,
So she loved with a whole heart,
   Neglecting man. . . .

Fade, fail, innocent stars
   On the green of May:
She has left our bournes for ever,
   Too fine to stay.

LOST LOVE

His eyes are quickened so with grief,
He can watch a grass or leaf
Every instant grow; he can
Clearly through a flint wall see,
Or watch the startled spirit flee
From the throat of a dead man.
   Across two counties he can hear
And catch your words before you speak.
The woodlouse or the maggot's weak
Clamour rings in his sad ear,
And noise so slight it would surpass
Credence—drinking sound of grass,
Worm talk, clashing jaws of moth
Chumbling holes in cloth;
The groan of ants who undertake
Gigantic loads for honour's sake
(Their sinews creak, their breath comes thin);
Whir of spiders when they spin,
And minute whispering, mumbling, sighs
Of idle grubs and flies.
   This man is quickened so with grief,
He wanders god-like or like thief
Inside and out, below, above,
Without relief seeking lost love.

VAIN AND CARELESS

Lady, lovely lady,
  Careless and gay!
Once, when a beggar called,
  She gave her child away.

The beggar took the baby,
    Wrapped it in a shawl—
'Bring him back,' the lady said,
    'Next time you call.'

Hard by lived a vain man,
    So vain and so proud
He would walk on stilts
    To be seen by the crowd,

Up above the chimney pots,
    Tall as a mast—
And all the people ran about
    Shouting till he passed.

'A splendid match surely,'
    Neighbours saw it plain,
'Although she is so careless,
    Although he is so vain.'

But the lady played bobcherry,
    Did not see or care,
As the vain man went by her,
    Aloft in the air.

This gentle-born couple
    Lived and died apart—
Water will not mix with oil,
    Nor vain with careless heart.

THE PIER-GLASS

Lost manor where I walk continually
A ghost, though yet in woman's flesh and blood.
Up your broad stairs mounting with outspread fingers
And gliding steadfast down your corridors
I come by nightly custom to this room,
And even on sultry afternoons I come
Drawn by a thread of time-sunk memory.

Empty, unless for a huge bed of state
Shrouded with rusty curtains drooped awry
(A puppet theatre where malignant fancy
Peoples the wings with fear). At my right hand
A ravelled bell-pull hangs in readiness
To summon me from attic glooms above
Service of elder ghosts; here, at my left,
A sullen pier-glass, cracked from side to side,
Scorns to present the face (as do new mirrors)
With a lying flush, but shows it melancholy
And pale, as faces grow that look in mirrors.

Is there no life, nothing but the thin shadow
And blank foreboding, never a wainscot rat
Rasping a crust? Or at the window-pane
No fly, no bluebottle, no starveling spider?
The windows frame a prospect of cold skies
Half-merged with sea, as at the first creation—
Abstract, confusing welter. Face about,
Peer rather in the glass once more, take note
Of self, the grey lips and long hair dishevelled,
Sleep-staring eyes. Ah, mirror, for Christ's love
Give me one token that there still abides
Remote—beyond this island mystery,
So be it only this side Hope, somewhere,
In streams, on sun-warm mountain pasturage—
True life, natural breath; not this phantasma.

APPLES AND WATER

Dust in a cloud, blinding weather,
  Drums that rattle and roar!
A mother and daughter stood together
  By their cottage door.

'Mother, the heavens are bright like brass,
  The dust is shaken high,
With labouring breath the soldiers pass,
  Their lips are cracked and dry.

'Mother, I'll throw them apples down,
  I'll fetch them cups of water.'
The mother turned with an angry frown,
  Holding back her daughter.

'But, mother, see, they faint with thirst,
  They march away to war.'
'Ay, daughter, these are not the first
  And there will come yet more.

'There is no water can supply them
  In western streams that flow;
There is no fruit can satisfy them
  On orchard-trees that grow.

'Once in my youth I gave, poor fool,
  A soldier apples and water;
And may I die before you cool
  Such drouth as his, my daughter.'

ANGRY SAMSON

Are they blind, the lords of Gaza
   In their strong towers,
Who declare Samson pillow-smothered
   And stripped of his powers?

O stolid Philistines,
   Stare now in amaze
At my foxes running in your cornfields
   With their tails ablaze,

At swung jaw-bone, at bees swarming
   In the stark lion's hide,
At these, the gates of well-walled Gaza
   A-clank to my stride.

DOWN

Downstairs a clock had chimed, two o'clock only.
Then outside from the hen-roost crowing came.
Why should the shift-wing call against the clock,
Three hours from dawn? Now shutters click and knock,
And he remembers a sad superstition
Unfitting for the sick-bed. . . . Turn aside,
Distract, divide, ponder the simple tales
That puzzled childhood; riddles, turn them over—
Half-riddles, answerless, the more intense.
Lost bars of music tinkling with no sense
Recur, drowning uneasy superstition.

Mouth open he was lying, this sick man,
And sinking all the while; how had he come
To sink? On better nights his dream went flying,
Dipping, sailing the pasture of his sleep,
But now (since clock and cock) had sunk him down
Through mattress, bed, floor, floors beneath, stairs, cellars,
Through deep foundations of the manse; still sinking
Through unturned earth. How had he magicked space
With inadvertent motion or word uttered
Of too-close-packed intelligence (such there are),
That he should penetrate with sliding ease
Dense earth, compound of ages, granite ribs
And groins? Consider: there was some word uttered,
Some abracadabra—then, like a stage-ghost,
Funereally with weeping, down, drowned, lost!

Oh, to be a child once more, sprawling at ease
On smooth turf of a ruined castle court!
Once he had dropped a stone between the slabs
That masked an ancient well, mysteriously
Plunging his mind down with it. Hear it go
Rattling and rocketing into secret void!
Count slowly: one, two, three! and echoes come
Fainter and fainter, merged in the general hum
Of bees and flies; only a thin draught rises
To chill the drowsy air. There he had lain
As if unborn, until life floated back
From the deep waters.
                            Oh, to renew now
That bliss of repossession, kindly sun
Forfeit for ever, and the towering sky!

Falling, falling! Day closed up behind him.
Now stunned by the violent subterrene flow
Of rivers, whirling down to hiss below
On the flame-axis of this terrible earth;
Toppling upon their waterfall, O spirit. . . .

IN PROCESSION

Often, half-way to sleep,
Not yet sunken deep—
The sudden moment on me comes
From a mountain shagged and steep,
With terrible roll of dream drums,
Reverberations, cymbals, horns replying,
When with standards flying,
Horsemen in clouds behind,
The coloured pomps unwind
Carnival wagons
With their saints and their dragons
On the scroll of my teeming mind:
The Creation and Flood
With our Saviour's Blood
And fat Silenus' flagons,
And every rare beast
From the South and East,
Both greatest and least,
On and on,
In endless, variant procession.
I stand at the top rungs
Of a ladder reared in the air,
And I rail in strange tongues,
So the crowds murmur and stare;
Then volleys again the blare
Of horns, and summer flowers
Fly scattering in showers,
And the sun leaps in the sky,
While the drums thumping by
Proclaim me. . . .

Oh, then, when I wake,
Could I courage take
To renew my speech,
Could I stretch and reach
The flowers and the ripe fruit
Laid out at the ladder's foot,
Could I rip a silken shred
From the banner tossed ahead,
Could I call a double-flam
From the drums, could the goat
Horned with gold, could the ram
With a flank like a barn-door,
The dwarf, the blackamoor,
Could Jonah and the Whale
And the Holy Grail,
The Ape with his platter
Going clitter-clatter,
The Nymphs and the Satyr,
And every marvellous matter
Come before me here,
Standing near and clear—
Could I make it so that you
Might wonder at them too!
—Glories of land and sea,
Of Heaven glittering free,
Castles hugely built in Spain,
Glories of Cockaigne,
Of that spicy kingdom, Cand,
Of the Delectable Land,
Of the Land of Crooked Stiles,
Of the Fortunate Isles,
Of the more than three-score miles
That to Babylon lead
(A pretty city indeed
Built on a four-square plan),
Of the Land of the Gold Man
Whose eager horses whinny
In their cribs of gold,
Of the Land of Whipperginny,
Of the land where none grows old. . . .

But cowardly I tell,
Rather, of the Town of Hell—
A huddle of dirty woes
And houses in fading rows
Straggled through space:
Hell has no market-place,
Nor point where four ways meet,
Nor principal street,
Nor barracks, nor Town Hall,
Nor shops at all,
Nor rest for weary feet,
Nor theatre, square, or park,
Nor lights after dark,
Nor churches, nor inns,
Nor convenience for sins—
Neither ends nor begins,
Rambling, limitless, hated well,
This Town of Hell
Where between sleep and sleep I dwell.

WARNING TO CHILDREN

Children, if you dare to think
Of the greatness, rareness, muchness,
Fewness of this precious only
Endless world in which you say
You live, you think of things like this:
Blocks of slate enclosing dappled
Red and green, enclosing tawny
Yellow nets, enclosing white
And black acres of dominoes,
Where a neat brown paper parcel
Tempts you to untie the string.
In the parcel a small island,
On the island a large tree,
On the tree a husky fruit.
Strip the husk and pare the rind off:
In the kernel you will see
Blocks of slate enclosed by dappled
Red and green, enclosed by tawny
Yellow nets, enclosed by white
And black acres of dominoes,
Where the same brown paper parcel—
Children, leave the string alone!
For who dares undo the parcel
Finds himself at once inside it,
On the island, in the fruit,
Blocks of slate about his head,
Finds himself enclosed by dappled
Green and red, enclosed by yellow
Tawny nets, enclosed by black
And white acres of dominoes,
With the same brown paper parcel
Still unopened on his knee.
And, if he then should dare to think
Of the fewness, muchness, rareness,
Greatness of this endless only
Precious world in which he says
He lives—he then unties the string.

ALICE

When that prime heroine of our nation, Alice,
Climbing courageously in through the Palace
Of Looking Glass, found it inhabited
By chessboard personages, white and red,
Involved in never-ending tournament,
She being of a speculative bent
Had long foreshadowed something of the kind,
Asking herself: 'Suppose I stood behind
And viewed the fireplace of Their drawing-room
From hearthrug level, why must I assume
That what I'd see would need to correspond
With what I now see? And the rooms beyond?'
Proved right, yet not content with what she had done,
Alice decided to prolong her fun:
She set herself, with truly British pride
In being a pawn and playing for her side,
And simple faith in simple stratagem,
To learn the rules and moves and perfect them.
So prosperously there she settled down
That six moves only and she'd won her crown—
A triumph surely! But her greater feat
Was rounding these adventures off complete:
Accepting them, when safe returned again,
As queer but true—not only in the main
True, but as true as anything you'd swear to,
The usual three dimensions you are heir to.
For Alice though a child could understand
That neither did this chance-discovered land
Make nohow or contrariwise the clean
Dull round of mid-Victorian routine,
Nor did Victoria's golden rule extend
Beyond the glass: it came to the dead end
Where empty hearses turn about; thereafter
Begins that lubberland of dream and laughter,
The red-and-white-flower-spangled hedge, the grass
Where Apuleius pastured his Gold Ass,
Where young Gargantua made whole holiday. . . .

But farther from our heroine not to stray,
Let us observe with what uncommon sense—
Though a secure and easy reference
Between Red Queen and Kitten could be found—
She made no false assumption on that ground
(A trap in which the scientist would fall)
That queens and kittens are identical.

RICHARD ROE AND JOHN DOE

Richard Roe wished himself Solomon,
Made cuckold, you should know, by one John Doe:
Solomon's neck was firm enough to bear
Some score of antlers more than Roe could wear.

Richard Roe wished himself Alexander,
Being robbed of house and land by the same hand:
Ten thousand acres or a principal town
Would have cost Alexander scarce a frown.

Richard Roe wished himself Job the prophet,
Sunk past reclaim in stinking rags and shame—
However ill Job's plight, his own was worse
He knew no God to call on or to curse.

He wished himself Job, Solomon, Alexander,
For patience, wisdom, power to overthrow
Misfortune; but with spirit so unmanned
That most of all he wished himself John Doe.

I'D DIE FOR YOU

I'd die for you, or you for me,
So furious is our jealousy—
And if you doubt this to be true
Kill me outright, lest I kill you.

ANCESTORS

My New Year's drink is mulled to-night
   And hot sweet vapours roofward twine.
The shades cry *Gloria!* with delight
   As down they troop to taste old wine.

They crowd about the crackling fire,
   Impatient as the rites begin;
Mulled porto is their souls' desire—
   Porto well aged with nutmeg in.

'Ha,' cries the first, 'my Alma wine
   Of one-and-seventy years ago!'
The second cheers 'God bless the vine!'
   The third and fourth like cockerels crow:

They crow and clap their arms for wings,
   They have small pride or breeding left—
Two grey-beards, a tall youth who sings,
   A soldier with his cheek-bone cleft.

O Gloria! for each ghostly shape,
   That whiffled like a candle smoke,
Now fixed and ruddy with the grape
   And mirrored in the polished oak.

I watch their brightening boastful eyes,
   I hear the toast their glasses clink:
'May this young man in drink grown wise
   Die, as we also died, in drink!'

Their reedy voices I abhor,
   I am alive at least, and young.
I dash their swill upon the floor:
   Let them lap grovelling, tongue to tongue.

THE CORONATION MURDER

Old Becker crawling in the night
  From his grave at the stair-foot,
Labours up the long flight,
  Feeble, dribbling, black as soot,
Quakes at his own ghostly fright.

A cat goes past with lantern eyes,
  Shooting splendour through the dark.
'Murder! Help!' a voice cries
  In nightmare; the son dreams that stark
In lead his vanished father lies.

A stair-top glimmer points the goal.
  Becker goes wavering up, tongue-tied,
Stoops, with eye to keyhole. . . .
  There, a tall candle by her side,
Delilah sits, serene and whole.

Her fingers turn the prayer-book leaves
  And, free from spiritual strife,
Soft and calm her breast heaves:
  Thus calmly with his cobbling knife
She stabbed him through; now never grieves.

Baffled, aghast with hate, mouse-poor,
  He glares and clatters the brass knob.
Through his heart it slid sure:
  He bowed, he fell with never a sob.
Again she stabbed, now sits secure,

Praying (as she has always prayed)
  For great Victoria's Majesty,
Droning prayer for God's aid
  To succour long dead Royalty,
The Consort Prince, Queen Adelaide. . . .

She falls asleep, the clocks chime two;
    Old Becker sinks to unquiet rest.
Loud and sad the cats mew.
    Lead weighs cruelly on his breast,
His bones are tufted with mildew.

CHILDREN OF DARKNESS

We spurred our parents to the kiss,
Though doubtfully they shrank from this—
Day had no courage to pursue
What lusty dark alone might do:
Then were we joined from their caress
In heat of midnight, one from two.

This night-seed knew no discontent:
In certitude our changings went.
Though there were veils about his face,
With forethought, even in that pent place,
Down toward the light his way we bent
To kingdoms of more ample space.

Is Day prime error, that regret
For Darkness roars unstifled yet?
That in this freedom, by faith won,
Only acts of doubt are done?
That unveiled eyes with tears are wet:
We loathe to gaze upon the sun?

THE COOL WEB

Children are dumb to say how hot the day is,
How hot the scent is of the summer rose,
How dreadful the black wastes of evening sky,
How dreadful the tall soldiers drumming by.

But we have speech, to chill the angry day,
And speech, to dull the rose's cruel scent.
We spell away the overhanging night,
We spell away the soldiers and the fright.

There's a cool web of language winds us in,
Retreat from too much joy or too much fear:
We grow sea-green at last and coldly die
In brininess and volubility.

But if we let our tongues lose self-possession,
Throwing off language and its watery clasp
Before our death, instead of when death comes,
Facing the wide glare of the children's day,
Facing the rose, the dark sky and the drums,
We shall go mad no doubt and die that way.

LOVE IN BARRENNESS

Below the ridge a raven flew
And we heard the lost curlew
Mourning out of sight below.
Mountain tops were touched with snow;
Even the long dividing plain
Showed no wealth of sheep or grain,
But fields of boulders lay like corn
And raven's croak was shepherd's horn
Where slow cloud-shadow strayed across
A pasture of thin heath and moss.

The North Wind rose: I saw him press
With lusty force against your dress,
Moulding your body's inward grace
And streaming off from your set face;
So now no longer flesh and blood
But poised in marble flight you stood.
O wingless Victory, loved of men,
Who could withstand your beauty then?

SONG OF CONTRARIETY

Far away is close at hand,
Close joined is far away,
Love shall come at your command
Yet will not stay.

At summons of your dream-despair
She might not disobey,
But slid close down beside you there,
And complaisant lay.

Yet now her flesh and blood consent
In the hours of day,
Joy and passion both are spent,
Twining clean away.

Is the person empty air,
Is the spectre clay,
That love, lent substance by despair,
Wanes and leaves you lonely there
On the bridal day?

THE PRESENCE

Why say 'death'? Death is neither harsh nor kind:
Other pleasures or pains could hold the mind
If she were dead. For dead is gone indeed,
Lost beyond recovery and need,
Discarded, ended, rotted underground—
Of whom no personal feature could be found
To stand out from the soft blur evenly spread
On memory, if she were truly dead.

But living still, barred from accustomed use
Of body and dress and motion, with profuse
Reproaches (since this anguish of her grew
Do I still love her as I swear I do?)
She fills the house and garden terribly
With her bewilderment, accusing me,
Till every stone and flower, table and book,
Cries out her name, pierces me with her look,
'You are deaf, listen!
You are blind, see!'
                    How deaf or blind,
When horror of the grave maddens the mind
With those same pangs that lately choked her breath,
Altered her substance, and made sport of death?

THE LAND OF WHIPPERGINNY

Come closer yet, my honeysuckle, my sweetheart Jinny:
    A low sun is gilding the bloom of the wood—
Is it Heaven, or Hell, or the Land of Whipperginny
    That holds this fairy lustre, not understood?

For stern proud psalms from the chapel on the moors
    Waver in the night wind, their firm rhythm broken,
Lugubriously twisted to a howling of whores
    Or lent an airy glory too strange to be spoken.

Soon the risen Moon will peer down with pity,
    Drawing us in secret by an ivory gate
To the fruit-plats and fountains of her silver city
    Where lovers need not argue the tokens of fate.

IN NO DIRECTION

To go in no direction
    Surely as carelessly,
Walking on the hills alone,
    I never found easy.

Either I sent leaf or stick
    Twirling in the air,
Whose fall might be prophetic,
    Pointing 'there',

Or in superstition
    Edged somewhat away
From a sure direction,
    Yet could not stray,

Or undertook the climb
    That I had avoided
Directionless some other time,
    Or had not avoided,

Or called as companion
    An eyeless ghost
And held his no direction
    Till my feet were lost.

THE CASTLE

Walls, mounds, enclosing corrugations
Of darkness, moonlight on dry grass.
Walking this courtyard, sleepless, in fever;
Planning to use—but by definition
There's no way out, no way out—
Rope-ladders, baulks of timber, pulleys,
A rocket whizzing over the walls and moat—
Machines easy to improvise.
                              No escape,
No such thing; to dream of new dimensions,
Cheating checkmate by painting the king's robe
So that he slides like a queen;
Or to cry, 'Nightmare, nightmare!'
Like a corpse in the cholera-pit
Under a load of corpses;
Or to run the head against these blind walls,
Enter the dungeon, torment the eyes
With apparitions chained two and two,
And go frantic with fear—
To die and wake up sweating by moonlight
In the same courtyard, sleepless as before.

RETURN

The seven years' curse is ended now
That drove me forth from this kind land,
From mulberry-bough and apple-bough
And gummy twigs the west wind shakes,
To drink the brine from crusted lakes
And grit my teeth on sand.

Now for your cold, malicious brain
And most uncharitable, cold heart,
You, too, shall clank the seven years' chain
On sterile ground for all time cursed
With famine's itch and flames of thirst,
The blank sky's counterpart.

The load that from my shoulder slips
Straightway upon your own is tied:
You, too, shall scorch your finger-tips
With scrabbling on the desert's face
Such thoughts I had of this green place,
Sent scapegoat for your pride.

Here, Robin on a tussock sits,
And Cuckoo with his call of hope
Cuckoos awhile, then off he flits,
While peals of dingle-dongle keep
Troop-discipline among the sheep
That graze across the slope.

A brook from fields of gentle sun
Through the glade its water heaves,
The falling cone would well-nigh stun
That Squirrel wantonly lets drop
When up he scampers to tree-top
And dives among the green.

But no, I ask a surer peace
Than vengeance on you could provide.
So fear no ill from my release:
Be off, elude the curse, disgrace
Some other green and happy place—
This world of fools is wide.

THE BARDS

The bards falter in shame, their running verse
Stumbles, with marrow-bones the drunken diners
Pelt them for their delay.
It is a something fearful in the song
Plagues them—an unknown grief that like a churl
Goes commonplace in cowskin
And bursts unheralded, crowing and coughing,
An unpilled holly-club twirled in his hand,
Into their many-shielded, samite-curtained,
Jewel-bright hall where twelve kings sit at chess
Over the white-bronze pieces and the gold;
And by a gross enchantment
Flails down the rafters and leads off the queens—
The wild-swan-breasted, the rose-ruddy-cheeked
Raven-haired daughters of their admiration—
To stir his black pots and to bed on straw.

NOBODY

Nobody, ancient mischief, nobody,
Harasses always with an absent body.

Nobody coming up the road, nobody,
Like a tall man in a dark cloak, nobody.

Nobody about the house, nobody,
Like children creeping up the stairs, nobody.

Nobody anywhere in the garden, nobody,
Like a young girl quiet with needlework, nobody.

Nobody coming, nobody, not yet here,
Incessantly welcomed by the wakeful ear.

Until this nobody shall consent to die
Under his curse must everyone lie—

The curse of his envy, of his grief and fright,
Of sudden rape and murder screamed in the night.

THE PROGRESS

There is a travelling fury in his feet
   (Scorn for the waters of his native spring)
    Which proves at last the downfall of this king:
Shame will not let him sound the long retreat.

Tormented by his progress he displays
   An open flank to the swarmed enemy
    Who, charging through and through, set his pride free
For death's impossible and footless ways.

FULL MOON

As I walked out that sultry night,
   I heard the stroke of One.
The moon, attained to her full height,
   Stood beaming like the sun:
She exorcized the ghostly wheat
To mute assent in love's defeat,
   Whose tryst had now begun.

The fields lay sick beneath my tread,
   A tedious owlet cried,
A nightingale above my head
   With this or that replied—
Like man and wife who nightly keep
Inconsequent debate in sleep
   As they dream side by side.

Your phantom wore the moon's cold mask,
    My phantom wore the same;
Forgetful of the feverish task
    In hope of which they came,
Each image held the other's eyes
And watched a grey distraction rise
    To cloud the eager flame—

To cloud the eager flame of love,
    The fog the shining gate;
They held the tyrannous queen above
    Sole mover of their fate,
They glared as marble statues glare
Across the tessellated stair
    Or down the halls of state.

And now warm earth was Arctic sea,
    Each breath came dagger-keen;
Two bergs of glinting ice were we,
    The broad moon sailed between;
There swam the mermaids, tailed and finned,
And love went by upon the wind
    As though it had not been.

VANITY

Be assured, the Dragon is not dead
But once more from the pools of peace
Shall rear his fabulous green head.

The flowers of innocence shall cease
And like a harp the wind shall roar
And the clouds shake an angry fleece.

'Here, here is certitude,' you swore,
'Below this lightning-blasted tree.
Where once it struck, it strikes no more.

'Two lovers in one house agree.
The roof is tight, the walls unshaken.
As now, so must it always be.'

Such prophecies of joy awaken
The toad who dreams away the past
Under your hearth-stone, light forsaken,

Who knows that certitude at last
Must melt away in vanity—
No gate is fast, no door is fast—

That thunder bursts from the blue sky,
That gardens of the mind fall waste,
That fountains of the heart run dry.

PURE DEATH

We looked, we loved, and therewith instantly
Death became terrible to you and me.
By love we disenthralled our natural terror
From every comfortable philosopher
Or tall, grey doctor of divinity:
Death stood at last in his true rank and order.

It happened soon, so wild of heart were we,
Exchange of gifts grew to a malady:
Their worth rose always higher on each side
Till there seemed nothing but ungivable pride
That yet remained ungiven, and this degree
Called a conclusion not to be denied.

Then we at last bethought ourselves, made shift
And simultaneously this final gift
Gave: each with shaking hands unlocks
The sinister, long, brass-bound coffin-box,
Unwraps pure death, with such bewilderment
As greeted our love's first acknowledgement.

SICK LOVE

O Love, be fed with apples while you may,
And feel the sun and go in royal array,
A smiling innocent on the heavenly causeway,

Though in what listening horror for the cry
That soars in outer blackness dismally,
The dumb blind beast, the paranoiac fury:

Be warm, enjoy the season, lift your head,
Exquisite in the pulse of tainted blood,
That shivering glory not to be despised.

Take your delight in momentariness,
Walk between dark and dark—a shining space
With the grave's narrowness, though not its peace.

IT WAS ALL VERY TIDY

When I reached his place,
The grass was smooth,
The wind was delicate,
The wit well timed,
The limbs well formed,
The pictures straight on the wall:
It was all very tidy.

He was cancelling out
The last row of figures,
He had his beard tied up in ribbons,
There was no dust on his shoe,
Everyone nodded:
It was all very tidy.

Music was not playing,
There were no sudden noises,
The sun shone blandly,
The clock ticked:
It was all very tidy.

'Apart from and above all this,'
I reassured myself,
'There is now myself.'
It was all very tidy.

Death did not address me,
He had nearly done:
It was all very tidy.
They asked, did I not think
It was all very tidy?

I could not bring myself
To laugh, or untie
His beard's neat ribbons,
Or jog his elbow,
Or whistle, or sing,
Or make disturbance.
I consented, frozenly,
He was unexceptionable:
It was all very tidy.

III

THIEF

To the galleys, thief, and sweat your soul out
With strong tugging under the curled whips,
That there your thievishness may find full play.
Whereas, before, you stole rings, flowers and watches,
Oaths, jests and proverbs,
Yet paid for bed and board like an honest man,
This shall be entire thiefdom: you shall steal
Sleep from chain-galling, diet from sour crusts,
Comradeship from the damned, the ten-year-chained—
And, more than this, the excuse for life itself
From a craft steered toward battles not your own.

THE FURIOUS VOYAGE

So, overmasterful, to sea!
But hope no distant view of sail,
No growling ice, nor weed, nor whale,
Nor breakers perilous on the lee.

Though you enlarge your angry mind
Three leagues and more about the ship
And stamp till every puncheon skip,
The wake runs evenly behind.

And it has width enough for you,
This vessel, dead from truck to keel,
With its unmanageable wheel,
A blank chart and a surly crew,

In ballast only due to fetch
The turning point of wretchedness
On an uncoasted, featureless
And barren ocean of blue stretch.

SONG: LIFT-BOY

Let me tell you the story of how I began:
I began as the boot-boy and ended as the boot-man,
With nothing in my pockets but a jack-knife and a button,
With nothing in my pockets but a jack-knife and a button,
With nothing in my pockets.

Let me tell you the story of how I went on:
I began as the lift-boy and ended as the lift-man,
With nothing in my pockets but a jack-knife and a button,
With nothing in my pockets but a jack-knife and a button,
With nothing in my pockets.

I found it very easy to whistle and play
With nothing in my head or my pockets all day,
With nothing in my pockets.
But along came Old Eagle, like Moses or David;
He stopped at the fourth floor and preached me Damnation:
'Not a soul shall be savèd, not one shall be savèd.
The whole First Creation shall forfeit salvation:
From knife-boy to lift-boy, from ragged to regal,
Not one shall be savèd, not you, not Old Eagle,
No soul on earth escapeth, even if all repent——'
So I cut the cords of the lift and down we went,
With nothing in our pockets.

THE NEXT TIME

And that inevitable accident
   On the familiar journey—roughly reckoned
By miles and shillings—in a cramped compartment
   Between a first hereafter and a second?

And when we passengers are given two hours,
   The wheels failing once more at Somewhere-Nowhere,
To climb out, stretch our legs and pick wild flowers—
   Suppose that this time I elect to stay there?

ULYSSES

To the much-tossed Ulysses, never done
   With woman whether gowned as wife or whore,
Penelope and Circe seemed as one:
She like a whore made his lewd fancies run,
   And wifely she a hero to him bore.

Their counter-changings terrified his way:
   They were the clashing rocks, Symplegades,
Scylla and Charybdis too were they;
Now angry storms frosting the sea with spray
   And now the lotus island's drunken ease.

They multiplied into the Sirens' throng,
   Forewarned by fear of whom he stood bound fast
Hand and foot helpless to the vessel's mast,
Yet would not stop his ears: daring their song
   He groaned and sweated till that shore was past.

One, two and many: flesh had made him blind,
   Flesh had one pleasure only in the act,
Flesh set one purpose only in the mind—
Triumph of flesh and afterwards to find
   Still those same terrors wherewith flesh was racked.

His wiles were witty and his fame far known,
Every king's daughter sought him for her own,
    Yet he was nothing to be won or lost.
    All lands to him were Ithaca: love-tossed
He loathed the fraud, yet would not bed alone.

THE SUCCUBUS

Thus will despair
In ecstasy of nightmare
Fetch you a devil-woman through the air,
    To slide below the sweated sheet
And kiss your lips in answer to your prayer
    And lock her hands with yours and your feet with her feet.

Yet why does she
Come never as longed-for beauty
Slender and cool, with limbs lovely to see,
    (The bedside candle guttering high)
And toss her head so the thick curls fall free
    Of halo'd breast, firm belly and long, slender thigh?

Why with hot face,
With paunched and uddered carcase,
Sudden and greedily does she embrace,
    Gulping away your soul, she lies so close,
Fathering brats on you of her own race?
    Yet is the fancy grosser than your lusts were gross?

THE READER OVER MY SHOULDER

You, reading over my shoulder, peering beneath
My writing arm—I suddenly feel your breath
   Hot on my hand or on my nape,
So interrupt my theme, scratching these few
Words on the margin for you, namely you,
   Too-human shape fixed in that shape:—

All the saying of things against myself
And for myself I have well done myself.
   What now, old enemy, shall you do
But quote and underline, thrusting yourself
Against me, as ambassador of myself,
   In damned confusion of myself and you?

For you in strutting, you in sycophancy,
Have played too long this other self of me,
   Doubling the part of judge and patron
With that of creaking grind-stone to my wit.
Know me, have done: I am a proud spirit
   And you for ever clay. Have done!

THE LEGS

There was this road,
And it led up-hill,
And it led down-hill,
And round and in and out.

And the traffic was legs,
Legs from the knees down,
Coming and going,
Never pausing.

And the gutters gurgled
With the rain's overflow,
And the sticks on the pavement
Blindly tapped and tapped.

What drew the legs along
Was the never-stopping,
And the senseless, frightening
Fate of being legs.

Legs for the road,
The road for legs,
Resolutely nowhere
In both directions.

My legs at least
Were not in that rout:
On grass by the roadside
Entire I stood,

Watching the unstoppable
Legs go by
With never a stumble
Between step and step.

Though my smile was broad
The legs could not see,
Though my laugh was loud
The legs could not hear.

My head dizzied, then:
I wondered suddenly,
Might I too be a walker
From the knees down?

Gently I touched my shins.
The doubt unchained them:
They had run in twenty puddles
Before I regained them.

GARDENER

Loveliest flowers, though crooked in their border,
And glorious fruit, dangling from ill-pruned boughs—
Be sure the gardener had not eye enough
To wheel a barrow between the broadest gates
Without a clumsy scraping.

Yet none could think it simple awkwardness;
And when he stammered of a garden-guardian,
Said the smooth lawns came by angelic favour,
The pinks and pears in spite of his own blunders,
They nudged at this conceit.

Well, he had something, though he called it nothing—
An ass's wit, a hairy-belly shrewdness
That would appraise the intentions of an angel
By the very yard-stick of his own confusion,
And bring the most to pass.

FRONT DOOR SOLILOQUY

'Yet from the antique heights or deeps of what
Or which was grandeur fallen, sprung or what
Or which, beyond doubt I am grandeur's grandson
True to the eagle nose, the pillared neck,
(Missed by the intervening generation)
Whom large hands, long face, and long feet sort out
From which and what, to wear my heels down even,
To be connected with all reigning houses,
Show sixteen quarterings or sixty-four
Or even more, with clear skin and eyes clear
To drive the nails in and not wound the wood,
With lungs and heart sound and with bowels easy:
An angry man, heaving the sacks of grain
From cart to loft and what and what and which
And even thus, and being no Rousseauist,
Nor artists-of-the-world-unite, or which,
Or what, never admitting, in effect,
Touch anything my touch does not adorn—
Now then I dung on my grandfather's doorstep,
Which is a reasonable and loving due
To hold no taint of spite or vassalage
And understood only by him and me—
But you, you bog-rat-whiskered, you psalm-griddling,
Lame, rotten-livered, which and what canaille,
You, when twin lackeys, with armorial shovels,
Unbolt the bossy gates and bend to the task,
Be off, work out your heads from between the railings,
Lest we unkennel the mastiff and the Dane—
This house is jealous of its nastiness.'

IN BROKEN IMAGES

He is quick, thinking in clear images;
I am slow, thinking in broken images.

He becomes dull, trusting to his clear images;
I become sharp, mistrusting my broken images.

Trusting his images, he assumes their relevance;
Mistrusting my images, I question their relevance.

Assuming their relevance, he assumes the fact;
Questioning their relevance, I question the fact.

When the fact fails him, he questions his senses;
When the fact fails me, I approve my senses.

He continues quick and dull in his clear images;
I continue slow and sharp in my broken images.

He in a new confusion of his understanding;
I in a new understanding of my confusion.

TRUDGE, BODY!

Trudge, body, and climb, trudge and climb,
But not to stand again on any peak of time:
Trudge, body!

I'll cool you, body, with a hot sun, that draws the sweat,
I'll warm you, body, with ice-water, that stings the blood,
I'll enrage you, body, with idleness, to do
And having done to sleep the long night through:
Trudge, body!

But in such cooling, warming, doing or sleeping,
No pause for satisfaction: henceforth you make address
Beyond heat to the heat, beyond cold to the cold,
Beyond enraged idleness to enraged idleness.
With no more hours of hope, and none of regret,
Before each sun may rise, you salute it for set:
Trudge, body!

THE CHRISTMAS ROBIN

The snows of February had buried Christmas
Deep in the woods, where grew self-seeded
The fir-trees of a Christmas yet unknown,
Without a candle or a strand of tinsel.

Nevertheless when, hand in hand, plodding
Between the frozen ruts, we lovers paused
And 'Christmas trees!' cried suddenly together,
Christmas was there again, as in December.

We velveted our love with fantasy
Down a long vista-row of Christmas trees,
Whose coloured candles slowly guttered down
As grandchildren came trooping round our knees.

But he knew better, did the Christmas robin—
The murderous robin with his breast aglow
And legs apart, in a spade-handle perched:
He prophesied more snow, and worse than snow.

ON RISING EARLY

Rising early and walking in the garden
Before the sun has properly climbed the hill—
His rays warming the roof, not yet the grass
That is white with dew still.

And not enough breeze to eddy a puff of smoke,
And out in the meadows a thick mist lying yet,
And nothing anywhere ill or noticeable—
Thanks indeed for that.

But was there ever a day with wit enough
To be always early, to draw the smoke up straight
Even at three o'clock of an afternoon,
To spare dullness or sweat?

Indeed, many such days I remember
That were dew-white and gracious to the last,
That ruled out meal-times, yet had no more hunger
Than was felt by rising a half-hour before breakfast,
Nor more fatigue—where was it that I went
So unencumbered, with my feet trampling
Like strangers on the past?

FLYING CROOKED

The butterfly, a cabbage-white,
(His honest idiocy of flight)
Will never now, it is too late,
Master the art of flying straight,
Yet has—who knows so well as I?—
A just sense of how not to fly:
He lurches here and here by guess
And God and hope and hopelessness.
Even the aerobatic swift
Has not his flying-crooked gift.

FRAGMENT OF A LOST POEM

O the clear moment, when from the mouth
A word flies, current immediately
Among friends; or when a loving gift astounds
As the identical wish nearest the heart;
Or when a stone, volleyed in sudden danger,
Strikes the rabid beast full on the snout!

Moments in never. . . .

BROTHER

It's odd enough to be alive with others,
But odder still to have sisters and brothers:
To make one of a characteristic litter—
The sisters puzzled and vexed, the brothers vexed and bitter
That this one wears, though flattened by abuse,
The family nose for individual use.

IV

THE DEVIL'S ADVICE TO STORY-TELLERS

Lest men suspect your tale to be untrue,
Keep probability—some say—in view.
But my advice to story-tellers is:
Weigh out no gross of probabilities,
Nor yet make diligent transcriptions of
Known instances of virtue, crime or love.
To forge a picture that will pass for true,
Do conscientiously what liars do—
Born liars, not the lesser sort that raid
The mouths of others for their stock-in-trade:
Assemble, first, all casual bits and scraps
That may shake down into a world perhaps;
People this world, by chance created so,
With random persons whom you do not know—
The teashop sort, or travellers in a train
Seen once, guessed idly at, not seen again;
Let the erratic course they steer surprise
Their own and your own and your readers' eyes;
Sigh then, or frown, but leave (as in despair)
Motive and end and moral in the air;
Nice contradiction between fact and fact
Will make the whole read human and exact.

SEA SIDE

Into a gentle wildness and confusion,
Of here and there, of one and everyone,
Of windy sandhills by an unkempt sea,
Came two and two in search of symmetry,
Found symmetry of two in sea and sand,
In left foot, right foot, left hand and right hand.

The beast with two backs is a single beast,
Yet by his love of singleness increased
To two and two and two and two again,
Until, instead of sandhills, see, a plain
Patterned in two and two, by two and two—
And the sea parts in horror at a view
Of rows of houses coupling, back to back,
While love smokes from their common chimney-stack
With two-four-eight-sixteenish single same
Re-registration of the duple name.

WM. BRAZIER

At the end of Tarriers' Lane, which was the street
We children thought the pleasantest in Town
Because of the old elms growing from the pavement
And the crookedness, when the other streets were straight,
[They were always at the lamp-post round the corner,
Those pugs and papillons and in-betweens,
Nosing and snuffling for the latest news]
Lived Wm. Brazier, with a gilded sign,
'Practical Chimney Sweep'. He had black hands,
Black face, black clothes, black brushes and white teeth;
He jingled round the town in a pony-trap,
And the pony's name was Soot, and Soot was black.

But the brass fittings on the trap, the shafts,
On Soot's black harness, on the black whip-butt,
Twinkled and shone like any guardsman's buttons.
Wasn't that pretty? And when we children jeered:
'Hello, Wm. Brazier! Dirty-face Wm. Brazier!'
He would crack his whip at us and smile and bellow,
'Hello, my dears!' [If he were drunk, but otherwise:
'Scum off, you damned young milliners' bastards, you!']

Let them copy it out on a pink page of their albums,
Carefully leaving out the bracketed lines.
It's an old story—f's for s's—
But good enough for them, the suckers.

WELSH INCIDENT

'But that was nothing to what things came out
From the sea-caves of Criccieth yonder.'
'What were they? Mermaids? dragons? ghosts?'
'Nothing at all of any things like that.'
'What were they, then?'
                              'All sorts of queer things,
Things never seen or heard or written about,
Very strange, un-Welsh, utterly peculiar
Things. Oh, solid enough they seemed to touch,
Had anyone dared it. Marvellous creation,
All various shapes and sizes, and no sizes,
All new, each perfectly unlike his neighbor,
Though all came moving slowly out together.'
'Describe just one of them.'
                              'I am unable.'
'What were their colours?'
                              'Mostly nameless colours,
Colours you'd like to see; but one was puce
Or perhaps more like crimson, but not purplish.
Some had no colour.'

'Tell me, had they legs?'
'Not a leg nor foot among them that I saw.'
'But did these things come out in any order?
What o'clock was it? What was the day of the week?
Who else was present? How was the weather?'
'I was coming to that. It was half-past three
On Easter Tuesday last. The sun was shining.
The Harlech Silver Band played *Marchog Jesu*
On thirty-seven shimmering instruments,
Collecting for Caernarvon's (Fever) Hospital Fund.
The populations of Pwllheli, Criccieth,
Portmadoc, Borth, Tremadoc, Penrhyndeudraeth,
Were all assembled. Criccieth's mayor addressed them
First in good Welsh and then in fluent English,
Twisting his fingers in his chain of office,
Welcoming the things. They came out on the sand,
Not keeping time to the band, moving seaward
Silently at a snail's pace. But at last
The most odd, indescribable thing of all,
Which hardly one man there could see for wonder,
Did something recognizably a something.'
'Well, what?'
                    'It made a noise.'
                                    'A frightening noise?'
'No, no.'
          'A musical noise? A noise of scuffling?'
'No, but a very loud, respectable noise—
Like groaning to oneself on Sunday morning
In Chapel, close before the second psalm.'
'What did the mayor do?'
                              'I was coming to that.'

INTERRUPTION

If ever against this easy blue and silver
Hazed-over countryside of thoughtfulness,
Far behind in the mind and above,
Boots from before and below approach trampling,
Watch how their premonition will display
A forward countryside, low in the distance—
A picture-postcard square of June grass;
Will warm a summer season, trim the hedges,
Cast the river about on either flank,
Start the late cuckoo emptily calling,
Invent a rambling tale of moles and voles,
Furnish a path with stiles.
Watch how the field will broaden, the feet nearing,
Sprout with great dandelions and buttercups,
Widen and heighten. The blue and silver
Fogs at the border of this all-grass.
Interruption looms gigantified,
Lurches against, treads thundering through,
Blots the landscape, scatters all,
Roars and rumbles like a dark tunnel,
Is gone.
       The picture-postcard grass and trees
Swim back to central: it is a large patch,
It is a modest, failing patch of green,
The postage-stamp of its departure,
Clouded with blue and silver, closing in now
To a plain countryside of less and less,
Unpeopled and unfeatured blue and silver,
Before, behind, above.

HELL

Husks, rags and bones, waste-paper, excrement,
    Denied a soul whether for good or evil
And casually consigned to unfulfilment,
    Are pronged into his bag by the great-devil.

Or words repeated, over and over and over,
    Until their sense sickens and all but dies,
These the same fellow like a ghoulish lover
    Will lay his hands upon and hypnotize.

From husks and rags and waste and excrement
    He forms the pavement-feet and the lift-faces;
He steers the sick words into parliament
    To rule a dust-bin world with deep-sleep phrases.

When healthy words or people chance to dine
    Together in this rarely actual scene,
There is a love-taste in the bread and wine,
    Nor is it asked: 'Do you mean what you mean?'

But to their table-converse boldly comes
    The same great-devil with his brush and tray,
To conjure plump loaves from the scattered crumbs,
    And feed his false five thousands day by day.

LEDA

Heart, with what lonely fears you ached,
    How lecherously mused upon
That horror with which Leda quaked
    Under the spread wings of the swan.

Then soon your mad religious smile
  Made taut the belly, arched the breast,
And there beneath your god awhile
  You strained and gulped your beastliest.

Pregnant you are, as Leda was,
  Of bawdry, murder and deceit;
Perpetuating night because
  The after-languors hang so sweet.

SYNTHETIC SUCH

'The sum of all the parts of Such—
  Of each laboratory scene—
Is Such.' While Science means this much
  And means no more, why, let it mean!

But were the science-men to find
  Some animating principle
Which gave synthetic Such a mind
  Vital, though metaphysical—

To Such, such an event, I think
  Would cause unscientific pain:
Science, appalled by thought, would shrink
  To its component parts again.

THE FLORIST ROSE

This wax-mannequin nude, the florist rose,
She of the long stem and too glossy leaf,
Is dead to honest greenfly and leaf-cutter:
Behind plate-glass watches the yellow fogs.

Claims kin with the robust male aeroplane
Whom eagles hate and phantoms of the air,
Who has no legend, as she breaks from legend—
From fellowship with sword and sail and crown.

Experiment's flower, scentless (he its bird);
Is dewed by the spray-gun; is tender-thorned;
Pouts, false-virginal, between bud and bloom;
Bought as a love-gift, droops within the day.

LOST ACRES

These acres, always again lost
   By every new ordnance-survey
And searched for at exhausting cost
   Of time and thought, are still away.

They have their paper-substitute—
   Intercalation of an inch
At the so-many-thousandth foot—
   And no one parish feels the pinch

But lost they are, despite all care,
   And perhaps likely to be bound
Together in a piece somewhere,
   A plot of undiscovered ground.

Invisible, they have the spite
   To swerve the tautest measuring-chain
And the exact theodolite
   Perched every side of them in vain.

Yet, be assured, we have no need
   To plot these acres of the mind
With prehistoric fern and reed
   And monsters such as heroes find.

Maybe they have their flowers, their birds,
   Their trees behind the phantom fence,
But of a substance without words:
   To walk there would be loss of sense.

AT FIRST SIGHT

'Love at first sight,' some say, misnaming
Discovery of twinned helplessness
Against the huge tug of procreation.

But friendship at first sight? This also
Catches fiercely at the surprised heart
So that the cheek blanches and then blushes.

DOWN, WANTON, DOWN!

Down, wanton, down! Have you no shame
That at the whisper of Love's name,
Or Beauty's, presto! up you raise
Your angry head and stand at gaze?

Poor bombard-captain, sworn to reach
The ravelin and effect a breach—
Indifferent what you storm or why,
So be that in the breach you die!

Love may be blind, but Love at least
Knows what is man and what mere beast;
Or Beauty wayward, but requires
More delicacy from her squires.

Tell me, my witless, whose one boast
Could be your staunchness at the post,
When were you made a man of parts
To think fine and profess the arts?

Will many-gifted Beauty come
Bowing to your bald rule of thumb,
Or Love swear loyalty to your crown?
Be gone, have done! Down, wanton, down!

A FORMER ATTACHMENT

And glad to find, on again looking at it,
It meant even less to me than I had thought—
You know the ship is moving when you see
The boxes on the quayside slide away
And become smaller—and feel a calm delight
When the port's cleared and the coast out of sight,
And ships are few, each on its proper course,
With no occasion for approach or discourse.

NATURE'S LINEAMENTS

When mountain rocks and leafy trees
And clouds and things like these,
With edges,

Caricature the human face,
Such scribblings have no grace
Nor peace—

The bulbous nose, the sunken chin,
The ragged mouth in grin
Of cretin.

Nature is always so: you find
That all she has of mind
Is wind,

Retching among the empty spaces,
Ruffling the idiot grasses,
The sheeps' fleeces.

Whose pleasures are excreting, poking,
Havocking and sucking,
Sleepy licking.

Whose griefs are melancholy,
Whose flowers are oafish,
Whose waters, silly,
Whose birds, raffish,
Whose fish, fish.

TIME

The vague sea thuds against the marble cliffs
And from their fragments age-long grinds
Pebbles like flowers.

Or the vague weather wanders in the fields,
And up spring flowers with coloured buds
Like marble pebbles.

The beauty of the flowers is Time, death-grieved;
The pebbles' beauty too is Time,
Life-wearied.

It is easy to admire a blowing flower
Or a smooth pebble flower-like freaked
By Time and vagueness.

Time is Time's lapse, the emulsive element coaxing
All obstinate locks and rusty hinges
To loving-kindness.

And am I proof against that lovesome pair,
Old age and childhood, twins in Time,
In sorrowful vagueness?

And will I not pretend the accustomed thanks:
Humouring age with filial flowers,
Childhood with pebbles?

THE PHILOSOPHER

Three blank walls, a barred window with no view,
A ceiling within reach of the raised hands,
A floor blank as the walls.

And, ruling out distractions of the body—
Growth of the hair and nails, a prison diet,
Thoughts of escape—

Ruling out memory and fantasy,
The distant tramping of a gaoler's boots,
Visiting mice and such,

What solace here for a laborious mind!
What a redoubtable and single task
One might attempt here:

Threading a logic between wall and wall,
Ceiling and floor, more accurate by far
Than the cob-spider's.

Truth captured without increment of flies:
Spinning and knotting till the cell became
A spacious other head

In which the emancipated reason might
Learn in due time to walk at greater length
And more unanswerably.

Robert Graves. (Humanities Research, The University of Texas at Austin, Austin, Texas)

above: Left to right–Rosaleen, Clarissa, and Robert about 1899 or 1900. *(The Malahat Review)*

opposite: Graves, at age nineteen. *(The Malahat Review)*

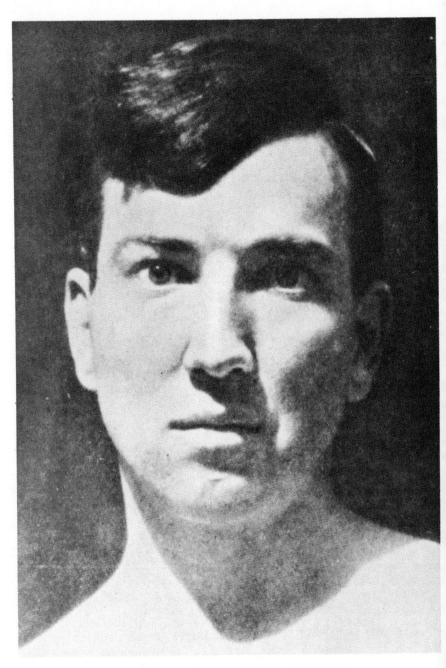
Robert Graves as a young man. (New York *Times*)

ON DWELLING

Courtesies of good-morning and good-evening
From rustic lips fail as the town encroaches:
Soon nothing passes but the cold quick stare
Of eyes that see ghosts, yet too many for fear.

Here I too walk, silent myself, in wonder
At a town not mine though plainly coextensive
With mine, even in days coincident:
In mine I dwell, in theirs like them I haunt.

And the green country, should I turn again there?
My bumpkin neighbours loom even ghostlier:
Like trees they murmur or like blackbirds sing
Courtesies of good-morning and good-evening.

OGRES AND PYGMIES

Those famous men of old, the Ogres—
They had long beards and stinking arm-pits,
They were wide-mouthed, long-yarded and great-bellied
Yet not of taller stature, Sirs, than you.
They lived on Ogre-Strand, which was no place
But the churl's terror of their vast extent,
Where every foot was three-and-thirty inches
And every penny bought a whole hog.
Now of their company none survive, not one,
The times being, thank God, unfavourable
To all but nightmare shadows of their fame;
Their images stand howling on the hill
(The winds enforced against those wide mouths),
Whose granite haunches country-folk salute
With May Day kisses, and whose knobbed knees.

So many feats they did to admiration:
With their enormous throats they sang louder
Than ten cathedral choirs, with their grand yards
Stormed the most rare and obstinate maidenheads,
With their strong-gutted and capacious bellies
Digested stones and glass like ostriches.
They dug great pits and heaped huge mounds,
Deflected rivers, wrestled with the bear
And hammered judgements for posterity—
For the sweet-cupid-lipped and tassel-yarded
Delicate-stomached dwellers
In Pygmy Alley, where with brooding on them
A foot is shrunk to seven inches
And twelve-pence will not buy a spare rib.
And who would judge between Ogres and Pygmies—
The thundering text, the snivelling commentary—
Reading between such covers he will marvel
How his own members bloat and shrink again.

SINGLE FARE

By way of Fishguard, all the lying devils
Are back to Holy Ireland whence they came.
Each took a single fare: which cost them less
And brought us comfort. The dumb devils too
Take single fares, return by rail to Scotland
Whence they came. So the air is cool and easy.
And if, in some quarter of some big city,
A little Eire or a little Scotland
Serves as a rallying-point for a few laggards,
No matter, we are free from taint of them.
And at the fire-side now (drinking our coffee),
If I ask, 'But to what township did they book,
Those dumb devils of Scotland?' you will answer:
'There's the Bass Rock, once more a separate kingdom,
Leagued with Ireland, the same cold grey crag
Screamed against by the gulls that are all devils.'
And of the Irish devils you will answer:
'In Holy Ireland many a country seat
Still stands unburned—as Cooper's Hill, Lisheen,
Cloghan Castle, or Killua in County Galway—
For the devils to enter, unlock the library doors
And write love-letters and long threatening letters
Even to us, if it so pleases them.'

TO WALK ON HILLS

To walk on hills is to employ legs
As porters of the head and heart
Jointly adventuring towards
Perhaps true equanimity.

To walk on hills is to see sights
And hear sounds unfamiliar.
When in wind the pine-tree roars,
When crags with bleatings echo,
When water foams below the fall,
Heart records that journey
As memorable indeed;
Head reserves opinion,
Confused by the wind.

A view of three shires and the sea!
Seldom so much at once appears
Of the coloured world, says heart.
Head is glum, says nothing.

Legs become weary, halting
To sprawl in a rock's shelter,
While the sun drowsily blinks
On head at last brought low—
This giddied passenger of legs
That has no word to utter.

Heart does double duty,
As heart, and as head,
With portentous trifling.
A castle, on its crag perched,
Across the miles between is viewed
With awe as across years.

Now a daisy pleases,
Pleases and astounds, even,
That on a garden lawn could blow
All summer long with no esteem.

And the buzzard's cruel poise,
And the plover's misery,
And the important beetle's
Blue-green-shiny back. . . .

To walk on hills is to employ legs
To march away and lose the day.
Tell us, have you known shepherds?
And are they not a witless race,
Prone to quaint visions?
Not thus from solitude
(Solitude sobers only)
But from long hilltop striding.

TO BRING THE DEAD TO LIFE

To bring the dead to life
Is no great magic.
Few are wholly dead:
Blow on a dead man's embers
And a live flame will start.

Let his forgotten griefs be now,
And now his withered hopes;
Subdue your pen to his handwriting
Until it prove as natural
To sign his name as yours.

Limp as he limped,
Swear by the oaths he swore;
If he wore black, affect the same;
If he had gouty fingers,
Be yours gouty too.

Assemble tokens intimate of him—
A seal, a cloak, a pen:
Around these elements then build
A home familiar to
The greedy revenant.

So grant him life, but reckon
That the grave which housed him
May not be empty now:
You in his spotted garments
Shall yourself lie wrapped.

TO EVOKE POSTERITY

To evoke posterity
Is to weep on your own grave,
Ventriloquizing for the unborn:
'Would you were present in flesh, hero!
What wreaths and junketings!'

And the punishment is fixed:
To be found fully ancestral,
To be cast in bronze for a city square,
To dribble green in times of rain
And stain the pedestal.

Spiders in the spread beard;
A life proverbial
On clergy lips a-cackle;
Eponymous institutes,
Their luckless architecture.

Two more dates of life and birth
For the hour of special study
From which all boys and girls of mettle
Twice a week play truant
And worn excuses try.

Alive, you have abhorred
The crowds on holiday
Jostling and whistling—yet would you air
Your death-mask, smoothly lidded,
Along the promenade?

ANY HONEST HOUSEWIFE

Any honest housewife could sort them out,
Having a nose for fish, an eye for apples.
Is it any mystery who are the sound,
And who the rotten? Never, by her lights.

Any honest housewife who, by ill-fortune,
Ever engaged a slut to scrub for her
Could instantly distinguish from the workers
The lazy, the liars, and the petty thieves.

Does this denote a sixth peculiar sense
Gifted to housewives for their vestal needs?
Or is it failure of the usual five
In all unthrifty writers on this head?

NEVER SUCH LOVE

Twined together and, as is customary,
For words of rapture groping, they
'Never such love,' swore, 'ever before was!'
Contrast with all loves that had failed or staled
Registered their own as love indeed.

And was this not to blab idly
The heart's fated inconstancy?
Better in love to seal the love-sure lips,
For truly love was before words were,
And no word given, no word broken.

When the name 'love' is uttered
(Love, the near-honourable malady
With which in greed and haste they
Each other do infect and curse)
Or, worse, is written down. . . .

69

Wise after the event, by love withered,
A 'never more!' most frantically
Sorrow and shame would proclaim
Such as, they'd swear, never before were:
True lovers even in this.

CERTAIN MERCIES

Now must all satisfaction
Appear mere mitigation
Of an accepted curse?

Must we henceforth be grateful
That the guards, though spiteful,
Are slow of foot and wit?

That by night we may spread
Over the plank bed
A thin coverlet?

That the rusty water
In the unclean pitcher
Our thirst quenches?

That the rotten, detestable
Food is yet eatable
By us ravenous?

That the prison censor
Permits a weekly letter?
(We may write: 'We are well.')

That, with patience and deference,
We do not experience
The punishment cell?

That each new indignity
Defeats only the body,
Pampering the spirit
With obscure, proud merit?

THE CUIRASSIERS OF THE FRONTIER

Goths, Vandals, Huns, Isaurian mountaineers,
Made Roman by our Roman sacrament,
We can know little (as we care little)
Of the Metropolis: her candled churches,
Her white-gowned pederastic senators,
The cut-throat factions of her Hippodrome,
The eunuchs of her draped saloons.

Here is the frontier, here our camp and place—
Beans for the pot, fodder for horses,
And Roman arms. Enough. He who among us
At full gallop, the bowstring to his ear,
Lets drive his heavy arrows, to sink
Stinging through Persian corslets damascened,
Then follows with the lance—he has our love.

The Christ bade Holy Peter sheathe his sword,
Being outnumbered by the Temple guard.
And this was prudence, the cause not yet lost
While Peter might persuade the crowd to rescue.
Peter renegued, breaking his sacrament.
With us the penalty is death by stoning,
Not to be made a bishop.

In Peter's Church there is no faith nor truth,
Nor justice anywhere in palace or court.
That we continue watchful on the rampart
Concerns no priest. A gaping silken dragon,
Puffed by the wind, suffices us for God.
We, not the City, are the Empire's soul:
A rotten tree lives only in its rind.

THE LAUREATE

Like a lizard in the sun, though not scuttling
When men approach, this wretch, this thing of rage,
Scowls and sits rhyming in his horny age.

His time and truth he has not bridged to ours,
But shrivelled by long heliotropic idling
He croaks at us his out-of-date humours.

Once long ago here was a poet; who died.
See how remorse twitching his mouth proclaims
It was no natural death, but suicide.

Arrogant, lean, unvenerable, he
Still turns for comfort to the western flames
That glitter a cold span above the sea.

A JEALOUS MAN

To be homeless is a pride
To the jealous man prowling
Hungry down the night lanes,

Who has no steel at his side,
No drink hot in his mouth,
But a mind dream-enlarged,

Who witnesses warfare,
Man with woman, hugely
Raging from hedge to hedge:

The raw knotted oak-club
Clenched in the raw fist,
The ivy-noose well flung,

The thronged din of battle,
Gaspings of the throat-snared,
Snores of the battered dying,

Tall corpses, braced together,
Fallen in clammy furrows,
Male and female,

Or, among haulms of nettle
Humped, in noisome heaps,
Male and female.

He glowers in the choked roadway
Between twin churchyards,
Like a turnip ghost.

(Here, the rain-worn headstone,
There, the celtic cross
In rank white marble.)

This jealous man is smitten,
His fear-jerked forehead
Sweats a fine musk;

A score of bats bewitched
By the ruttish odour
Swoop singing at his head;

Nuns bricked up alive
Within the neighbouring wall
Wail in cat-like longing.

Crow, cocks, crow loud,
Reprieve the doomed devil—
Has he not died enough?

Now, out of careless sleep,
She wakes and greets him coldly,
The woman at home,

She, with a private wonder
At shoes bemired and bloody—
His war was not hers.

THE CLOAK

Into exile with only a few shirts,
Some gold coin and the necessary papers.
But winds are contrary: the Channel packet
Time after time returns the sea-sick peer
To Sandwich, Deal or Rye. He does not land,
But keeps his cabin; so at last we find him
In humble lodgings maybe at Dieppe,
His shirts unpacked, his night-cap on a peg,
Passing the day at cards and swordsmanship
Or merry passages with chambermaids,
By night at his old work. And all is well—
The country wine wholesome although so sharp,
And French his second tongue; a faithful valet
Brushes his hat and brings him newspapers.
This nobleman is at home anywhere,
His castle being, the valet says, his title.
The cares of an estate would incommode
Such tasks as now his Lordship has in hand.
His Lordship, says the valet, contemplates
A profitable absence of some years.
Has he no friend at Court to intercede?
He wants none: exile's but another name
For an old habit of non-residence
In all but the recesses of his cloak.
It was this angered a great personage.

THE FOREBODING

Looking by chance in at the open window
   I saw my own self seated in his chair
With gaze abstracted, furrowed forehead,
   Unkempt hair.

I thought that I had suddenly come to die,
   That to a cold corpse this was my farewell,
Until the pen moved slowly upon paper
   And tears fell.

He had written a name, yours, in printed letters:
   One word on which bemusedly to pore—
No protest, no desire, your naked name,
   Nothing more.

Would it be tomorrow, would it be next year?
   But the vision was not false, this much I knew;
And I turned angrily from the open window
   Aghast at you.

Why never a warning, either by speech or look,
   That the love you cruelly gave me could not last?
Already it was too late: the bait swallowed,
   The hook fast.

WITH HER LIPS ONLY

This honest wife, challenged at dusk
At the garden gate, under a moon perhaps,
In scent of honeysuckle, dared to deny
Love to an urgent lover: with her lips only,
Not with her heart. It was no assignation;
Taken aback, what could she say else?
For the children's sake, the lie was venial;
'For the children's sake', she argued with her conscience.

75

Yet a mortal lie must follow before dawn:
Challenged as usual in her own bed,
She protests love to an urgent husband,
Not with her heart but with her lips only;
'For the children's sake', she argues with her conscience,
'For the children'—turning suddenly cold towards them.

THE HALLS OF BEDLAM

Forewarned of madness:
In three days' time at dusk
The fit masters him.

How to endure those days?
(Forewarned is foremad)
'—Normally, normally.'

He will gossip with children,
Argue with elders,
Check the cash account.

'I shall go mad that day—'
The gossip, the argument,
The neat marginal entry.

His case is not uncommon,
The doctors pronounce;
But prescribe no cure.

To be mad is not easy,
Will earn him no more
Than a niche in the news.

Then to-morrow, children,
To-morrow or the next day
He resigns from the firm.

His boyhood's ambition
Was to become an artist—
Like any City man's.

To the walls and halls of Bedlam
The artist is welcome—
Bold brush and full palette.

Through the cell's grating
He will watch his children
To and from school.

'Suffer the little children
To come unto me
With their Florentine hair!'

A very special story
For their very special friends—
They burst in the telling:

Of an evil thing, armed,
Tap-tapping on the door,
Tap-tapping on the floor,
'On the third day at dusk.'

Father in his shirt-sleeves
Flourishing a hatchet—
Run, children, run!

No one could stop him,
No one understood;
And in the evening papers. . . .

(Imminent genius,
Troubles at the office,
Normally, normally,
As if already mad.)

OR TO PERISH BEFORE DAY

The pupils of the eye expand
And from near-nothings build up sight;
The pupil of the heart, the ghost,
Swelling parades the dewy land:

With cowardice and with self-esteem
Makes terror in the track that through
The fragrant spotted pasture runs;
And a bird wails across the dream.

Now, if no heavenly window shines
Nor angel-voices cheer the way,
The ghost will overbear the man
And mark his head with fever-signs.

The flowers of dusk that he has pulled
To wonder at when morning's here
Are snail-shells upon straws of grass—
So easily the eye is gulled.

The sounding words that his mouth fill
Upon to-morrow's lip shall droop;
The legs that slide with skating ease
Be stiff to the awakened will.

Or, should he perish before day,
He leaves his lofty ghost behind
Perpetuating uncontrolled
This hour of glory and dismay.

A COUNTRY MANSION

This ancient house so notable
For its gables and great staircase,
Its mulberry-trees and alleys of clipped yew,
Humbles the show of every near demesne.

At the beginning it acknowledged owners—
Father, son, grandson—
But then, surviving the last heirs of the line,
Became a place for life-tenancy only.

At the beginning, no hint of fate,
No rats and no hauntings;
In the garden, then, the fruit-trees grew
Slender and similar in long rows.

A bedroom with a low ceiling
Caused little fret at first;
But gradual generations of discomfort
Have bred an anger there to stifle sleep.

And the venerable dining-room,
Where port in Limerick glasses
Glows twice as red reflected
In the memory-mirror of the waxed table—

For a time with paint and flowered paper
A mistress tamed its walls,
But pious antiquarian hands, groping,
Rediscovered the grey panels beneath.

Children love the old house tearfully,
And the parterres, how fertile!
Married couples under the testers hugging
Enjoy carnality's bliss as nowhere else.

A smell of mould from loft to cellar,
Yet sap still brisk in the oak
Of the great beams: if ever they use a saw
It will stain, as cutting a branch from a green tree.

. . . Old Parr had lived one hundred years and five
(So to King Charles he bragged)
When he did open penance, in a sheet,
For fornication with posterity.

Old Parr died; not so the mansion
Whose inhabitants, bewitched,
Pour their fresh blood through its historic veins
And, if a tile blow from the roof, tremble.

The last-born of this race of sacristans
Broke the long spell, departed;
They lay his knife and fork at every meal
And every evening warm his bed;

Yet cannot draw him back from the far roads
For trifling by the lily-pool
Or wine at the hushed table where they meet,
The guests of genealogy.

It was his childhood's pleasure-ground
And still may claim his corpse,
Yet foster-cradle or foster-grave
He will not count as home.

This rebel does not hate the house,
Nor its dusty joys impugn:
No place less reverend could provoke
So proud an absence from it.

He has that new malaise of time:
Gratitude choking with vexation
That he should opulently inherit
The goods and titles of the extinct.

LOVERS IN WINTER

The posture of the tree
  Shows the prevailing wind;
And ours, long misery
  When you are long unkind.

But forward, look, we lean—
  Not backward as in doubt—
And still with branches green
  Ride our ill weather out.

ADVOCATES

Fugitive firs and larches for a moment
Caught, past midnight, by our headlight beam
On that mad journey through unlasting lands
I cannot put a name to, years ago,
(And my companions drowsy-drunk)—those trees
Resume again their sharp appearance, perfect
Of spur and tassel, claiming memory,
Claiming affection: 'Will we be included
In the catalogue? Yes, yes?' they plead.

Green things, you are already there enrolled
And should a new resentment gnaw in me
Against my dear companions of that journey
(Strangers already then, in thought and deed)
You shall be advocates, charged to deny
That all the good I lived with them is lost.

ON PORTENTS

If strange things happen where she is,
So that men say that graves open
And the dead walk, or that futurity
Becomes a womb and the unborn are shed,
Such portents are not to be wondered at,
Being tourbillions in Time made
By the strong pulling of her bladed mind
Through that ever-reluctant element.

THE TERRACED VALLEY

In a deep thought of you and concentration
I came by hazard to a new region:
The unnecessary sun was not there,
The necessary earth lay without care—
For more than sunshine warmed the skin
Of the round world that was turned outside-in.

Calm sea beyond the terraced valley
Without horizon easily was spread,
As it were overhead,
Washing the mountain-spurs behind me:
The unnecessary sky was not there,
Therefore no heights, no deeps, no birds of the air.

Neat outside-inside, neat below-above,
Hermaphrodizing love.
Neat this-way-that-way and without mistake:
On the right hand could slide the left glove.
Neat over-under: the young snake
Through an unyielding shell his path could break.
Singing of kettles, like a singing brook,
Made out-of-doors a fireside nook.

But you, my love, where had you then your station?
Seeing that on this counter-earth together
We got not distant from each other;
I knew you near me in that strange region,
So searched for you, in hope to see you stand
On some near olive-terrace, in the heat,
The left-hand glove drawn on your right hand,
The empty snake's egg perfect at your feet—
But found you nowhere in the wide land,
And cried disconsolately, until you spoke
Immediate at my elbow, and your voice broke
This trick of time, changing the world about
To once more inside-in and outside-out.

THE CHINK

A sunbeam on the well-waxed oak,
    In shape resembling not at all
The ragged chink by which it broke
    Into this darkened hall,
Swims round and golden over me,
The sun's plenipotentiary.

So may my round love a chink find:
    With such address to break
Into your grief-occluded mind
    As you shall not mistake
    But, rising, open to me for truth's sake.

THE AGES OF OATH

To find a garden-tulip growing
Among wild primroses of a wild field,
Or a cuckoo's egg in a blackbird's nest,
Or a giant mushroom, a whole basketful—
The memorable feats of childhood!
Once, by the earthworks, scratching in the soil,
My stick turned up a Roman amber bead. . . .

The lost, the freakish, the unspelt
Drew me: for simple sights I had no eye.
And did I swear allegiance then
To wildness, not (as I thought) to truth—
Become a virtuoso, and this also,
Later, of simple sights, when tiring
Of unicorn and upas?

Did I forget how to greet plainly
The especial sight, how to know deeply
The pleasure shared by upright hearts?
And is this to begin afresh, with oaths
On the true book, in the true name,
Now stammering out my praise of you,
Like a boy owning his first love?

NEW LEGENDS

Content in you,
Andromeda serene,
Mistress of air and ocean
And every fiery dragon,
Chained to no cliff,
Asking no rescue of me.

84

Content in you,
Mad Atalanta,
Stooping unpausing,
Ever ahead,
Acquitting me of rivalry.

Content in you
Who made King Proteus marvel,
Showing him singleness
Past all variety.

Content in you,
Niobe of no children,
Of no calamity.

Content in you,
Helen, foiler of beauty.

LIKE SNOW

She, then, like snow in a dark night,
Fell secretly. And the world waked
With dazzling of the drowsy eye,
So that some muttered 'Too much light',
And drew the curtains close.
Like snow, warmer than fingers feared,
And to soil friendly;
Holding the histories of the night
In yet unmelted tracks.

END OF PLAY

We have reached the end of pastime, for always,
Ourselves and everyone, though few confess it
Or see the sky other than, as of old,
A foolish smiling Mary-mantle blue;

Though life may still seem to dawdle golden
In some June landscape among giant flowers,
The grass to shine as cruelly green as ever,
Faith to descend in a chariot from the sky—

May seem only: a mirror and an echo
Mediate henceforth with vision and sound.
The cry of faith, no longer mettlesome,
Sounds as blind man's pitiful plea of 'blind'.

We have at last ceased idling, which to regret
Were as shallow as to ask our milk-teeth back;
As many forthwith do, and on their knees
Call lugubriously upon chaste Christ.

We tell no lies now, at last cannot be
The rogues we were—so evilly linked in sense
With what we scrutinized that lion or tiger
Could leap from every copse, strike and devour us.

No more shall love in hypocritic pomp
Conduct its innocents through a dance of shame,
From timid touching of gloved fingers
To frantic laceration of naked breasts.

Yet love survives, the word carved on a sill
Under antique dread of the headsman's axe;
It is the echoing mind, as in the mirror
We stare on our dazed trunks at the block kneeling.

THE CLIMATE OF THOUGHT

The climate of thought has seldom been described.
It is no terror of Caucasian frost,
Nor yet that brooding Hindu heat
For which a loin-rag and a dish of rice
Suffice until the pestilent monsoon.
But, without winter, blood would run too thin;
Or, without summer, fires would burn too long.
In thought the seasons run concurrently.

Thought has a sea to gaze, not voyage, on;
And hills, to rough the edge of the bland sky,
Not to be climbed in search of blander prospect;
Few birds, sufficient for such caterpillars
As are not fated to turn butterflies;
Few butterflies, sufficient for such flowers
As are the luxury of a full orchard;
Wind, sometimes, in the evening chimneys; rain
On the early morning roof, on sleepy sight;
Snow streaked upon the hilltop, feeding
The fond brook at the valley-head
That greens the valley and that parts the lips;
The sun, simple, like a country neighbour;
The moon, grand, not fanciful with clouds.

THE FALLEN TOWER OF SILOAM

Should the building totter, run for an archway!
We were there already—already the collapse
Powdered the air with chalk, and shrieking
Of old men crushed under the fallen beams
Dwindled to comic yelps. How unterrible
When the event outran the alarm
And suddenly we were free—

Free to forget how grim it stood,
That tower, and what wide fissures ran
Up the west wall, how rotten the under-pinning
At the south-eastern angle. Satire
Had curled a gentle wind around it,
As if to buttress the worn masonry;
Yet we, waiting, had abstained from satire.

It behoved us, indeed, as poets
To be silent in Siloam, to foretell
No visible calamity. Though kings
Were crowned and gold coin minted still and horses
Still munched at nose-bags in the public streets,
All such sad emblems were to be condoned:
An old wives' tale, not ours.

THE GREAT-GRANDMOTHER

That aged woman with the bass voice
And yellowing white hair: believe her.
Though to your grandfather, her son, she lied
And to your father disingenuously
Told half the tale as the whole,
Yet she was honest with herself,
Knew disclosure was not yet due,
Knows it is due now.

She will conceal nothing of consequence
From you, her great-grandchildren
(So distant the relationship,
So near her term),
Will tell you frankly, she has waited
Only for your sincere indifference
To exorcize that filial regard
Which has estranged her, seventy years,
From the folk of her house.

Confessions of old distaste
For music, sighs and roses—
Their false-innocence assaulting her,
Breaching her hard heart;
Of the pleasures of a full purse,
Of clean brass and clean linen,
Of being alone at last;
Disgust with the ailing poor
To whom she was bountiful;
How the prattle of young children
Vexed more than if they whined;
How she preferred cats.

She will say, yes, she acted well,
Took such pride in the art
That none of them suspected, even,
Her wrathful irony
In doing what they asked
Better than they could ask it. . . .
But, ah, how grudgingly her will returned
After the severance of each navel-cord,
And fled how far again,
When again she was kind!

She has outlasted all man-uses,
As was her first resolve:
Happy and idle like a port
After the sea's recession,
She does not misconceive the nature
Of shipmen or of ships.
Hear her, therefore, as the latest voice;
The intervening generations (drifting
On tides of fancy still), ignore.

NO MORE GHOSTS

The patriarchal bed with four posts
Which was a harbourage of ghosts
Is hauled out from the attic glooms
And cut to wholesome furniture for wholesome rooms;

Where they (the ghosts) confused, abused, thinned,
Forgetful how they sighed and sinned,
Cannot disturb our ordered ease
Except as summer dust tickles the nose to sneeze.

We are restored to simple days, are free
From cramps of dark necessity,
And one another recognize
By an immediate love that signals at our eyes.

No new ghosts can appear. Their poor cause
Was that time freezes, and time thaws;
But here only such loves can last
As do not ride upon the weathers of the past.

VI

A LOVE STORY

The full moon easterly rising, furious,
Against a winter sky ragged with red;
The hedges high in snow, and owls raving—
Solemnities not easy to withstand:
A shiver wakes the spine.

In boyhood, having encountered the scene,
I suffered horror: I fetched the moon home,
With owls and snow, to nurse in my head
Throughout the trials of a new Spring,
Famine unassuaged.

But fell in love, and made a lodgement
Of love on those chill ramparts.
Her image was my ensign: snows melted,
Hedges sprouted, the moon tenderly shone,
The owls trilled with tongues of nightingale.

These were all lies, though they matched the time,
And brought me less than luck: her image
Warped in the weather, turned beldamish.
Then back came winter on me at a bound,
The pallid sky heaved with a moon-quake.

Dangerous it had been with love-notes
To serenade Queen Famine.
In tears I recomposed the former scene,
Let the snow lie, watched the moon rise, suffered the owls
Paid homage to them of unevent.

DAWN BOMBARDMENT

Guns from the sea open against us:
The smoke rocks bodily in the casemate
And a yell of doom goes up.
We count and bless each new, heavy concussion—
Captives awaiting rescue.

Visiting angel of the wild-fire hair
Who in dream reassured us nightly
Where we lay fettered,
Laugh at us, as we wake—our faces
So tense with hope the tears run down.

THE SHOT

The curious heart plays with its fears:
To hurl a shot through the ship's planks,
Being assured that the green angry flood
Is charmed and dares not dance into the hold—
Nor first to sweep a lingering glance around
For land or shoal or cask adrift.
'So miracles are done; but madmen drown.'

O weary luxury of hypothesis—
For human nature, honest human nature
(Which the fear-pampered heart denies)
Knows its own miracle: not to go mad.
Will pitch the shot in fancy, hint the fact,
Will bore perhaps a meagre auger hole
But stanch the spurting with a tarred rag,
And will not drown, nor even ride the cask.

THE THIEVES

Lovers in the act dispense
With such meum-tuum sense
As might warningly reveal
What they must not pick or steal,
And their nostrum is to say:
'I and you are both away.'

After, when they disentwine
You from me and yours from mine,
Neither can be certain who
Was that I whose mine was you.
To the act again they go
More completely not to know.

Theft is theft and raid is raid
Though reciprocally made.
Lovers, the conclusion is
Doubled sighs and jealousies
In a single heart that grieves
For lost honour among thieves.

LOLLOCKS

By sloth on sorrow fathered,
These dusty-featured Lollocks
Have their nativity in all disordered
Backs of cupboard drawers.

They play hide and seek
Among collars and novels
And empty medicine bottles,
And letters from abroad
That never will be answered.

Every sultry night
They plague little children,
Gurgling from the cistern,
Humming from the air,
Skewing up the bed-clothes,
Twitching the blind.

When the imbecile agèd
Are over-long in dying
And the nurse drowses,
Lollocks come skipping
Up the tattered stairs
And are nasty together
In the bed's shadow.

The signs of their presence
Are boils on the neck,
Dreams of vexation suddenly recalled
In the middle of the morning,
Languor after food.

Men cannot see them,
Men cannot hear them,
Do not believe in them—
But suffer the more
Both in neck and belly.

Women can see them—
O those naughty wives
Who sit by the fireside
Munching bread and honey,
Watching them in mischief
From corners of their eyes,
Slily allowing them to lick
Honey-sticky fingers.

Sovereign against Lollocks
Are hard broom and soft broom,
To well comb the hair,
To well brush the shoe,
And to pay every debt
As it falls due.

TO SLEEP

The mind's eye sees as the heart mirrors:
Loving in part, I did not see you whole,
Grew flesh-enraged that I could not conjure
A whole you to attend my fever-fit
In the doubtful hour between a night and day
And be Sleep that had kept so long away.

Of you sometimes a hand, a brooch, a shoe
Wavered beside me, unarticulated—
As the vexed insomniac dream-forges;
And the words I chose for your voice to speak
Echoed my own voice with its dry creak.

Now that I love you, now that I recall
All scattered elements of will that swooped
By night as jealous dreams through windows
To circle above the beds like bats,
Or as dawn-birds flew blindly at the panes
In curiosity rattling out their brains—

Now that I love you, as not before,
Now you can be and say, as not before:
The mind clears and the heart true-mirrors you
Where at my side an early watch you keep
And all self-bruising heads loll into sleep.

DESPITE AND STILL

Have you not read
The words in my head,
And I made part
Of your own heart?
We have been such as draw
The losing straw—
You of your gentleness,
I of my rashness,
Both of despair—
Yet still might share
This happy will:
To love despite and still.
Never let us deny
The thing's necessity,
But, O, refuse
To choose
Where chance may seem to give
Loves in alternative.

THE SUICIDE IN THE COPSE

The suicide, far from content,
Stared down at his own shattered skull:
Was this what he meant?

Had not his purpose been
To liberate himself from duns and dolts
By a change of scene?

From somewhere came a roll of laughter:
He had looked so on his wedding-day,
And the day after.

There was nowhere at all to go,
And no diversion now but to peruse
What literature the winds might blow

Into the copse where his body lay:
A year-old sheet of sporting news,
A crumpled schoolboy essay.

FRIGHTENED MEN

We were not ever of their feline race,
Never had hidden claws so sharp as theirs
In any half-remembered incarnation;
Have only the least knowledge of their minds
Through a grace on their part in thinking aloud;
And we remain mouse-quiet when they begin
Suddenly in their unpredictable way
To weave an allegory of their lives,
Making each point by walking round it—
Then off again, as interest is warmed.
What have they said? Or unsaid? What?
We understood the general drift only.

They are punctilious as implacable,
Most neighbourly to those who love them least.
A shout will scare them. When they spring, they seize.
The worst is when they hide from us and change
To something altogether other:
We meet them at the door, as who returns
After a one-hour-seeming century
To a house not his own.

THE OATH

The doubt and the passion
Falling away from them,
  In that instant both
Take timely courage
From the sky's clearness
  To confirm an oath.

Her loves are his loves,
His trust is her trust;
  Else all were grief
And they, lost ciphers
On a yellowing page,
  Death overleaf.

Rumour of old battle
Growls across the air;
  Then let it growl
With no more terror
Than the creaking stair
  Or the calling owl.

She knows, as he knows,
Of a faithful-always
  And an always-dear
By early emblems
Prognosticated,
  Fulfilled here.

LANGUAGE OF THE SEASONS

Living among orchards, we are ruled
By the four seasons necessarily:
This from unseasonable frosts we learn
Or from usurping suns and haggard flowers—
Legitimist our disapproval.

Weather we knew, not seasons, in the city
Where, seasonless, orange and orchid shone,
Knew it by heavy overcoat or light,
Framed love in later terminologies
Than here, where we report how weight of snow,
Or weight of fruit, tears branches from the tree.

MID-WINTER WAKING

Stirring suddenly from long hibernation,
I knew myself once more a poet
Guarded by timeless principalities
Against the worm of death, this hillside haunting;
And presently dared open both my eyes.

O gracious, lofty, shone against from under,
Back-of-the-mind-far clouds like towers;
And you, sudden warm airs that blow
Before the expected season of new blossom,
While sheep still gnaw at roots and lambless go—

Be witness that on waking, this mid-winter,
I found her hand in mine laid closely
Who shall watch out the Spring with me.
We stared in silence all around us
But found no winter anywhere to see.

THE BEACH

Louder than gulls the little children scream
Whom fathers haul into the jovial foam;
But others fearlessly rush in, breast high,
Laughing the salty water from their mouths—
Heroes of the nursery.

The horny boatman, who has seen whales
And flying fishes, who has sailed as far
As Demerara and the Ivory Coast,
Will warn them, when they crowd to hear his tales,
That every ocean smells alike of tar.

THE VILLAGERS AND DEATH

The Rector's pallid neighbour at The Firs,
Death, did not flurry the parishioners.
Yet from a weight of superstitious fears
Each tried to lengthen his own term of years.
He was congratulated who combined
Toughness of flesh and weakness of the mind
In consequential rosiness of face.
This dull and not ill-mannered populace
Pulled off their caps to Death, as they slouched by,
But rumoured him both atheist and spy.
All vowed to outlast him (though none ever did)
And hear the earth drum on his coffin-lid.
Their groans and whispers down the village street
Soon soured his nature, which was never sweet.

THE DOOR

When she came suddenly in
It seemed the door could never close again,
Nor even did she close it—she, she—
The room lay open to a visiting sea
Which no door could restrain.

Yet when at last she smiled, tilting her head
To take her leave of me,
Where she had smiled, instead
There was a dark door closing endlessly,
The waves receded.

UNDER THE POT

Sulkily the sticks burn, and though they crackle
　　With scorn under the bubbling pot, or spout
Magnanimous jets of flame against the smoke,
　　At each heel end a dirty sap breaks out.

Confess, creatures, how sulkily ourselves
　　We hiss with doom, fuel of a sodden age—
Not rapt up roaring to the chimney stack
　　On incandescent clouds of spirit or rage.

THROUGH NIGHTMARE

Never be disenchanted of
That place you sometimes dream yourself into,
Lying at large remove beyond all dream,
Or those you find there, though but seldom
In their company seated—

The untameable, the live, the gentle.
Have you not known them? Whom? They carry
Time looped so river-wise about their house
There's no way in by history's road
To name or number them.

In your sleepy eyes I read the journey
Of which disjointedly you tell; which stirs
My loving admiration, that you should travel
Through nightmare to a lost and moated land,
Who are timorous by nature.

TO LUCIA AT BIRTH

Though the moon beaming matronly and bland
   Greets you, among the crowd of the new-born,
With 'welcome to the world' yet understand
   That still her pale, lascivious unicorn
And bloody lion are loose on either hand:
   With din of bones and tantarará of horn
Their fanciful cortège parades the land—
   Pest on the high road, wild-fire in the corn.

Outrageous company to be born into,
   Lunatics of a royal age long dead.
Then reckon time by what you are or do,
   Not by the epochs of the war they spread.
   Hark how they roar; but never turn your head.
Nothing will change them, let them not change you.

DEATH BY DRUMS

If I cried out in anger against music,
   It was not that I cried
Against the wholesome bitter arsenic
   Necessary for suicide:
For suicide in the drums' racking riot
   Where horned moriscoes wailing to their bride
Scare every Lydian songster from the spot.

SHE TELLS HER LOVE WHILE HALF ASLEEP

She tells her love while half asleep,
   In the dark hours,
      With half-words whispered low:
As Earth stirs in her winter sleep
   And puts out grass and flowers
      Despite the snow,
      Despite the falling snow.

THESEUS AND ARIADNE

High on his figured couch beyond the waves
He dreams, in dream recalling her set walk
Down paths of oyster-shell bordered with flowers,
Across the shadowy turf below the vines.
He sighs: 'Deep sunk in my erroneous past
She haunts the ruins and the ravaged lawns.'

Yet still unharmed it stands, the regal house
Crooked with age and overtopped by pines
Where first he wearied of her constancy.
And with a surer foot she goes than when
Dread of his hate was thunder in the air,
When the pines agonized with flaws of wind
And flowers glared up at her with frantic eyes.
Of him, now all is done, she never dreams
But calls a living blessing down upon
What he supposes rubble and rank grass;
Playing the queen to nobler company.

PENTHESILEIA

Penthesileia, dead of profuse wounds,
Was despoiled of her arms by Prince Achilles
Who, for love of that fierce white naked corpse,
Necrophily on her committed
In the public view.

Some gasped, some groaned, some bawled their indignation,
Achilles nothing cared, distraught by grief,
But suddenly caught Thersites' obscene snigger
And with one vengeful buffet to the jaw
Dashed out his life.

This was a fury few might understand,
Yet Penthesileia, hailed by Prince Achilles
On the Elysian plain, pauses to thank him
For avenging her insulted womanhood
With sacrifice.

THE DEATH ROOM

Look forward, truant, to your second childhood.
The crystal sphere discloses
Wall-paper roses mazily repeated
In pink and bronze, their bunches harbouring
Elusive faces, under an inconclusive
Circling, spidery, ceiling craquelure,
And, by the window-frame, the well-loathed, lame.
Damp-patch, cross-patch, sleepless L-for-Lemur
Who, puffed to giant size,
Waits jealously till children close their eyes.

TO JUAN AT THE WINTER SOLSTICE

There is one story and one story only
That will prove worth your telling,
Whether as learned bard or gifted child;
To it all lines or lesser gauds belong
That startle with their shining
Such common stories as they stray into.

Is it of trees you tell, their months and virtues,
Or strange beasts that beset you,
Of birds that croak at you the Triple will?
Or of the Zodiac and how slow it turns
Below the Boreal Crown,
Prison of all true kings that ever reigned?

Water to water, ark again to ark,
From woman back to woman:
So each new victim treads unfalteringly
The never altered circuit of his fate,
Bringing twelve peers as witness
Both to his starry rise and starry fall.

Or is it of the Virgin's silver beauty,
All fish below the thighs?
She in her left hand bears a leafy quince;
When with her right she crooks a finger, smiling,
How may the King hold back?
Royally then he barters life for love.

Or of the undying snake from chaos hatched,
Whose coils contain the ocean,
Into whose chops with naked sword he springs,
Then in black water, tangled by the reeds,
Battles three days and nights,
To be spewed up beside her scalloped shore?

Much snow is falling, winds roar hollowly,
The owl hoots from the elder,
Fear in your heart cries to the loving-cup:
Sorrow to sorrow as the sparks fly upward.
The log groans and confesses:
There is one story and one story only.

Dwell on her graciousness, dwell on her smiling,
Do not forget what flowers
The great boar trampled down in ivy time.
Her brow was creamy as the crested wave,
Her sea-grey eyes were wild
But nothing promised that is not performed.

TO BE CALLED A BEAR

Bears gash the forest trees
    To mark the bounds
    Of their own hunting grounds;
They follow the wild bees
    Point by point home
    For love of honeycomb;
They browse on blueberries.

Then should I stare
If I am called a bear,
And it is not the truth?
Unkempt and surly with a sweet tooth
I tilt my muzzle toward the starry hub
Where Queen Callisto guards her cub;

But envy those that here
    All winter breathing slow
    Sleep warm under the snow,
That yawn awake when the skies clear,
    And lank with longing grow
No more than one brief month a year.

VII

MY NAME AND I

The impartial Law enrolled a name
  For my especial use:
My rights in it would rest the same
Whether I puffed it into fame
  Or sank it in abuse.

Robert was what my parents guessed
  When first they peered at me,
And *Graves* an honourable bequest
With Georgian silver and the rest
  From my male ancestry.

They taught me: 'You are *Robert Graves*
  (Which you must learn to spell),
But see that *Robert Graves* behaves,
Whether with honest men or knaves,
  Exemplarily well.'

Then though my I was always I,
  Illegal and unknown,
With nothing to arrest it by—
As will be obvious when I die
  And *Robert Graves* lives on—

I cannot well repudiate
  This noun, this natal star,
This gentlemanly self, this mate
So kindly forced on me by fate,
  Time and the registrar;

And therefore hurry him ahead
   As an ambassador
To fetch me home my beer and bread
Or commandeer the best green bed,
   As he has done before.

Yet, understand, I am not he
   Either in mind or limb;
My name will take less thought for me,
In worlds of men I cannot see,
   Than ever I for him.

1805

At Viscount Nelson's lavish funeral,
   While the mob milled and yelled about St Paul's,
A General chatted with an Admiral:

'One of your Colleagues, Sir, remarked today
   That Nelson's *exit*, though to be lamented,
Falls not inopportunely, in its way.'

'He was a thorn in our flesh,' came the reply—
   'The most bird-witted, unaccountable,
Odd little runt that ever I did spy.

'One arm, one peeper, vain as Pretty Poll,
   A meddler, too, in foreign politics
And gave his heart in pawn to a plain moll.

'He would dare lecture us Sea Lords, and then
   Would treat his ratings as though men of honour
And play at leap-frog with his midshipmen!

'We tried to box him down, but up he popped,
   And when he'd banged Napoleon at the Nile
Became too much the hero to be dropped.

'You've heard that Copenhagen "blind eye" story?
    We'd tied him to Nurse Parker's apron-strings—
By G—d, he snipped them through and snatched the glory!'

'Yet,' cried the General, 'six-and-twenty sail
    Captured or sunk by him off Tráfalgár—
That writes a handsome *finis* to the tale.'

'Handsome enough. The seas are England's now.
    That fellow's foibles need no longer plague us.
He died most creditably, I'll allow.'

'And, Sir, the secret of his victories?'
    'By his unServicelike, familiar ways, Sir,
He made the whole Fleet love him, damn his eyes!'

THE PERSIAN VERSION

Truth-loving Persians do not dwell upon
The trivial skirmish fought near Marathon.
As for the Greek theatrical tradition
Which represents that summer's expedition
Not as a mere reconnaissance in force
By three brigades of foot and one of horse
(Their left flank covered by some obsolete
Light craft detached from the main Persian fleet)
But as a grandiose, ill-starred attempt
To conquer Greece—they treat it with contempt;
And only incidentally refute
Major Greek claims, by stressing what repute
The Persian monarch and the Persian nation
Won by this salutary demonstration:
Despite a strong defence and adverse weather
All arms combined magnificently together.

THE WEATHER OF OLYMPUS

Zeus was once overheard to shout at Hera:
   'You hate it, do you? Well, I hate it worse—
East wind in May, sirocco all the Summer.
   Hell take this whole impossible Universe!'

A scholiast explains his warm rejoinder,
   Which sounds too man-like for Olympic use,
By noting that the snake-tailed Chthonian winds
   Were answerable to Fate alone, not Zeus.

APOLLO OF THE PHYSIOLOGISTS

Despite this learned cult's official
And seemingly sincere denial
That they either reject or postulate
God, or God's scientific surrogate,
Prints of a deity occur *passim*
Throughout their extant literature. They make him
A dumb, dead-pan Apollo with a profile
Drawn in Victorian-Hellenistic style—
The pallid, bald, partitioned head suggesting
Wholly abstract cerebral functioning;
Or nude and at full length, this deity
Displays digestive, venous, respiratory
And nervous systems painted in bold colour
On his immaculate exterior.
Sometimes, *in verso*, a bald, naked Muse,
His consort, flaunts her arteries and sinews,
While, upside-down, crouched in her chaste abdomen,
Adored by men and wondered at by women,
Hangs a Victorian-Hellenistic foetus—
Fruit of her academic god's afflatus.

THE OLDEST SOLDIER

The sun shines warm on seven old soldiers
   Paraded in a row,
Perched like starlings on the railings—
   Give them plug-tobacco!

They'll croon you the Oldest-Soldier Song:
   Of Harry who took a holiday
From the sweat of ever thinking for himself
   Or going his own bloody way.

It was arms-drill, guard and kit-inspection,
   Like dreams of a long train-journey,
And the barrack-bed that Harry dossed on
   Went rockabye, rockabye, rockabye.

Harry kept his rifle and brasses clean,
   But Jesus Christ, what a liar!
He won the Military Medal
   For his coolness under fire.

He was never the last on parade
   Nor the first to volunteer,
And when Harry rose to be storeman
   He seldom had to pay for his beer.

Twenty-one years, and out Harry came
   To be odd-job man, or janitor,
Or commissionaire at a picture-house,
   Or, some say, bully to a whore.

But his King and Country calling Harry,
   He reported again at the Depôt,
To perch on this railing like a starling,
   The oldest soldier of the row.

GROTESQUES

I

My Chinese uncle, gouty, deaf, half-blinded,
And more than a trifle absent-minded,
Astonished all St James's Square one day
By giving long and unexceptionably exact directions
To a little coolie girl, who'd lost her way.

II

The Lion-faced Boy at the Fair
And the Heir Apparent
Were equally slow at remembering people's faces.
But whenever they met, incognito, in the Brazilian
Pavilion, the Row and such-like places,
They exchanged, it is said, their sternest nods—
Like gods of dissimilar races.

Dr Newman with the crooked pince-nez
Had studied in Vienna and Chicago.
Chess was his only relaxation.
And Dr Newman remained unperturbed
By every nastier manifestation
Of pluto-democratic civilization:
All that was cranky, corny, ill-behaved,
Unnecessary, askew or orgiastic
Would creep unbidden to his side-door (hidden
Behind a poster in the Tube Station,
Nearly half-way up the moving stairs),
Push its way in, to squat there undisturbed
Among box-files and tubular steel-chairs.
He was once seen at the Philharmonic Hall
Noting the reactions of two patients,
With pronounced paranoiac tendencies,
To old Dutch music. He appeared to recall
A tin of lozenges in his breast-pocket,
Put his hand confidently in—
And drew out a black imp, or sooterkin,
Six inches long, with one ear upside-down,
Licking at a vanilla ice-cream cornet—
Then put it back again with a slight frown.

IV

A Royal Duke, with no campaigning medals
To dignify his Orders, he would speak
Nostalgically at times of Mozambique
Where once the ship he cruised in ran aground:
How he drank cocoa, from a sailor's mug,
Poured from the cinnamon jug,
While loyal toasts went round.

Sir John addressed the Snake-god in his temple,
Which was full of bats, not as a votary
But with the somewhat cynical courtesy,
Just short of condescension,
He might have paid the Governor-General
Of a small, hot, backward colony.
He was well versed in primitive religion,
But found this an embarrassing occasion:
The God was immense, noisy and affable,
Began to tickle him with a nervous chuckle,
Unfobbed a great gold clock for him to listen,
Hissed like a snake, and swallowed him at one mouthful.

All horses on the racecourse of Tralee
  Have four more legs in gallop than in trot—
  Two pairs fully extended, two pairs not;
And yet no thoroughbred with either three
  Or five legs but is mercilessly shot.
I watched a filly gnaw her fifth leg free,
Warned by a speaking mare since turned silentiary.

BEAUTY IN TROUBLE

Beauty in trouble flees to the good angel
  On whom she can rely
To pay her cab-fare, run a steaming bath,
  Poultice her bruised eye;

Will not at first, whether for shame or caution,
  Her difficulty disclose;
Until he draws a cheque book from his plumage,
  Asking how much she owes.

(Breakfast in bed: coffee and marmalade,
    Toast, eggs, orange-juice,
After a long, sound sleep—the first since when?—
    And no word of abuse.)

Loves him less only than her saint-like mother,
    Promises to repay
His loans and most seraphic thoughtfulness
    A million-fold one day.

Beauty grows plump, renews her broken courage
    And, borrowing ink and pen,
Writes a news-letter to the evil angel
    (Her first gay act since when?):

The fiend who beats, betrays and sponges on her,
    Persuades her white is black,
Flaunts vespertilian wing and cloven hoof;
    And soon will fetch her back.

Virtue, good angel, is its own reward:
    Your guineas were well spent.
But would you to the marriage of true minds
    Admit impediment?

SIROCCO AT DEYÁ

How most unnatural-seeming, yet how proper;
The sea like a cat with fur rubbed the wrong way,
As the sirocco with its furnace flavour
Dashes at full tilt around the village
['From every-which-a-way, hot as a two-buck pistol']
Stripping green olives from the blown-back boughs,
Scorching the roses, blinding the eyes with sand;
While slanderous tongues in the small cafés
And in the tightly-shuttered limestone houses
Clack defamation, incite and invite
Knives to consummate their near-murders. . . .
Look up, a great grey cloud broods nonchalant
On the mountain-top nine hundred feet above us,
Motionless and turgid, blotting out the sun,
And from it sneers a supercilious Devil:
'Mere local wind: no messenger of mine!'

FROM THE EMBASSY

I, an ambassador of Otherwhere
To the unfederated states of Here and There
Enjoy (as the phrase is)
Extra-territorial privileges.
With heres and theres I seldom come to blows
Or need, as once, to sandbag all my windows.
And though the Otherwhereish currency
Cannot be quoted yet officially,
I meet less hindrance now with the exchange
Nor is my garb, even, considered strange;
And shy enquiries for literature
Come in by every post, and the side door.

VIII

THE WHITE GODDESS

All saints revile her, and all sober men
Ruled by the God Apollo's golden mean—
In scorn of which we sailed to find her
In distant regions likeliest to hold her
Whom we desired above all things to know,
Sister of the mirage and echo.

It was a virtue not to stay,
To go our headstrong and heroic way
Seeking her out at the volcano's head,
Among pack ice, or where the track had faded
Beyond the cavern of the seven sleepers:
Whose broad high brow was white as any leper's,
Whose eyes were blue, with rowan-berry lips,
With hair curled honey-coloured to white hips.

Green sap of Spring in the young wood a-stir
Will celebrate the Mountain Mother,
And every song-bird shout awhile for her;
But we are gifted, even in November
Rawest of seasons, with so huge a sense
Of her nakedly worn magnificence
We forget cruelty and past betrayal,
Heedless of where the next bright bolt may fall.

THE SONG OF BLODEUWEDD

[Reassembled from the deliberately confused mediaeval poem medley *Câd Goddeu*, in the *Red Book of Hergest*, hitherto regarded as nonsensical.]

Not of father nor of mother
Was my blood, was my body.
I was spellbound by Gwydion,
Prime enchanter of the Britons,
When he formed me from nine blossoms,
  Nine buds of various kind:
From primrose of the mountain,
Broom, meadow-sweet and cockle,
  Together intertwined,
From the bean in its shade bearing
A white spectral army
  Of earth, of earthy kind,
From blossoms of the nettle,
Oak, thorn and bashful chestnut—
Nine powers of nine flowers,
  Nine powers in me combined,
    Nine buds of plant and tree.
Long and white are my fingers
    As the ninth wave of the sea.

INSTRUCTIONS TO THE ORPHIC ADEPT

[In part translated from the *Timpone Grande* and *Campagno* Orphic tablets.]

So soon as ever your mazed spirit descends
From daylight into darkness, Man, remember
What you have suffered here in Samothrace,
What you have suffered.

After your passage through Hell's seven floods,
Whose fumes of sulphur will have parched your throat,
The Halls of Judgement shall loom up before you,
A miracle of jasper and of onyx.
To the left hand there bubbles a black spring
Overshadowed with a great white cypress.
Avoid this spring, which is Forgetfulness;
Though all the common rout rush down to drink,
Avoid this spring!

To the right hand there lies a secret pool
Alive with speckled trout and fish of gold;
A hazel overshadows it. Ophion,
Primaeval serpent straggling in the branches,
Darts out his tongue. This holy pool is fed
By dripping water; guardians stand before it.
Run to this pool, the pool of Memory,
Run to this pool!

Then will the guardians scrutinize you, saying:
'Who are you, who? What have you to remember?
Do you not fear Ophion's flickering tongue?
Go rather to the spring beneath the cypress,
Flee from this pool!'

Then you shall answer: 'I am parched with thirst.
Give me to drink. I am a child of Earth,
But of Sky also, come from Samothrace.
Witness the glint of amber on my brow.
Out of the Pure I come, as you may see.
I also am of your thrice-blessèd kin,
Child of the three-fold Queen of Samothrace;
Have made full quittance for my deeds of blood,
Have been by her invested in sea-purple,
And like a kid have fallen into milk.
Give me to drink, now I am parched with thirst,
Give me to drink!'

But they will ask you yet: 'What of your feet?'
You shall reply: 'My feet have borne me here
Out of the weary wheel, the circling years,
To that still, spokeless wheel:—Persephone.
Give me to drink!'

Then they will welcome you with fruit and flowers,
And lead you toward the ancient dripping hazel,
Crying: 'Brother of our immortal blood,
Drink and remember glorious Samothrace!'
Then you shall drink.

You shall drink deep of that refreshing draught,
To become lords of the uninitiated
Twittering ghosts, Hell's countless populace—
To become heroes, knights upon swift horses,
Pronouncing oracles from tall white tombs
By the nymphs tended. They with honey water
Shall pour libations to your serpent shapes,
That you may drink.

LAMENT FOR PASIPHAË

Dying sun, shine warm a little longer!
My eye, dazzled with tears, shall dazzle yours,
Conjuring you to shine and not to move.
You, sun, and I all afternoon have laboured
Beneath a dewless and oppressive cloud—
A fleece now gilded with our common grief
That this must be a night without a moon.
Dying sun, shine warm a little longer!

Faithless she was not: she was very woman,
Smiling with dire impartiality,
Sovereign, with heart unmatched, adored of men,
Until Spring's cuckoo with bedraggled plumes
Tempted her pity and her truth betrayed.
Then she who shone for all resigned her being,
And this must be a night without a moon.
Dying sun, shine warm a little longer!

RETURN OF THE GODDESS

Under your Milky Way
  And slow-revolving Bear
Frogs from the alder thicket pray
In terror of your judgement day,
  Loud with repentance there.

The log they crowned as king
  Grew sodden, lurched and sank;
An owl floats by on silent wing
Dark water bubbles from the spring;
  They invoke you from each bank.

At dawn you shall appear,
  A gaunt red-leggèd crane,
You whom they know too well for fear,
Lunging your beak down like a spear
  To fetch them home again.

                Sufficiunt
                Tecum,
                Caryatis,
                Domnia
                Quina.

IX

COUNTING THE BEATS

You, love, and I,
(He whispers) you and I,
And if no more than only you and I
What care you or I?

Counting the beats,
Counting the slow heart beats,
The bleeding to death of time in slow heart beats,
Wakeful they lie.

Cloudless day,
Night, and a cloudless day,
Yet the huge storm will burst upon their heads one day
From a bitter sky.

Where shall we be,
(She whispers) where shall we be,
When death strikes home, O where then shall we be
Who were you and I?

Not there but here,
(He whispers) only here,
As we are, here, together, now and here,
Always you and I.

Counting the beats,
Counting the slow heart beats,
The bleeding to death of time in slow heart beats,
Wakeful they lie.

THE YOUNG CORDWAINER

SHE: Love, why have you led me here
   To this lampless hall,
  A place of despair and fear
   Where blind things crawl?

HE: Not I, but your complaint
   Heard by the riverside
  That primrose scent grew faint
   And desire died.

SHE: Kisses had lost virtue
   As yourself must know;
  I declared what, alas, was true
   And still shall do so.

HE: Mount, sweetheart, this main stair
   Where bandogs at the foot
  Their crooked gilt teeth bare
   Between jaws of soot.

SHE: I loathe them, how they stand
   Like prick-eared spies.
  Hold me fast by the left hand;
   I walk with closed eyes.

HE: Primrose has periwinkle
   As her mortal fellow:
  Five leaves, blue and baleful,
   Five of true yellow.

SHE: Overhead, what's overhead?
   Where would you take me?
  My feet stumble for dread,
   My wits forsake me.

HE: Flight on flight, floor above floor,
        In suspense of doom
    To a locked secret door
      And a white-walled room.

SHE: Love, have you the pass-word,
       Or have you the key,
    With a sharp naked sword
     And wine to revive me?

HE: Enter: here is starlight,
        Here the state bed
    Where your man lies all night
      With blue flowers garlanded.

SHE: Ah, the cool open window
       Of this confessional!
    With wine at my elbow,
    And sword beneath the pillow,
     I shall perfect all.

YOUR PRIVATE WAY

Whether it was your way of walking
Or of laughing moved me,
At sight of you a song wavered
Ghostly on my lips; I could not voice it,
Uncertain what the notes or key.

Be thankful I am no musician,
Sweet Anonymity, to madden you
With your own private walking-laughing way
Imitated on a beggar's fiddle
Or blared across the square on All Fools' Day.

THE SURVIVOR

To die with a forlorn hope, but soon to be raised
By hags, the spoilers of the field, to elude their claws
And stand once more on a well-swept parade-ground,
Scarred and bemedalled, sword upright in fist
At head of a new undaunted company:

Is this joy?—to be doubtless alive again,
And the others dead? Will your nostrils gladly savour
The fragrance, always new, of a first hedge-rose?
Will your ears be charmed by the thrush's melody
Sung as though he had himself devised it?

And is this joy: after the double suicide
(Heart against heart) to be restored entire,
To smooth your hair and wash away the life-blood,
And presently seek a young and innocent bride,
Whispering in the dark: 'for ever and ever'?

QUESTIONS IN A WOOD

The parson to his pallid spouse,
    The hangman to his whore,
Do both not mumble the same vows,
    Both knock at the same door?

And when the fury of their knocks
    Has waned, and that was that,
What answer comes, unless the pox
    Or one more parson's brat?

Tell me, my love, my flower of flowers,
    True woman to this man,
What have their deeds to do with ours
    Or any we might plan?

Your startled gaze, your restless hand,
    Your hair like Thames in flood,
And choked voice, battling to command
    The insurgence of your blood:

How can they spell the dark word said
    Ten thousand times a night
By women as corrupt and dead
    As you are proud and bright?

And how can I, in the same breath,
    Though warned against the cheat,
Vilely deliver love to death
    Wrapped in a rumpled sheet?

Yet, if from delicacy of pride
    We choose to hold apart,
Will no blue hag appear, to ride
    Hell's wager in each heart?

DARIEN

It is a poet's privilege and fate
To fall enamoured of the one Muse
Who variously haunts this island earth.

She was your mother, Darien,
And presaged by the darting halcyon bird
Would run green-sleeved along her ridges,
Treading the asphodels and heather-trees
With white feet bare.

Often at moonrise I had watched her go,
And a cold shudder shook me
To see the curved blaze of her Cretan axe.
Averted her set face, her business
Not yet with me, long-striding,
She would ascend the peak and pass from sight.
But once at full moon, by the sea's verge,
I came upon her without warning.

Unrayed she stood, with long hair streaming,
A cockle-shell cupped in her warm hands,
Her axe propped idly on a stone.

No awe possessed me, only a great grief;
Wanly she smiled, but would not lift her eyes
(As a young girl will greet the stranger).
I stood upright, a head taller than she.
'See who has come,' said I.

She answered: 'If I lift my eyes to yours
And our eyes marry, man, what then?
Will they engender my son Darien?
Swifter than wind, with straight and nut-brown hair,
Tall, slender-shanked, grey-eyed, untameable;
Never was born, nor ever will be born
A child to equal my son Darien,
Guardian of the hid treasures of your world.'

I knew then by the trembling of her hands
For whom that flawless blade would sweep:
My own oracular head, swung by its hair.

'Mistress,' I cried, 'the times are evil
And you have changed me with their remedy.
O, where my head is now, let nothing be
But a clay counterfeit with nacre blink:
Only look up, so Darien may be born!

'He is the northern star, the spell of knowledge,
Pride of all hunters and all fishermen,
Your deathless fawn, an eaglet of your eyrie,
The topmost branch of your unfellable tree,
A tear streaking the summer night,
The new green of my hope.'
                              Lifting her eyes,
She held mine for a lost eternity.
'Sweetheart,' said I, 'strike now, for Darien's sake!'

THE PORTRAIT

She speaks always in her own voice
Even to strangers; but those other women
Exercise their borrowed, or false, voices
Even on sons and daughters.

She can walk invisibly at noon
Along the high road; but those other women
Gleam phosphorescent—broad hips and gross fingers—
Down every lampless alley.

She is wild and innocent, pledged to love
Through all disaster; but those other women
Decry her for a witch or a common drab
And glare back when she greets them.

Here is her portrait, gazing sidelong at me,
The hair in disarray, the young eyes pleading:
'And you, love? As unlike those other men
As I those other women?'

PROMETHEUS

Close bound in a familiar bed
All night I tossed, rolling my head;
Now dawn returns in vain, for still
The vulture squats on her warm hill.

I am in love as giants are
That dote upon the evening star,
And this lank bird is come to prove
The intractability of love.

Yet still, with greedy eye half shut,
Rend the raw liver from its gut:
Feed, jealousy, do not fly away—
If she who fetched you also stay.

THE STRAW

Peace, the wild valley streaked with torrents,
A hoopoe perched on his warm rock. Then why
This tremor of the straw between my fingers?

What should I fear? Have I not testimony
In her own hand, signed with her own name
That my love fell as lightning on her heart?

These questions, bird, are not rhetorical.
Watch how the straw twitches and leaps
As though the earth quaked at a distance.

Requited love; but better unrequited
If this chance instrument gives warning
Of cataclysmic anguish far away.

Were she at ease, warmed by the thought of me,
Would not my hand stay steady as this rock?
Have I undone her by my vehemence?

CRY FAUGH!

Caria and Philistia considered
Only pre-marital adventures wise;
The bourgeois French argue contrariwise.

Socrates and Plato burked the issue
(Namely, how man-and-woman love should be)
With homosexual ideology.

Apocalyptic Israelites, foretelling
The Imminent End, called only for a chaste
Sodality: all dead below the waist.

Curious, various, amoral, moral—
Tell me, what elegant square or lumpish hamlet
Lives free from nymphological disquiet?

'Yet males and females of the lower species
Contrive to eliminate the sexual problem,'
Scientists ponder: 'Why not learn from them?'

Cry faugh! on science, ethics, metaphysics,
On antonyms of sacred and profane—
Come walk with me, love, in a golden rain

Past toppling colonnades of glory,
The moon alive on each uptilted face:
Proud remnants of a visionary race.

HERCULES AT NEMEA

Muse, you have bitten through my fool's-finger.
Fierce as a lioness you seized it
In your white teeth most amorously;
And I stared back, dauntless and fiery-eyed,
Challenging you to maim me for my pride.

See me a fulvous hero of nine fingers—
Sufficient grasp for bow and arrow.
My beard bristles in exultation:
Let all Nemea look and understand
Why you have set your mark on this right hand.

DIALOGUE ON THE HEADLAND

SHE: You'll not forget these rocks and what I told you?
HE: How could I? Never: whatever happens.
SHE: What do you think might happen?
    Might you fall out of love?—did you mean that?
HE: Never, never! 'Whatever' was a sop
    For jealous listeners in the shadows.
SHE: You haven't answered me. I asked:
    'What do you think might happen?'
HE: Whatever happens: though the skies should fall
    Raining their larks and vultures in our laps—
SHE: 'Though the seas turn to slime'—say that—
    'Though water-snakes be hatched with six heads.'
HE: Though the seas turn to slime, or tower
    In an arching wave above us, three miles high—
SHE: 'Though she should break with you'—dare you say that?
    'Though she deny her words on oath.'
HE: I had that in my mind to say, or nearly;
    It hurt so much I choked it back.
SHE: How many other days can't you forget?
    How many other loves and landscapes?

HE:	You are jealous?
SHE:	Damnably.
HE:	The past is past.
SHE:	And this?
HE:	Whatever happens, this goes on.
SHE:	Without a future? Sweetheart, tell me now:
	What do you want of me? I must know that.
HE:	Nothing that isn't freely mine already.
SHE:	Say what is freely yours and you shall have it.
HE:	Nothing that, loving you, I could dare take.
SHE:	O, for an answer with no 'nothing' in it!
HE:	Then give me everything that's left.
SHE:	Left after what?
HE:	After whatever happens:
	Skies have already fallen, seas are slime,
	Watersnakes poke and peer six-headedly—
SHE:	And I lie snugly in the Devil's arms.
HE:	I said: 'Whatever happens.' Are you crying?
SHE:	You'll not forget me—ever, ever, ever?

LIADAN AND CURITHIR

Even in childhood
Liadan never would
  Accept love simply,
But stifled longing
And went away to sing
  In strange company.

Alas, for Liadan!
To fear perfection
  Was her ill custom:
Choosing a scruple
That might seem honourable,
  For retreat therefrom.

Herself she enticed
To be nunned for Christ,
   Though in marriage sought
By a master-poet
On whom her heart was set—
   Curithir of Connaught;

And raised a wall
As it were of crystal
   Her grief around.
He might not guess
The cause of her fickleness
   Nor catch one sound.

She was walled soon after
Behind stones and mortar,
   From whence too late
He heard her keening,
Sighing and complaining
   Of her dire self-hate.

THE SEA HORSE

Since now in every public place
Lurk phantoms who assume your walk and face,
You cannot yet have utterly abjured me
Nor stifled the insistent roar of sea.

Do as I do: confide your unquiet love
(For one who never owed you less than love)
To this indomitable hippocamp,
Child of your element, coiled a-ramp,
Having ridden out worse tempests than you know of;
Under his horny ribs a blood-red stain
Portends renewal of our pain.
Sweetheart, make much of him and shed
Tears on his taciturn dry head.

CAT-GODDESSES

A perverse habit of cat-goddesses—
Even the blackest of them, black as coals
Save for a new moon blazing on each breast,
With coral tongues and beryl eyes like lamps,
Long-legged, pacing three by three in nines—
This obstinate habit is to yield themselves,
In verisimilar love-ecstasies,
To tatter-eared and slinking alley-toms
No less below the common run of cats
Than they above it; which they do for spite,
To provoke jealousy—not the least abashed
By such gross-headed, rabbit-coloured litters
As soon they shall be happy to desert.

THE BLUE-FLY

Five summer days, five summer nights,
The ignorant, loutish, giddy blue-fly
Hung without motion on the cling peach,
Humming occasionally: 'O my love, my fair one!'
    As in the *Canticles*.

Magnified one thousand times, the insect
Looks farcically human; laugh if you will!
Bald head, stage-fairy wings, blear eyes,
A caved-in chest, hairy black mandibles,
    Long spindly thighs.

The crime was detected on the sixth day.
What then could be said or done? By anyone?
It would have been vindictive, mean and what-not
To swat that fly for being a blue-fly,
    For debauch of a peach.

Is it fair, either, to bring a microscope
To bear on the case, even in search of truth?
Nature, doubtless, has some compelling cause
To glut the carriers of her epidemics—
 Nor did the peach complain.

A LOST JEWEL

Who on your breast pillows his head now,
Jubilant to have won
The heart beneath on fire for him alone,

At dawn will hear you, plagued by nightmare,
Mumble and weep
About some blue jewel you were sworn to keep.

Wake, blink, laugh out in reassurance,
Yet your tears will say:
'It was not mine to lose or give away.

'For love it shone—never for the madness
Of a strange bed—
Light on my finger, fortune in my head.'

Roused by your naked grief and beauty,
For lust he will burn:
'Turn to me, sweetheart! Why do you not turn?'

THE WINDOW SILL

Presage and caveat not only seem
To come in dream,
But do so come in dream.

When the cock crew and phantoms floated by,
This dreamer I
Out of the house went I,

Down long unsteady streets to a queer square;
And who was there,
Or whom did I know there?

Julia, leaning on her window sill.
'I love you still,'
She said, 'O love me still!'

I answered: 'Julia, do you love me best?'
'What of this breast,'
She mourned, 'this flowery breast?'

Then a wild sobbing spread from door to door,
And every floor
Cried shame on every floor,

As she unlaced her bosom to disclose
Each breast a rose,
A white and cankered rose.

SPOILS

When all is over and you march for home,
The spoils of war are easily disposed of:
Standards, weapons of combat, helmets, drums
May decorate a staircase or a study,
While lesser gleanings of the battlefield—
Coins, watches, wedding-rings, gold teeth and such—
Are sold anonymously for solid cash.

The spoils of love present a different case,
When all is over and you march for home:
That lock of hair, these letters and the portrait
May not be publicly displayed; nor sold;
Nor burned; nor returned (the heart being obstinate)—
Yet never dare entrust them to a safe
For fear they burn a hole through two-foot steel.

RHEA

On her shut lids the lightning flickers,
Thunder explodes above her bed,
An inch from her lax arm the rain hisses;
Discrete she lies,

Not dead but entranced, dreamlessly
With slow breathing, her lips curved
In a half-smile archaic, her breast bare,
Hair astream.

The house rocks, a flood suddenly rising
Bears away bridges: oak and ash
Are shivered to the roots—royal green timber.
She nothing cares.

(Divine Augustus, trembling at the storm,
Wrapped sealskin on his thumb; divine Gaius
Made haste to hide himself in a deep cellar,
Distraught by fear.)

Rain, thunder, lighting: pretty children.
'Let them play,' her mother-mind repeats;
'They do no harm, unless from high spirits
Or by mishap.'

X

THE FACE IN THE MIRROR

Grey haunted eyes, absent-mindedly glaring
From wide, uneven orbits; one brow drooping
Somewhat over the eye
Because of a missile fragment still inhering,
Skin deep, as a foolish record of old-world fighting.

Crookedly broken nose—low tackling caused it;
Cheeks, furrowed; coarse grey hair, flying frenetic;
Forehead, wrinkled and high;
Jowls, prominent; ears, large; jaw, pugilistic;
Teeth, few; lips, full and ruddy; mouth, ascetic.

I pause with razor poised, scowling derision
At the mirrored man whose beard needs my attention,
And once more ask him why
He still stands ready, with a boy's presumption,
To court the queen in her high silk pavilion.

GRATITUDE FOR A NIGHTMARE

His appearances are incalculable,
His strength terrible,
I do not know his name.

Huddling pensive for weeks on end, he
Gives only random hints of life, such as
Strokes of uncomfortable coincidence.

To eat heartily, dress warmly, lie snugly
And earn respect as a leading citizen
Granted long credit at all shops and inns—

How dangerous! I had feared this shag demon
Would not conform with my conformity
And in some leaner belly make his lair.

But now in dream he suddenly bestrides me. . . .
'All's well,' I groan, and fumble for a light,
Brow bathed in sweat, heart pounding.

FRIDAY NIGHT

Love, the sole Goddess fit for swearing by,
Concedes us graciously the little lie:
The white lie, the half-lie, the lie corrective
Without which love's exchange might prove defective,
Confirming hazardous relationships
By kindly *maquillage* of Truth's pale lips.

This little lie was first told, so they say,
On the sixth day (Love's planetary day)
When, meeting her full-bosomed and half dressed,
Jove roared out suddenly: 'Hell take the rest!
Six hard days of Creation are enough'—
And clasped her to him, meeting no rebuff.

Next day he rested, and she rested too.
The busy little lie between them flew:
'If this be not perfection,' Love would sigh,
'Perfection is a great, black, thumping lie. . . .'
Endearments, kisses, grunts, and whispered oaths;
But were her thoughts on breakfast, or on clothes?

THE NAKED AND THE NUDE

For me, the naked and the nude
(By lexicographers construed
As synonyms that should express
The same deficiency of dress
Or shelter) stand as wide apart
As love from lies, or truth from art.

Lovers without reproach will gaze
On bodies naked and ablaze;
The Hippocratic eye will see
In nakedness, anatomy;
And naked shines the Goddess when
She mounts her lion among men.

The nude are bold, the nude are sly
To hold each treasonable eye.
While draping by a showman's trick
Their dishabille in rhetoric,
They grin a mock-religious grin
Of scorn at those of naked skin.

The naked, therefore, who compete
Against the nude may know defeat;
Yet when they both together tread
The briary pastures of the dead,
By Gorgons with long whips pursued,
How naked go the sometime nude!

WOMAN AND TREE

To love one woman, or to sit
    Always beneath the same tall tree,
Argues a certain lack of wit
    Two steps from imbecility.

A poet, therefore, sworn to feed
   On every food the senses know,
Will claim the inexorable need
   To be Don Juan Tenorio.

Yet if, miraculously enough,
   (And why set miracles apart?)
Woman and tree prove of a stuff
   Wholly to glamour his wild heart?

And if such visions from the void
   As shone in fever there, or there,
Assemble, hold and are enjoyed
   On climbing one familiar stair . . . ?

To change and chance he took a vow,
   As he thought fitting. None the less,
What of a phoenix on the bough,
   Or a sole woman's fatefulness?

FORBIDDEN WORDS

There are some words carry a curse with them:
Smooth-trodden, abstract, slippery vocables.
They beckon like a path of stepping stones;
But lift them up and watch what writhes or scurries!

Concepts barred from the close language of love—
Darling, you use no single word of the list,
Unless ironically in truth's defence
To volley it back against the abstractionist.

Which is among your several holds on my heart;
For you are no uninstructed child of Nature,
But passed in schools and attained the laurel wreath:
Only to trample it on Apollo's floor.

A SLICE OF WEDDING CAKE

Why have such scores of lovely, gifted girls
    Married impossible men?
Simple self-sacrifice may be ruled out,
    And missionary endeavour, nine times out of ten.

Repeat 'impossible men': not merely rustic,
    Foul-tempered or depraved
(Dramatic foils chosen to show the world
    How well women behave, and always have behaved).

Impossible men: idle, illiterate,
    Self-pitying, dirty, sly,
For whose appearance even in City parks
    Excuses must be made to casual passers-by.

Has God's supply of tolerable husbands
    Fallen, in fact, so low?
Or do I always over-value woman
    At the expense of man?
                    Do I?
                        It might be so.

A PLEA TO BOYS AND GIRLS

You learned Lear's *Nonsense Rhymes* by heart, not rote;
    You learned Pope's *Iliad* by rote, not heart;
These terms should be distinguished if you quote
    My verse, children—keep them poles apart—
And call the man a liar who says I wrote
    All that I wrote in love, for love of art.

NOTHING

NOTHING is circular,
Like the empty centre
Of a smoke-ring's shadow:
That colourless zero
Marked on a bare wall—
Nothing at all
And reflected in a mirror.

Then need you wonder
If the trained philosopher
Who seeks to define NOTHING
As absence of anything,
A world more logistically
Than, above, I
(Though my terms are cosier),

And claims he has found
That NOTHING is not round
Or hardly ever,
Will run a brain-fever
To the precise degree
Of one hundred and three
On Fahrenheit's thermometer?

CALL IT A GOOD MARRIAGE

Call it a good marriage—
For no one ever questioned
Her warmth, his masculinity,
Their interlocking views;
Except one stray graphologist
Who frowned in speculation
At her h's and her s's,
His p's and w's.

Though few would still subscribe
To the monogramic axiom
That strife below the hip-bones
Need not estrange the heart,
Call it a good marriage:
More drew those two together,
Despite a lack of children,
Than pulled them apart.

Call it a good marriage:
They never fought in public,
They acted circumspectly
And faced the world with pride;
Thus the hazards of their love-bed
Were none of our damned business—
Till as jurymen we sat upon
Two deaths by suicide.

THE SECOND-FATED

My stutter, my cough, my unfinished sentences,
Denote an inveterate physical reluctance
To use the metaphysical idiom.
Forgive me: what I am saying is, perhaps this:—

Your accepted universe, by Jove's naked hand
Or Esmun's, or Odomankoma's, or Marduk's—
Choose which name jibes—formed scientifically
From whatever there was before Time was,
And begging the question of perfect consequence,
May satisfy the general run of men
(If 'run' be an apt term for patent paralytics)
That blueprints destine all they suffer here,
But does not satisfy certain few else.

Fortune enrolled me among the second-fated
Who have read their own obituaries in *The Times*,
Have heard 'Where, death, thy sting? Where, grave, thy victory.'
Intoned with unction over their still clay,
Have seen two parallel red-ink lines drawn
Under their manic-depressive bank accounts,
And are therefore strictly forbidden to walk in grave-yards
Lest they scandalise the sexton and his bride.

We, to be plain with you, taking advantage
Of a brief demise, visited first the Pit,
A library of shades, completed characters;
And next the silver-bright Hyperborean Queendom,
Basking under the sceptre of Guess Whom?
Where pure souls matrilineally foregather.

We were then shot through by merciful lunar shafts.
Until hearts tingled, heads sang, and praises flowed;
And learned to scorn your factitious universe
Ruled by the death which we had flouted;
Acknowledging only that from the Dove's egg hatched
Before aught was, but wind—unpredictable
As our second birth would be, or our second love:
A moon-warmed world of discontinuance.

THE TWIN OF SLEEP

Death is the twin of Sleep, they say:
    For I shall rise renewed,
Free from the cramps of yesterday,
    Clear-eyed and supple-thewed.

But though this bland analogy
    Helps other folk to face
Decrepitude, senility,
    Madness, disease, disgrace,

I do not like Death's greedy looks:
    Give me his twin instead—
Sleep never auctions off my books,
    My boots, my shirts, my bed.

AROUND THE MOUNTAIN

Some of you may know, others perhaps can guess
    How it is to walk all night through summer rain
(Thin rain that shrouds a beneficent full moon),
    To circle a mountain, and then limp home again.

The experience varies with a traveller's age
    And bodily strength, and strength of the love affair
That harries him out of doors in steady drizzle,
    With neither jacket nor hat, and holds him there.

Still, let us concede some common elements:
    Wild-fire that, until midnight, burns his feet;
And surging rankly up, strong on the palate,
    Scents of July, imprisoned by long heat.

Add: the sub-human, black tree-silhouettes
    Against a featureless pale pall of sky;
Unseen, gurgling water; the bulk and menace
    Of entranced houses; a wraith wandering by.

Milestones, each one witness of a new mood—
    Anger, desperation, grief, regret;
Her too-familiar face that whirls and totters
    In memory, never willing to stay set.

Whoever makes the desired turning-point,
    Which means another fifteen miles to go,
Learns more from dawn than love, so far, has taught him:
    Especially the false dawn, when cocks first crow.

Those last few miles are easy: being assured
    Of the truth, why should he fabricate fresh lies?
His house looms up; the eaves drip drowsily;
    The windows blaze to a resolute sunrise.

LEAVING THE REST UNSAID

Finis, apparent on an earlier page,
With fallen obelisk for colophon,
Must this be here repeated?

Death has been ruefully announced
And to die once is death enough,
Be sure, for any life-time.

Must the book end, as you would end it,
With testamentary appendices
And graveyard indices?

But no, I will not lay me down
To let your tearful music mar
The decent mystery of my progress.

So now, my solemn ones, leaving the rest unsaid,
Rising in air as on a gander's wing
At a careless comma,

XI

LYCEIA

All the wolves of the forest
Howl for Lyceia,
Crowding together
In a close circle,
Tongues a-loll.

A silver serpent
Coiled at her waist
And a quiver at knee,
She combs fine tresses
With a fine comb:

Wolf-like, woman-like,
Gazing about her,
Greeting the wolves;
Partial to many,
Yet masked in pride.

The young wolves snarl,
They snap at one another
Under the moon.
'Beasts, be reasonable,
My beauty is my own!'

Lyceia has a light foot
For a weaving walk.
Her archer muscles
Warn them how tightly
She can stretch the string.

I question Lyceia,
Whom I find posted
Under the pine trees
One early morning:
'What do the wolves learn?'

'They learn only envy,'
Lyceia answers,
'Envy and hope.
Hope and chagrin.
Would you howl too
In that wolfish circle?'
She laughs as she speaks.

SYMPTOMS OF LOVE

Love is a universal migraine,
A bright stain on the vision
Blotting out reason.

Symptoms of true love
Are leanness, jealousy,
Laggard dawns;

Are omens and nightmares—
Listening for a knock,
Waiting for a sign:

For a touch of her fingers
In a darkened room,
For a searching look.

Take courage, lover!
Could you endure such grief
At any hand but hers?

THE SHARP RIDGE

Since now I dare not ask
Any gift from you, or gentle task,
Or lover's promise—nor yet refuse
Whatever I can give and you dare choose—
Have pity on us both: choose well
On this sharp ridge dividing death from hell.

UNDER THE OLIVES

We never would have loved had love not struck
Swifter than reason, and despite reason:
Under the olives, our hands interlocked,
We both fell silent:
Each listened for the other's answering
Sigh of unreasonableness—
Innocent, gentle, bold, enduring, proud.

THE VISITATION

Drowsing in my chair of disbelief
I watch the door as it slowly opens—
A trick of the night wind?

Your slender body seems a shaft of moonlight
Against the door as it gently closes.
Do you cast no shadow?

Your whisper is too soft for credence,
Your tread like blossom drifting from a bough,
Your touch even softer.

You wear that sorrowful and tender mask
Which on high mountain tops in heather-flow
Entrances lonely shepherds;

And though a single word scatters all doubts
I quake for wonder at your choice of me:
Why, why and why?

FRAGMENT

Are you shaken, are you stirred
By a whisper of love?
Spell-bound to a word
Does Time cease to move,
Till her calm grey eye
Expands to a sky
And the clouds of her hair
Like storms go by?

APPLE ISLAND

Though cruel seas like mountains fill the bay,
Wrecking the quayside huts,
Salting our vineyards with tall showers of spray;

And though the moon shines dangerously clear,
Fixed in another cycle
Than the sun's progress round the felloe'd year;

And though I may not hope to dwell apart
With you on Apple Island
Unless my breast be docile to the dart—

Why should I fear your element, the sea,
Or the full moon, your mirror,
Or the halved apple from your holy tree?

THE FALCON WOMAN

It is hard to be a man
Whose word is his bond
In love with such a woman,

When he builds on a promise
She lightly let fall
In carelessness of spirit.

The more sternly he asks her
To stand by that promise
The faster she flies.

But is it less hard
To be born such a woman
With wings like a falcon
And in carelessness of spirit
To love such a man?

TROUGHS OF SEA

'Do you delude yourself?' a neighbour asks,
Dismayed by my abstraction.
But though love cannot question love
Nor need deny its need,

Pity the man who finds a rebel heart
Under his breastbone drumming
Which reason warns him he should drown
In midnight wastes of sea.

Now as he stalks between tormented pines
(The moon in her last quarter)
A lissom spectre glides ahead
And utters not a word.

Waves tasselled with dark weed come rearing up
Like castle walls, disclosing
Deep in their troughs a ribbed sea-floor
To break his bones upon.

—Clasp both your hands under my naked foot
And press hard, as I taught you:
A trick to mitigate the pangs
Either of birth or love.

THE LAUGH

Your sudden laugh restored felicity—
Everything grew clear that before would not:
The impossible genies, the extravagants,
Swung in to establish themselves fairly
As at last manageable elements
In a most daylight-simple plot.
It was the identity of opposites
Had so confused my all too sober wits.

THE DEATH GRAPPLE

Lying between your sheets, I challenge
A watersnake in a swoln cataract
Or a starved lioness among drifts of snow.

Yet dare it out, for after each death grapple,
Each gorgon stare borrowed from very hate,
A childish innocent smile touches your lips,
Your eyelids droop, fearless and careless,
And sleep remoulds the lineaments of love.

154

THE STARRED COVERLET

A difficult achievement for true lovers
Is to lie mute, without embrace or kiss,
Without a rustle or a smothered sigh,
Basking each in the other's glory.

Let us not undervalue lips or arms
As reassurances of constancy,
Or speech as necessary communication
When troubled hearts go groping through the dusk;

Yet lovers who have learned this last refinement—
To lie apart, yet sleep and dream together
Motionless under their starred coverlet—
Crown love with wreaths of myrtle.

PATIENCE

Almost I could prefer
A flare of anger
To your dumb signal of displeasure.

Must it be my task
To assume the mask
Of not desiring what I may not ask?

On a wide bed,
Both arms outspread,
I watch the spites do battle in my head,

Yet know this sickness
For stubborn weakness
Unconsonant with your tenderness.

O, to be patient
As you would have me patient:
Patient for a thousand nights, patient!

THE CURE

No lover ever found a cure for love
Except so cruel a thrust under the heart
(By her own hand delivered)
His wound was nine long years in healing,
Purulent with dead hope,
And ached yet longer at the moon's changes . . .
More tolerable the infection than its cure.

HAG-RIDDEN

I awoke in profuse sweat, arms aching,
Knees bruised and soles cut to the raw—
Preserved no memory of that night
But whipcracks and my own voice screaming.
Through what wild, flinty wastes of fury,
Hag of the Mill,
Did you ride your madman?

TURN OF THE MOON

Never forget who brings the rain
In swarthy goatskin bags from a far sea:
It is the Moon as she turns, repairing
Damages of long drought and sunstroke.

Never count upon rain, never foretell it,
For no power can bring rain
Except the Moon as she turns; and who can rule her?

She is prone to delay the necessary floods,
Lest such a gift might become obligation,
A month, or two, or three; then suddenly
Not relenting but by way of whim
Will perhaps conjure from the cloudless west
A single rain-drop to surprise with hope
Each haggard, upturned face.

Were the Moon a Sun, we would count upon her
To bring rain seasonably as she turned;
Yet no one thinks to thank the regular Sun
For shining fierce in summer, mild in winter—
Why should the Moon so drudge?

But if one night she brings us, as she turns,
Soft, steady, even, copious rain
That harms no leaf nor flower, but gently falls
Hour after hour, sinking to the tap roots,
And the sodden earth exhales at dawn
A long sigh scented with pure gratitude,
Such rain—the first rain of our lives, it seems,
Neither foretold, cajoled, nor counted on—
Is woman giving as she loves.

THE SECRET LAND

Every woman of true royalty owns
A secret land more real to her
Than this pale outer world:

At midnight when the house falls quiet
She lays aside needle or book
And visits it unseen.

Shutting her eyes, she improvises
A five-barred gate among tall birches,
Vaults over, takes possession.

Then runs, or flies, or mounts a horse
(A horse will canter up to greet her)
And travels where she will;

Can make grass grow, coax lilies up
From bud to blossom as she watches,
Lets fish eat from her palm.

Has founded villages, planted groves
And hallowed valleys for brooks running
Cool to a land-locked bay.

I never dared question my love
About the government of her queendom
Or its geography,

Nor followed her between those birches,
Setting one leg astride the gate,
Spying into the mist.

Yet she has pledged me, when I die,
A lodge beneath her private palace
In a level clearing of the wood
Where gentians grow and gillyflowers
And sometimes we may meet.

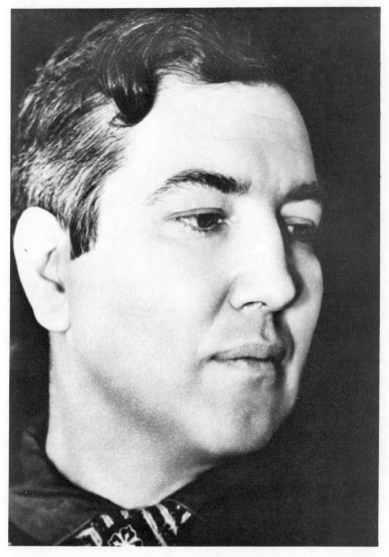

Robert Graves, 1939.

opposite: Graves in the doorway of his house in Majorca.
(The Granger Collection)

below: Graves at work in Majorca. (The Granger Collection)

Graves at his home in Majorca. (New York *Times*)

SELDOM YET NOW

Seldom yet now: the quality
Of this fierce love between us—
Seldom the encounter,
The presence always,
Free of oath or promise.

And if we were not so
But birds of similar plumage caged
In the peace of every day,
Would we still conjure wildfire up
From common earth, as now?

XII

A LOST WORLD

'Dear love, why should you weep
 For time's remorseless way?
Though today die in sleep
 And be called yesterday,
 We love, we stay.'

'I weep for days that died
 With former love that shone
On a world true and wide
 Before this newer one
 Which yours shines on.'

'Is this world not as true
 As that one ever was
Which now has fled from you
 Like shadows from the grass
 When the clouds pass?'

'Yet for that would I weep
 Kindly, before we kiss:
Love has a faith to keep
 With past felicities
 That weep for this.'

THE DANGEROUS GIFT

Were I to cut my hand
    On that sharp knife you gave me
    (That dangerous knife, your beauty),
I should know what to do:
    Bandage the wound myself
And hide the blood from you.

A murderous knife it is,
    As often you have warned me:
    For if I looked for pity
Or tried a wheedling note
    Either I must restore it
Or turn it on my throat.

TWICE OF THE SAME FEVER

No one can die twice of the same fever?
    Tell them it is untrue:
Have we not died three deaths, and three again,
    You of me, I of you?

The chill, the frantic pulse, brows burning,
    Lips broken by thirst—
Until, in darkness, a ghost grieves:
    'It was I died the first.'

Worse than such death, even, is resurrection.
    Do we dare laugh away
Disaster, and with a callous madrigal
    Salute the new day?

SURGICAL WARD: MEN

Something occurred after the operation
To scare the surgeons (though no fault of theirs),
Whose reassurance did not fool me long.
Beyond the shy, concerned faces of nurses
A single white-hot eye, focusing on me,
Forced sweat in rivers down from scalp to belly.
I whistled, gasped or sang, with blanching knuckles
Clutched at my bed-grip almost till it cracked:
Too proud, still, to let loose Bedlamite screeches
And bring the charge-nurse scuttling down the aisle
With morphia-needle levelled. . . .
                                        Lady Morphia—
Her scorpion kiss and dark gyrating dreams—
She in mistrust of whom I dared out-dare,
Two minutes longer than seemed possible,
Pain, that unpurposed, matchless elemental
Stronger than fear or grief, stranger than love.

THE TWO WITCHES

O sixteen hundred and ninety-one,
Never was year so well begun,
Backsy-forsy and inside out,
The best of years to ballad about.

On the first fine day of January
I ran to my sweetheart Margery
And tossed her over the roof so far
That down she fell like a shooting star.

But when we two had frolicked and kissed
She clapped her fingers about my wrist
And tossed me over the chimney stack,
And danced on me till my bones did crack.

Then, when she had laboured to ease my pain,
We sat by the stile of Robin's Lane,
She in a hare and I in a toad
And puffed at the clouds till merry they glowed.

We spelled our loves until close of day.
I wished her good-night and walked away,
But she put out a tongue that was long and red
And swallowed me down like a crumb of bread.

THE QUIET GLADES OF EDEN

All such proclivities are tabulated—
By trained pathologists, in detail too—
The obscener parts of speech compulsively
Shrouded in Classic Latin.

But though my pleasure in your feet and hair
Is ungainsayable, let me protest
(Dear love) I am no trichomaniac
And no foot-fetichist.

If it should please you, for your own best reasons,
To take and flog me with a rawhide whip,
I might (who knows?) surprisedly accept
This earnest of affection.

Nothing, agreed, is alien to love
When pure desire has overflowed its baulks;
But why must private sportiveness be viewed
Through public spectacles?

Enough, I will not claim a heart unfluttered
By these case-histories of aberrancy;
Nevertheless a long cool draught of water,
Or a long swim in the bay,

Serves to restore my wholesome appetite
For you and what we do at night together:
Which is no more than Adam did with Eve
In the quiet glades of Eden.

JOAN AND DARBY

My friends are those who find agreement with me
In large measure, but not absolutely.
Little children, parasites and God
May flatter me with absolute agreement—
For no one lives more cynical than God.

As for my love, I gifted my heart to her
Twenty years ago, without proviso,
And in return she gifted hers to me;
Yet still they beat as two, unyielding in
Their honest, first reluctance to agree.

Other seasons, other thoughts and reasons,
Other fears or phases of the moon:
In loving-kindness we grow grey together—
Like Joan and Darby in their weather-lodge
Who never venture out in the same weather.

SONG: COME, ENJOY YOUR SUNDAY!

Into your outstretched hands come pouring
Gifts by the cornucopiaful—
    What else is lacking?
Come, enjoy your Sunday
While yet you may!

Cease from unnecessary labours,
Saunter into the green world stretching far,
     Light a long cigar,
Come, enjoy your Sunday
While yet you may!

What more, what more? You fended off disaster
In a long war, never acknowledging
     Any man as master;
Come, enjoy your Sunday
While yet you may!

Are you afraid of death? But death is nothing:
The leaden seal set on a filled flask.
     If it be life you ask,
Come, enjoy your Sunday
While yet you may!

On a warm sand dune now, sprawling at ease
With little in mind, learn to despise the sea's
     Unhuman restlessness:
Come, enjoy your Sunday
While yet you may!

XIII

RUBY AND AMETHYST

Two women: one as good as bread,
    Bound to a sturdy husband.
Two women: one as rare as myrrh,
    Bound only to herself.

Two women: one as good as bread,
    Faithful to every promise.
Two women: one as rare as myrrh,
    Who never pledges faith.

The one a flawless ruby wears
    But with such innocent pleasure
A stranger's eye might think it glass
    And take no closer look.

Two women: one as good as bread,
    The noblest of the city.
Two women: one as rare as myrrh,
    Who needs no public praise.

The pale rose-amethyst on her breast
    Has such a garden in it
Your eye could trespass there for hours,
    And wonder, and be lost.

About her head a swallow wheels
    Nor ever breaks the circuit:
Glory and awe of womanhood
    Still undeclared to man.

Two women: one as good as bread,
    Resistant to all weathers.
Two women: one as rare as myrrh,
    Her weather still her own.

RECOGNITION

When on the cliffs we met, by chance,
    I startled at your quiet voice
And watched the swallows round you dance
    Like children that had made a choice.

Simple it was, as I stood there,
    To penetrate the mask you wore,
Your secret lineage to declare
    And your lost dignities restore.

Yet thus I earned a poet's fee
    So far out-distancing desire
That swallows yell in rage at me
    As who would set their world on fire.

VARIABLES OF GREEN

Grass-green and aspen-green,
Laurel-green and sea-green,
Fine-emerald-green,
And many another hue:
As green commands the variables of green
So love my loves of you.

THE WATCH

Since the night in which you stole
    Like a phantom to my bed,
Seized my throat and from it wrung
    Vows that could not be unsaid,

Here beneath my arching ribs
    Red-hot embers, primed to be
Blown upon by winds of love,
    Scorch away mortality.

Like sledgehammers my two fists,
    My broad forehead grim with pride,
Muscles corded on my calves
    And my frame gigantified.

Yet your watching for an hour
    That our mutual stars will bless
Proves you more entranced than I
    Who go parched in hope of less.

NAME DAY

Tears of delight that on my name-day
She gave me nothing, and in return
Accepted every gift I heaped upon her—
Call me the richest poet alive!

UNCALENDARED LOVE

The first name cut on a rock, a King's,
Marked the beginning of time's annals;
And each new year would recapitulate
The unkind sloughings and renewals
Of the death-serpent's chequered coat.

But you with me together, together, together,
Survive ordeals never before endured:
We snatch the quill out of Enoch's hand
To obliterate our names from his black scroll—
Twin absentees of time.

Ours is uncalendared love, whole life,
As long or brief as befalls. Alone, together,
Recalling little, prophesying less,
We watch the serpent, crushed by your bare heel,
Rainbow his scales in a deathward agony.

THE MEETING

We, two elementals, woman and man,
Approached each other from far away:
I on the lower wind, she on the upper.

And the faith with which we came invested
By the blind thousands of our twin worlds
Formed thunder clouds about us.

Never such uproar as when we met,
Nor such forked lightning; rain in a cataract
Tumbled on deserts dry these thousand years.

What of the meteorologists?
They said nothing, turned their faces away,
Let the event pass unrecorded.

And what of us? We also said nothing.
Is it not the height of silent humour
To cause an unknown change in the earth's climate?

LACK

Born from ignoble stock on a day of dearth
He tramps the roads, trailing his withered branch,
And grudges every beauty of the wide earth.

Lack is his name, and although in gentleness
You set him honourably at the high table
And load his plate with luxury of excess,

Crying: 'Eat well, brother, and drink your fill,'
Yet with hunger whetted only, he boasts aloud:
'I have never begged a favour, nor ever will!'

His clothes are sad, but a burly wretch is he,
Of lustreless look, slack mouth, a borrowed wit,
And a sigh that would charm the song-bird from her tree.

Now he casts his eye in greed upon your demesne
With open mockery of a heart so open
It dares this gallows-climber to entertain.

NOT AT HOME

Her house loomed at the end of a Berkshire lane,
Tall but retired. She was expecting me;
And I approached with light heart and quick tread,
Having already seen from the garden gate
How bright her knocker shone—in readiness
For my confident rap?—and the steps holystoned.
I ran the last few paces, rapped and listened
Intently for the rustle of her approach. . . .

No reply, no movement. I waited three long minutes,
Then, in surprise, went down the path again
To observe the chimney stacks. No smoke from either.
And the curtains: were they drawn against the sun?
Or against what, then? I glanced over a wall
At her well-tended orchard, heavy with bloom
(Easter fell late that year, Spring had come early),
And found the gardener, bent over cold frames.

'Her ladyship is not at home?'
                              'No, sir.'
'She was expecting me. My name is Lion.
Did she leave a note?'
                      'No, sir, she left no note.'
'I trust nothing has happened. . . ?'
                                      'No, sir, nothing. . . .
And yet she seemed preoccupied: we guess
Some family reason.'
                    '*Has* she a family?'
'That, sir, I could not say. . . . She seemed distressed—
Not quite herself, if I may venture so.'
'But she left no note?'
                        'Only a verbal message:
Her ladyship will be away some weeks
Or months, hopes to return before midsummer,
And, please, you are not to communicate.
There was something else: about the need for patience.'

The sun went in, a bleak wind shook the blossom,
Dust flew, the windows glared in a blank row. . . .
And yet I felt, when I turned slowly away,
Her eyes boring my back, as it might be posted
Behind a curtain slit, and still in love.

HORIZON

On a clear day how thin the horizon
Drawn between sea and sky,
Between sea-love and sky-love;
And after sunset how debatable
Even for an honest eye.

'Do as you will tonight,'
Said she, and so he did
By moonlight, candlelight,
Candlelight and moonlight,
While pillowed clouds the horizon hid.

Knowing-not-knowing that such deeds must end
In a curse which lovers long past weeping for
Had heaped upon him: she would be gone one night
With his familiar friend.
Granting him leave her beauty to explore
By moonlight, candlelight,
Candlelight and moonlight.

GOLDEN ANCHOR

Gone: and to an undisclosed region,
Free as the wind, if less predictable.
Why should I grieve, who have no claim on her?
My ring circles her finger, from her neck
Dangles my powerful jade. All is not lost
While still she wears those evident tokens
And no debts lie between us except love.

Or does the golden anchor plague her
As a drag on woman's liberty? Longing
To cut the cable, run grandly adrift,
Is she warned by a voice what wide misfortune
Ripples from ill faith?—therefore temporizes
And fears to use the axe, although consorting
With lovelessness and evil?

What should I say or do? It was she chose me,
Not contrariwise. Moreover, if I lavished
Extravagant praise on her, she deserved all.
I have been honest in love, as is my nature;
She secret, as is hers. I cannot grieve
Unless for having vexed her by unmasking
A jewelled virtue she was loth to use.

LION LOVER

You chose a lion to be your lover—
Me, who in joy such doom greeting
Dared jealously undertake
Cruel ordeals long foreseen and known,
Springing a trap baited with flesh: my own.

Nor would I now exchange this lion heart
For a less furious other,
Though by the Moon possessed
I gnaw at dry bones in a lost lair
And, when clouds cover her, roar my despair.

Gratitude and affection I disdain
As cheap in any market:
Your naked feet upon my scarred shoulders,
Your eyes naked with love,
Are all the gifts my beasthood can approve.

IBYCUS IN SAMOS

The women of Samos are lost in love for me:
Nag at their men, neglect their looms,
And send me secret missives, to my sorrow.

I am the poet Ibycus, known by the cranes,
Each slender Samian offers herself moon-blanched
As my only bride, my heart's belovèd;

And when I return a calm salute, no more,
Or a brotherly kiss, will heap curses upon me:
Do I despise her warm myrrh-scented bosom?

She whom I honour has turned her face away
A whole year now, and in pride more than royal
Lacerates my heart and hers as one.

Wherever I wander in this day-long fever,
Sprigs of the olive-trees are touched with fire
And stones twinkle along my devious path.

Who here can blame me if I alone am poet,
If none other has dared to accept the fate
Of death and again death in the Muse's house?

Or who can blame me if my hair crackles
Like thorns under a pot, if my eyes flash
As it were sheets of summer lightning?

POSSESSED

To be possessed by her is to possess—
Though rooted in this thought
Build nothing on it.

Unreasonable faith becomes you
And mute endurance
Even of betrayal.

Never expect to be brought wholly
Into her confidence.
Being natural woman

She knows what she must do, not why;
Balks your anticipation
Of pleasure vowed;

Yet, no less vulnerable than you,
Suffers the dire pangs
Of your self-defeat.

THE WINGED HEART

Trying to read the news, after your visit,
When the words made little sense, I let them go;
And found my heart suddenly sprouting feathers.

Alone in the house, and the full honest rain
After a devil's own four-day sirocco
Still driving down in sheets across the valley—

How it hissed, how the leaves of the olives shook!
We had suffered drought since earliest April;
Here we were already in October.

I have nothing more to tell you. What has been said
Can never possibly be retracted now
Without denial of the large universe.

Some curse has fallen between us, a dead hand,
An inhalation of evil sucking up virtue:
Which left us no recourse, unless we turned

Improvident as at our first encounter,
Deriding practical care of how or where:
Your certitude must be my certitude.

And the tranquil blaze of sky etherializing
The circle of rocks and our own rain-wet faces,
Was that not worth a lifetime of pure grief?

IN TRANCE AT A DISTANCE

It is easy, often, and natural even,
To commune with her in trance at a distance;
To attest those deep confessionary sighs
Otherwise so seldom heard from her;
To be assured by a single shudder
Wracking both hearts, and underneath the press
Of clothes by a common nakedness.

Hold fast to the memory, lest a cold fear
Of never again here, of nothing good coming,
Should lure you into self-delusive trade
With demonesses who dare masquerade
As herself in your dreams, and who after a while
Skilfully imitate her dancing gait,
Borrow her voice and vocables and smile.

It is no longer—was it ever?—in your power
To catch her close to you at any hour:
She has raised a wall of nothingness in between
(Were it something known and seen, to be torn apart,
You could grind its heartless fragments into the ground);
Yet, taken in trance, would she still deny
That you are hers, she yours, till both shall die?

THE WREATH

A bitter year it was. What woman ever
Cared for me so, yet so ill-used me,
Came in so close and drew so far away,
So much promised and performed so little,
So murderously her own love dared betray?
Since I can never be clear out of your debt,
Queen of ingratitude, to my dying day,
You shall be punished with a deathless crown
For your dark head, resist it how you may.

IN HER PRAISE

This they know well: the Goddess yet abides.
Though each new lovely woman whom she rides,
Straddling her neck a year or two or three,
Should sink beneath such weight of majesty
And, groping back to humankind, gainsay
The headlong power that whitened all her way
With a broad track of trefoil—leaving you,
Her chosen lover, ever again thrust through
With daggers, your purse rifled, your rings gone—
Nevertheless they call you to live on
To parley with the pure, oracular dead,
To hear the wild pack whimpering overhead,
To watch the moon tugging at her cold tides.
Woman is mortal woman. She abides.

A RESTLESS GHOST

Alas for obstinate doubt: the dread
Of error in supposing my heart freed,
All care for her stone dead!
Ineffably will shine the hills and radiant coast
Of early morning when she is gone indeed,
Her divine elements disbanded, disembodied
And through the misty orchards in love spread—
When she is gone indeed—
But still among them moves her restless ghost.

BETWEEN MOON AND MOON

In the last sad watches of night
Hardly a sliver of light will remain
To edge the guilty shadow of a waned moon
That dawn must soon devour.
                              Thereafter, another
Crescent queen shall arise with power—
So wise a beauty never yet seen, say I:
A true creature of moon, though not the same
In nature, name or feature—
Her innocent eye rebuking inconstancy
As if Time itself should die and disappear.

So was it ever. She is here again, I sigh.

XIV

BEWARE, MADAM!

Beware, madam, of the witty devil,
The arch intriguer who walks disguised
In a poet's cloak, his gay tongue oozing evil.

Would you be a Muse? He will so declare you,
Pledging his blind allegiance,
Yet remain secret and uncommitted.

Poets are men: are single-hearted lovers
Who adore and trust beyond all reason,
Who die honourably at the gates of hell.

The Muse alone is licensed to do murder
And to betray: weeping with honest tears
She thrones each victim in her paradise.

But from this Muse the devil borrows an art
That ill becomes a man. Beware, madam:
He plots to strip you bare of woman-pride.

He is capable of seducing your twin-sister
On the same pillow, and neither she nor you
Will suspect the act, so close a glamour he sheds.

Alas, being honourably single-hearted,
You adore and trust beyond all reason,
Being no more a Muse than he a poet.

THE CLIFF EDGE

Violence threatens you no longer:
It was your innocent temerity
Caused us to tremble: veterans discharged
From the dirty wars of life.

Forgive us this presumption: we are abashed—
As when a child, straying on the cliff's edge,
Turns about to ask her white-faced brothers:
'Do you take me for a child?'

THE MILLER'S MAN

The imperturbable miller's man
Whose help the boy implored, drowning,
Drifting slowly past the mill,
Was a stout swimmer, yet would not come between
The river-god and his assured victim.

Soon he, too, swimming in the sun,
Is caught with cramp: and the boy's ghost
Jeers from the reeds and rushes.
But he drowns valiantly in silence,
This being no one's business but his own.

Let us not reckon the miller's man
With Judas or with Jesus,
But with the cattle, who endure all weathers,
Or with the mill-wheel foolishly creaking,
Incurious of the grain in the bins.

ACROBATS

Poised impossibly on the high tight-rope
    Of love, in spite of all,
They still preserve their dizzying balance
And smile this way or that,
    As though uncertain on which side to fall.

OUZO UNCLOUDED

Here is ouzo (she said) to try you:
Better not drowned in water,
Better not chilled with ice,
Not sipped at thoughtfully,
Nor toped in secret.
Drink it down (she said) unclouded
At a blow, this tall glass full,
But keep your eyes on mine
Like a true Arcadian acorn-eater.

THE BROKEN GIRTH

Bravely from Fairyland he rode, on furlough,
Astride a tall bay given him by the Queen
From whose couch he had leaped not a half-hour since,
Whose lilies-of-the-valley shone from his helm.

But alas, as he paused to assist five Ulstermen
Sweating to raise a recumbent Ogham pillar,
Breach of a saddle-girth tumbled Oisín
To common Irish earth. And at once, it is said,
Old age came on him with grief and frailty.

St Patrick asked: would he not confess the Christ?—
Which for that Lady's sake he loathed to do,
But northward loyally turned his eyes in death.
It was Fenians bore the unshriven corpse away
For burial, keening.
                         Curse me all squint-eyed monks
Who misconstrue the passing of Finn's son:
Old age, not Fairyland, was his delusion.

INKIDOO AND THE QUEEN OF BABEL

When I was a callant, born far hence,
You first laid hand on my innocence,
But sent your champion into a boar
That my fair young body a-pieces tore.

When I was a lapwing, crowned with gold,
Your lust and liking for me you told,
But plucked my feathers and broke my wing—
Wherefore all summer for grief I sing.

When I was a lion of tawny fell,
You stroked my mane and you combed it well,
But pitfalls seven you dug for me
That from one or other I might not flee.

When I was a courser, proud and strong,
That like the wind would wallop along,
You bated my pride with spur and bit
And many a rod on my shoulder split.

When I was a shepherd that for your sake
The bread of love at my hearth would bake,
A ravening wolf did you make of me
To be thrust from home by my brothers three.

When I tended your father's orchard close
I brought you plum, pear, apple, and rose,
But my lusty manhood away you stole
And changed me into a grovelling mole.

When I was simple, when I was fond,
Thrice and thrice did you wave your wand,
But now you vow to be leal and true
And softly ask, will I wed with you?

THREE SONGS FOR THE LUTE

I

Truth Is Poor Physic

A wild beast falling sick
Will find his own best physic—
    Herb, berry, root of tree
Or wholesome salt to lick—
    And so run free.

But this I know at least
Better than a wild beast:
    That should I fall love-sick
And the wind veer to East,
    Truth is poor physic.

II

In Her Only Way

When her need for you dies
    And she wanders apart,
Never rhetoricize
    On the faithless heart,

But with manlier virtue
    Be content to say
She both loved you and hurt you
    In her only way.

III

Hedges Freaked with Snow

No argument, no anger, no remorse,
    No dividing of blame.
There was poison in the cup—why should we ask
    From whose hand it came?

No grief for our dead love, no howling gales
    That through darkness blow,
But the smile of sorrow, a wan winter landscape,
    Hedges freaked with snow.

THE AMBROSIA OF DIONYSUS AND SEMELE

Little slender lad, toad-headed,
For whom ages and leagues are dice to throw with,
Smile back to where entranced I wander
Gorged with your bitter flesh,
Drunk with your Virgin Mother's lullaby.

Little slender lad, lightning engendered,
Grand master of magicians:
When pirates stole you at Icaria
Wild ivy gripped their rigging, every oar
Changed to a serpent, panthers held the poop,
A giant vine sprouted from the mast crotch
And overboard they plunged, the whey-faced crew!

Lead us with your song, tall Queen of earth!
Twinned to the god, I follow comradely
Through a first rainbow-limbo, webbed in white,
Through chill Tyrrhenian grottoes, under water,
Where dolphins wallow between marble rocks,
Through sword-bright jungles, tangles of unease,
Through halls of fear ceilinged with incubi,
Through blazing treasure-chambers walled with garnet,
Through domes pillared with naked Caryatids—
Then mount at last on wings into pure air,
Peering down with regal eye upon
Five-fruited orchards of Elysium,
In perfect knowledge of all knowledges.

And still she drowsily chants
From her invisible bower of stars.
Gentle her voice, her notes come linked together
In intricate golden chains paid out
Slowly across brocaded cramoisy,
Or unfold like leaves from the jade-green shoot
Of a rising bush whose blossoms are her tears. . . .
O, whenever she pauses, my heart quails
Until the sound renews.

Little slender lad, little secret god,
Pledge her your faith in me,
Who have ambrosia eaten and yet live.

THE UNNAMED SPELL

Let us never name that royal certitude,
That simultaneous recognition
When first we stood together,

When I saw you as a child astonished,
Years before, under tall trees
By a marching sound of wind:

Your heart sown with a headlong wisdom
Which every grief or joy thereafter
Rooted still more strongly.

Naming is treacherous, names divide
Truth into lesser truths, enclosing them
In a coffin of counters—

Give the spell no name, liken it only
To the more than tree luxuriating
Seven ells above earth:

All heal, golden surprise of a kiss,
Wakeful glory while the grove winters,
A branch Hell-harrowing,

Of no discoverable parentage,
Strangeling scion of varied stocks
Yet true to its own leaf,

Secret of secrets disclosed only
To who already share it,
Who themselves sometimes raised an arch—
Pillared with honour; its lintel, love—
And passed silently through.

XV

A TIME OF WAITING

The moment comes when my sound senses
Warn me to keep the pot at a quiet simmer,
Conclude no rash decisions, enter into
No random friendships, check the runaway tongue
And fix my mind in a close caul of doubt—
Which is more difficult, maybe, than to face
Night-long assaults of lurking furies.

The pool lies almost empty; I watch it nursed
By a thin stream. Such idle intervals
Are from waning moon to the new—a moon always
Holds the cords of my heart. Then patience, hands;
Dabble your nerveless fingers in the shallows;
A time shall come when she has need of them.

EXPECT NOTHING

Give, ask for nothing, hope for nothing,
Subsist on crumbs, though scattered casually
Not for you (she smiles) but for the birds.
Though only a thief's diet, it staves off
Dire starvation, nor does she grow fat
On the bread she crumbles, while the lonely truth
Of love is honoured, and her word pledged.

NO LETTER

Be angry yourself, as well you may,
But why with her? She is no party to
Those avaricious dreams that pester you.
Why knot your fists as though plotting to slay
Even our postman George (whose only due
Is a small Christmas box on Christmas Day)
If his delivery does not raise the curse
Of doubt from your impoverished universe?

THE WHY OF THE WEATHER

Since no one knows the why of the weather
Or can authoritatively forecast
More than twelve hours of day or night, at most,
Every poor fool is licensed to explain it
As Heaven's considered judgement on mankind,
And I to account for its vagaries, Myrto,
By inklings of your unaccountable mind.

IN TIME

In time all undertakings are made good,
All cruelties remedied,
Each bond resealed more firmly than before—
Befriend us, Time, Love's gaunt executor!

FIRE WALKER

To be near her is to be near the furnace.
Fortunate boy who could slip idly through,
Basket in hand, culling the red-gold blossom,
Then wander on, untaught that flowers were flame,
With no least smell of scorching on his clothes!
I, at a greater distance, charred to coal,
Earn her reproach for my temerity.

DEED OF GIFT

After close, unembittered meditation
    She gave herself to herself, this time for good;
    Body and heart re-echoed gratitude
For such a merciful repudiation
    Of debts claimed from them by the neighbourhood—

Not only friends, and friends of friends, but lovers
    Whom in the circumstances few could blame
    (Her beauty having singed them like a flame)
If they had hoarded under legal covers
    Old promissory notes signed with her name.

And though to stand once more on the firm road
    From which by misadventure she had strayed,
    So that her journey was that much delayed,
Justified the default of duties owed,
    What debt of true love did she leave unpaid?

AT BEST, POETS

Woman with her forests, moons, flowers, waters,
And watchful fingers:
We claim no magic comparable to hers—
At best, poets; at worst, sorcerers.

SHE IS NO LIAR

She is no liar, yet she will wash away
Honey from her lips, blood from her shadowy hand,
And, dressed at dawn in clean white robes will say,
Trusting the ignorant world to understand:
'Such things no longer are; this is today.'

A LAST POEM

A last poem, and a very last, and yet another—
O, when can I give over?
Must I drive the pen until blood bursts from my nails
And my breath fails and I shake with fever,
Or sit well wrapped in a many-coloured cloak
Where the moon shines new through Castle Crystal?
Shall I never hear her whisper softly:
'But this is truth written by you only,
And for me only; therefore, love, have done'?

THE PEARL

When, wounded by her anger at some trifle,
I imitate the oyster, rounding out
A ball of nacre about the intrusive grit,
Why should she charge me with perversity
As one rejoicing in his own torn guts
Or in the lucent pearl resultant
Which she disdainfully strings for her neck?
Such anger I admire; but could she swear
That I am otherwise incorrigible?

THE LEAP

Forget the rest: my heart is true
And in its waking thought of you
Gives the same wild and sudden leap
That jerks it from the brink of sleep.

BANK ACCOUNT

Never again remind me of it:
There are no debts between us.
Though silences, half-promises, evasions
Curb my impatient spirit
And freeze the regular currency of love,
They do not weaken credit. Must I demand
Sworn attestations of collateral,
Forgetting how you looked when first you opened
Our joint account at the Bank of Fate?

JUDGEMENT OF PARIS

What if Prince Paris, after taking thought,
Had not adjudged the apple to Aphrodite
But, instead, had favoured buxom Hera,
Divine defendress of the marriage couch?
What if Queen Helen had been left to squander
Her beauty upon the thralls of Menelaus,
Hector to die unhonoured in his bed,
Penthesileia to hunt a poorer quarry,
The bards to celebrate a meaner siege?
Could we still have found the courage, you and I,
To embark together for Cranaë
And consummate our no less fateful love?

MAN DOES, WOMAN IS

Studiously by lamp-light I appraised
The palm of your hand, its heart-line
Identical with its head-line;
And you appraised the approving frown.

I spread my cards face-upwards on the table,
Not challenging you for yours.
Man does; but woman is—
Can a gamester argue with his luck?

THE AMPLE GARDEN

However artfully you transformed yourself
Into bitch, vixen, tigress,
I knew the woman behind.

Light as a bird now, you descend at dawn
From the poplar bough or ivy bunch
To peck my strawberries,

And have need indeed of an ample garden:
All my fruits, fountains, arbours, lawns
In fief to your glory.

You, most unmetaphorically you:
Call me a Catholic, so devout in faith
I joke of love, as Catholics do of God,
And scorn all exegesis.

TO MYRTO ABOUT HERSELF

Fierce though your love of her may be,
	What man alive can doubt
I love her more? Come now, agree
Not to turn rivalrous of me,
	Lest you and I fall out!

And should her law make little sense
	Even at times to you,
Love has its own sure recompense:
To love beyond all reason—hence
	Her fondness for us two.

What she pursues we neither know
	Nor can we well inquire;
But if you carelessly bestow
A look on me she did not owe
	It comes at her desire.

THE THREE-FACED

Who calls her two-faced? Faces, she has three:
The first inscrutable, for the outer world;
The second shrouded in self-contemplation;
The third, her face of love,
Once for an endless moment turned on me.

DAZZLE OF DARKNESS

The flame guttered, flared impossibly high,
Went out for good; yet in the dazzle of darkness
I saw her face ashine like an angel's:
Beauty too memorable for lamentation,
Though doomed to rat and maggot.

MYRRHINA

O, why judge Myrrhina
As though she were a man?
She obeys a dark wisdom
(As Eve did before her)
Which never can fail,
Being bound by no pride
Of armorial bearings
Bequeathed in tail male.

And though your blood brother
Who dared to do you wrong
In his greed of Myrrhina
Might plead a like wisdom
The fault to excuse,
Myrrhina is just:
She has hanged the poor rogue
By the neck from her noose.

FOOD OF THE DEAD

Blush as you stroke the curves—chin, lips and brow—
Of your scarred face, Prince Orpheus: for she has called it
Beautiful, nor would she stoop to flattery.
Yet are you patient still, when again she has eaten
Food of the dead, seven red pomegranate seeds,
And once more warmed the serpent at her thighs
For a new progress through new wards of hell?

EURYDICE

'I am oppressed, I am oppressed, I am oppressed'—
Once I utter the curse, how can she rest:
No longer able, weeping, to placate me
With renewed auguries of celestial beauty?

Speak, fly in her amber ring; speak, horse of gold!
What gift did I ever grudge her, or help withhold?
In a mirror I watch blood trickling down the wall—
Is it mine? Yet still I stand here, proud and tall.

Look where she shines, with a borrowed blaze of light
Among the cowardly, faceless, lost, unright,
Clasping a naked imp to either breast—
Am I not oppressed, oppressed, three times oppressed?

She has gnawn at corpse-flesh till her breath stank,
Paired with a jackal, grown distraught and lank,
Crept home, accepted solace, but then again
Flown off to chain truth back with an iron chain.

My own dear heart, dare you so war on me
As to strangle love in a mad perversity?
Is ours a fate can ever be forsworn
Though my lopped head sing to the yet unborn?

TO BEGUILE AND BETRAY

To beguile and betray, though pardonable in women,
Slowly quenches the divine need-fire
By true love kindled in them. Have you not watched
The immanent Goddess fade from their brows
When they make private to her mysteries
Some whip-scarred rogue from the hulks, some painted clown
From the pantomime—and afterwards accuse you
Of jealous hankering for the mandalot
Rather than horror and sick foreboding
That she will never return to the same house?

I WILL WRITE

He had done for her all that a man could,
And, some might say, more than a man should.
Then was ever a flame so recklessly blown out
Or a last goodbye so negligent as this?
'I will write to you,' she muttered briefly,
Tilting her cheek for a polite kiss;
Then walked away, nor ever turned about. . . .

Long letters written and mailed in her own head—
There are no mails in a city of the dead.

XVI

BIRD OF PARADISE

At sunset, only to his true love,
The bird of paradise opened wide his wings
Displaying emerald plumage shot with gold
Unguessed even by him.
                        True, that wide crest
Had blazoned royal estate, and the tropic flowers
Through which he flew had shown example
Of what brave colours gallantry might flaunt,
But these were other. She asked herself, trembling:
'What did I do to awake such glory?'

THE METAPHOR

The act of love seemed a dead metaphor
For love itself, until the timeless moment
When fingers trembled, heads clouded,
And love rode everywhere, too numinous
To be expressed or greeted calmly:
O, then it was, deep in our own forest,
We dared revivify the metaphor,
Shedding the garments of this epoch
In scorn of time's wilful irrelevancy;
So at last understood true nakedness
And the long debt to silence owed.

SONG: A PHOENIX FLAME

In my heart a phoenix flame
   Darts and scorches me all day—
Should a fierce sun do the same,
   I die away.

O for pools with sunken rocks,
   Minnow-haunted mountain brooks,
Blustering gales of Equinox,
   Cold, green nooks.

Who could boast a careless wit,
   Doubly roasted, heart and hide,
Turning on the Sun's red spit,
   Consumed inside?

SECRECY

Lovers are happy
When favoured by chance,
But here is blessedness
Beyond all happiness,

Not to be gainsaid
By any gust of chance,
Harvest of one vine,
Gold from the same mine:

To keep which sacred
Demands a secrecy
That the world might blame
As deceit and shame;

Yet to publish which
Would make a him and her
Out of me and you
That were both untrue.

Let pigeons couple
Brazenly on the bough,
But royal stag and hind
Are of our own mind.

JOSEPH AND MARY

They turned together with a shocked surprise—
He, old and fabulous; she, young and wise—
Both having heard a newborn hero weep
In convalescence from the stroke of sleep.

AN EAST WIND

Beware the giddy spell, ground fallen away
Under your feet, wings not yet beating steady:
An ignorant East Wind tempts you to deny
Faith in the twofold glory of your being—
You with a thousand leagues or more to fly.

'Poised in air between earth and paradise,
Paradise and earth, confess which pull
Do you find the stronger? Is it of homesickness
Or of passion? Would you be rather loyal or wise?
How are these choices reconcilable?'

Turn from him without anger. East Wind knows
Only one wall of every foursquare house,
Has never viewed your northern paradise
Nor watched its queen tending her jewelled boughs,
But always from the same sick quarter blows.

DANCE OF WORDS

To make them move, you should start from lightning
And not forecast the rhythm: rely on chance,
Or so-called chance for its bright emergence
Once lightning interpenetrates the dance.

Grant them their own traditional steps and postures
But see they dance it out again and again
Until only lightning is left to puzzle over—
The choreography plain, and the theme plain.

A BLIND ARROW

Though your blind arrow, shot in time of need
Among the shadowy birches, did indeed
Strike, as you knew it must, the assassin's heart,
Never disparage a trained bowman's art.

THE OLEASTER

Each night for seven nights beyond the gulf
A storm raged, out of hearing, and crooked flashes
Of lightning animated us. Before day-break
Rain fell munificently for the earth's need. . . .

No, here they never plant the sweet olive
As some do (bedding slips in a prepared trench),
But graft it on the club of Hercules
The savage, inexpugnable oleaster
Whose roots and bole bunching from limestone crannies
Sprout impudent shoots born only to be lopped
Spring after Spring. Theirs is a loveless berry. . . .

By mid-day we walk out, with naked feet,
Through pools on the road, gazing at waterfalls
Or a line of surf, but mostly at the trees
Whose elegant branches rain has duly blackened
And pressed their crowns to a sparkling silver.

Innumerable, plump with promise of oil,
The olives hang grass-green, in thankfulness
For a bitter sap and bitter New Year snows
That cleansed their bark. . . .
                            Forgive me, dearest love,
If nothing I can say be strange or new.
I am no child of the hot South like you,
Though in rock rooted like an oleaster.

THE SEPTUAGENARIAN

Youth is the ruggedest burden that can score
Your septuagenarian shoulder:
If you should threaten, as before, to powder
Rocks with bare heels, or rend the oak asunder
With naked fingers, you can now no more
Plead youthful benefit of metaphor.
Such unsubstantiated boasts will be
Substantial evidence of senility.

NON COGUNT ASTRA

Come, live in Now and occupy it well.
Prediction's no alternative to forethought
Despite at least four hundred arts of scrying
The dubious future, such as to study birds,
Or bull's guts, or sheep droppings, or wine lees
In an alabaster cup. True, the most ancient,
Most exact discipline, astrology,
Comes hallowed by a college of gowned mantics
Who still cast horoscopes only by stars
Apparent to the still unaided eye—
And of whom a few, the best, focus their powers
On exact horary configurations, then
At an agreed moment brusquely sweep away
Zodiacal signs, conjunctions, trines,
And reinduce a pure, archaic vision;
Yet disregard all false astrologers
Who dare lay greedy or compulsive hands
On the stars you sped at your nativity
Along their courses and forbad to canker
The rose of love or blunt the blade of honour:
No public hangmen these, but servants chosen
To wear bright livery at your house gate;
And favour you the more, the less you fear them.

SONG: SWORD AND ROSE

The King of Hearts a broadsword bears,
    The Queen of Hearts, a rose—
Though why, not every gambler cares
    Or cartomancer knows.

Be beauty yours, be honour mine,
    Yet sword and rose are one:
Great emblems that in love combine
    Until the dealing's done;

For no card, whether small or face,
    Shall overtrump our two
Except that Heart of Hearts, the Ace,
    To which their title's due.

ENDLESS PAVEMENT

In passage along an endless, eventless pavement,
None but the man in love, as he turns to stare
At the glazed eyes flickering past, will remain aware
Of his own, assured, meticulous, rustic tread—
As if pavement were pebbles, or rocks overgrown by grasses;
And houses, trees with birds flying overhead.

IN DISGUISE

Almost I welcome the dirty subterfuges
Of this unreal world closing us in,
That present you as a lady of high fashion
And me as a veteran on the pensioned list.

Our conversation is infinitely proper,
With a peck on either cheek as we meet or part—
Yet the seven archons of the heavenly stair
Tremble at the disclosure of our seals.

A MEASURE OF CASUALNESS

Too fierce the candlelight; your gentle voice
Roars as in dream; my shoulder-nooks flower;
A scent of honeysuckle invades the house,
And my fingertips are so love-enhanced
That sailcloth feels like satin to them.
Teach me a measure of casualness
Though you stalk into my room like Venus naked.

IN TIME OF ABSENCE

Lovers in time of absence need not signal
With call and answering call:
By sleight of providence each sends the other
A clear, more than coincidental answer
To every still unformulated puzzle,
Or a smile at a joke harboured, not yet made,
Or power to be already wise and unafraid.

THE GREEN CASTLE

The first heaven is a flowery plain;
The second, a glass mountain;
The third, likewise terrestrial,
Is an orchard-close unclouded
By prescience of death or change
Or the blood-sports of desire:
Our childhood paradise.

The next three heavens, known as celestial,
Are awkward of approach.
Mind is the prudent rider; body, the ass
Disciplined always by a harsh bit,
Accepts his daily diet of thorns
And frugal, brackish water;
Holds converse with archangels.

The seventh heaven, most unlike those others,
We once contrived to enter
By a trance of love; it is a green castle
Girdled with ramparts of blue sea
And silent but for the waves' leisured wash.
There Adam rediscovered Eve:
She wrapped him in her arms.

An afterglow of truth, still evident
When we had fallen earthward,
Astonished all except the born blind.
Strangers would halt us in the roadway:
'Confess where you have been.'
And, at a loss, we replied stumblingly:
'It was here, it was nowhere—
Last night we lodged at a green castle,
Its courtyard paved with gold.'

NOT TO SLEEP

Not to sleep all the night long, for pure joy,
Counting no sheep and careless of chimes,
Welcoming the dawn confabulation
Of birds, her children, who discuss idly
Fanciful details of the promised coming—
Will she be wearing red, or russet, or blue,
Or pure white?—whatever she wears, glorious:
Not to sleep all the night long, for pure joy,
This is given to few but at last to me,
So that when I laugh and stretch and leap from bed
I shall glide downstairs, my feet brushing the carpet
In courtesy to civilized progression,
Though, did I wish, I could soar through the open window
And perch on a branch above, acceptable ally
Of the birds still alert, grumbling gently together.

THE HEARTH

Here it begins: the worm of love breeding
Among red embers of a hearth-fire
Turns to a chick, is slowly fledged,
And will hop from lap to lap in a ring
Of eager children basking at the blaze.

But the luckless man who never sat there,
Nor borrowed live coals from the sacred source
To warm a hearth of his own making,
Nor bedded lay under pearl-grey wings
In dutiful content,

How shall he watch at the stroke of midnight
Dove become phoenix, plumed with green and gold?
Or be caught up by jewelled talons
And haled away to a fastness of the hills
Where an unveiled woman, black as Mother Night,
Teaches him a new degree of love
And the tongues and songs of birds?

THAT OTHER WORLD

Fatedly alone with you once more
As before Time first creaked:
Sole woman and sole man.

Others admire us as we walk this world:
We show them kindliness and mercy,
So be it none grow jealous
Of the truth that echoes between us two,
Or of that other world, in the world's cradle,
Child of your love for me.

THE BEDS OF GRAINNE AND DIARMUID

How many secret nooks in copse or glen
We sained for ever with our pure embraces,
No man shall know; though indeed master poets
Reckon one such for every eve of the year,
To sain their calendar.
                              But this much is true:
That children stumbling on our lairs by chance
In quest of hazel-nuts or whortleberries
Will recognize the impress of twin bodies
On the blue-green turf, starred with diversity
Of alien flowers, and shout astonishment.
Yet should some amorous country pair, presuming
To bask in joy on any bed of ours,
Offend against the love by us exampled,
Long ivy roots will writhe up from beneath
And bitterly fetter ankle, wrist and throat.

CONSORTIUM OF STONES

The stones you have gathered, of diverse shapes,
Chosen from sea strand, lake strand, mountain gully:
Lay them all out on a basalt slab together
But allow intervals for light and air,
These being human souls; and reject any
With crumpled calceous edges and no feature
That awakes loving correspondence.

Start at this pair: blue flint, grey ironstone,
Which you ring around with close affinities
In every changeless colour, hatched, patched, plain—
Curve always answering curve; and angle, angle.

Gaps there may be, which next year or the next
Will fill to a marvel: never jog Time's arm,
Only narrow your eyes when you walk about
Lest they miss what is missing. The agreed intent
Of each consortium, whether of seven stones,
Or of nineteen, or thirty-three, or more,
Must be a circle, with firm edges outward,
Each various element aware of the sum.

THE BLACK GODDESS

Silence, words into foolishness fading,
Silence prolonged, of thought so secret
We hush the sheep-bells and the loud cicada.

And your black agate eyes, wide open, mirror
The released firebird beating his way
Down a whirled avenue of blues and yellows.

Should I not weep? Profuse the berries of love,
The speckled fish, the filberts and white ivy
Which you, with a half-smile, bestow
On your delectable broad land of promise
For me, who never before went gay in plumes.

XVII

BROKEN NECK

'Some forty years ago or maybe more,'
Pronounced the radiologist, 'you broke
Your neck: that is to say, contrived to fracture
Your sixth cervical vertebra—see here,
The picture's clear—and between sixth and seventh
Flattened this cartilage to uselessness:
Hence rheumatism. Surely you recall
Some incident? We all do foolish things
While young, and obstinately laugh them off—
Till they catch up with us in God's good time.
Let me prescribe you a Swiss analgesic
Which should at least. . . .'
                                          Love, I still laugh it off
And all Swiss mercenary alleviations,
For though I broke my neck in God's good time
It is in yours alone I choose to live.

O

'*O per se O, O per se O!*',
The moribund grammarian cried
To certain scholars grouped at his bedside,
Spying the round, dark pit a-gape below:
'*O per se O!*'

WOMAN OF GREECE

By your knees they rightly clasp you,
    Strong sons of your bed,
Whom you get, kneeling; and bear, kneeling;
    Kneeling, mourn for dead.

THE COLOURS OF NIGHT

The Moon never makes use of the Sun's palette.
Admire her silvery landscapes, but abstain
From record of them: lest you be later tempted
To counterfeit the dangerous colours of Night
Which are man's blood spurted on moving cloud.

BETWEEN TRAINS

Arguing over coffee at the station,
Neither of us noticed her dark beauty,
Though she sat close by, until suddenly
Three casual words—does it matter what they were?—
Spoken without remarkable intonation
Or accent, so bewildered him and me,
As it were catching the breath of our conversation,
That each set down his coffee-cup, to stare.
'You have come for us?' my lips cautiously framed—
Her eyes were almost brighter than I could bear—
But she rose and left, unready to be named.

TO THE TEUMESSIAN VIXEN

Do not mistake me: I was never a rival
  Of that poor fox who pledged himself to win
Your heart by gnawing away his brush. Who ever
  Proved love was love except by a whole skin?

THE HUNG WU VASE

With women like Marie no holds are barred.
Where do they get the gall? How can they do it?

She stormed out, slamming the hall door so hard
That a vase on the gilt shelf above—you knew it,
Loot from the Summer Palace at Pekin
And worth the entire contents of my flat—
Toppled and fell. . . .
                         I poured myself straight gin,
Downing it at a gulp. 'So that was that!'

The bell once more. . . . Marie walked calmly in,
Observed broken red porcelain on the mat,
Looked up, looked down again with condescension,
Then, gliding past me to retrieve a glove
(Her poor excuse for this improper call),
Muttered: 'And one thing I forget to mention:
Your Hung Wu vase was phoney, like your love!'

How can they do it? Where do they get the gall?

LA MEJICANA

Perfect beneath an eight-rayed sun you lie,
    Rejoiced at his caresses. Yours is a land
For pumas, chillis, and men dark of eye;
    Yet summon me with no derisive hand
From these remote moon-pastures drenched in dew—
And watch who burns the blacker: I or you.

LAMIA IN LOVE

Need of this man was her ignoble secret:
Desperate for love, yet loathing to deserve it,
She wept pure tears of sorrow when his eyes
Betrayed mistrust in her impeccable lies.

AFTER THE FLOOD

Noah retrieves the dove again,
    Which bears him in its bill
A twig of olive to explain
That, if God sends them no more rain,
    The world may prosper still.

Shem, Ham and Japheth raise a shout,
    But weeks on end must wait
Till Father Noah, venturing out,
Can view the landscape all about
    And prophesy their fate.

'Where have the waters of God's Flood
    Dispersed?' God only knew.
What Noah saw was miles of mud.
Drowned rogues, and almond trees in bud
    With blossom peeping through.

'Bold lads, in patience here abide!
    This mire around the ark
By wind or sun must well be dried
Before we set against her side
    The planks to disembark.'

Obedient sons, a virtuous wife,
    Flocks, cattle, jars of seeds,
Crook, coulter, halter, pruning-knife—
Noah forecasts a brave new life
    Agreeable to his needs.

Exult with him at the clear sky,
    Proud Noahs of today,
For though we here and there descry
Morasses that no sun can dry
    (Regret them how we may),

God's rainbow is a glorious toy,
    His wine a cheerful drink,
And since He chooses to destroy
Folk better dead, we wish Him joy,
    While choking at the stink.

ALL I TELL YOU FROM MY HEART

I begged my love to wait a bit
    Although the sky was clear:
'I smell a shower of rain,' said I,
    'And you'll be caught, I fear.'
'You want to keep me trapped,' she said,
    'And hold my hand again. . . .'
But not ten minutes had she gone
    When how the rain did rain!

'Alas, dear love, so wet you are—
  You should have trusted me!
For all I tell you from my heart
  Is sure as prophecy.'

I begged my love to wait a bit
  And watch the faggots blaze.
'There's a music on the march,' said I,
  'To cheer whoever stays.'
'You want to keep me trapped,' she said,
  'O, every night's the same. . . .'
But not ten minutes had she gone
  When in the fiddlers came!

'Alas, dear love, what tunes they played—
  You should have trusted me!
For all I tell you from my heart
  Is sure as prophecy.'

I begged my love to take good heed
  When walking through the wood,
And warned her of a random rogue
  Who brought the world no good.
'You want to keep me trapped,' she said,
  'And roll me in your bed. . . .'
But scarce a hundred yards from home
  She lost her maidenhead.

'Alas, dear love, it is too late—
  You should have trusted me!
For all I told you from my heart
  Was sure as prophecy.'

THE UNDEAD

To be the only woman alive in a vast hive of death
Is a strange predicament, granted! Innumerable zombies
With glazed eyes shuffle around at their diurnal tasks,
Keep the machines whirring, drudge idly in stores and bars,
Bear still-born zombie children, pack them off to school
For education in science and the dead languages,
Divert themselves with moribund travesties of living,
Lay mountainous bets on horses never seen to run,
Speed along highways in conveyor-belt automobiles
But, significantly enough, often dare overshoot
The traffic signals and *boing!* destroy themselves again,
Earning expensive funerals. (These, if at last they emerge
From the select green cemetery plots awarded them
On their twenty-first death-days by sombre uncles and aunts,
Will become zombies of the second degree, reverenced
Nationwide in church or synagogue.)
                                            Nevertheless,
Let none of this daunt you, child! Accept it as your fate
To live, to love, knowingly to cause true miracles,
Nor ever to find your body possessed by a cold corpse.
For one day, as you choose an unfamiliar side-street
Keeping both eyes open, alert, not apprehensive,
You shall suddenly (this is a promise) come to a brief halt:
For striding towards you on the same sidewalk will appear
A young man with the halo of life around his head,
Will catch you reassuringly by both hands, asseverating
In phrases utterly unintelligible to a zombie
That all is well: you are neither diseased, deranged, nor mistaken,
But merely undead. He will name others like you, no less alive:
Two girls and a man, all moneyless immigrants arrived
Lately at a new necropolitan conurbation.

216

'Come with me, girl, and join them! The dead, you will observe,
Can exercise no direct sanctions against the living
And therefore doggedly try to omit them from all the records.
Still, they cannot avoid a certain morbid fascination
With what they call our genius. They will venture questions
But never wait for an answer—being doubtless afraid
That it will make their ears burn, or their eyes prick with tears—
Nor can they countermand what orders we may issue.'

Nod your assent, go with him, do not even return to pack!
When five live people room together, each rates as a million—
But encourage the zombies to serve you, the honest creatures,
For though one cannot ameliorate their way of death
By telling them true stories or singing them real songs,
They will feel obscurely honoured by your warm presence.

GRACE NOTES

It was not the words, nor the melody,
    Not the beat, nor the pace;
It was that slow suspension of our breathing
    As we watched your face,
And the grace-notes, unrecordable on the clef,
    Sung only by a spirit in grace.

GOOD NIGHT TO THE OLD GODS

Good night, old gods, all this long year so faint
You propped your heavy eyelids up with shells!
Though once we honoured you who ruled this land
One hundred generations and ten more,
Our mood has changed: you dribble at the mouth,
Your dark-blue fern-tattoos are faded green,
Your thunderous anger wanes to petulance,
And love to groanings of indifference.
What most you crave is rest in a rock-cave,
Seasonally aroused by raucous gulls
Or swallows, nodding off once more to sleep.

We lay you in a row with cool palm wine
Close at your elbows, should you suffer thirst,
And breadfruit piled on rushes by your feet;
But will not furnish you a standing guard—
We have fish to net and spear, taro to hoe,
Pigs to fatten, coco-trees to climb;
Nor are our poets so bedulled in spirit
They would mount a platform, praising in worn verse
Those fusillades of lightning hurled by you
At giants in a first day-break of time:
Whom you disarmed and stretched in a rock-cave
Not unlike this—you have forgotten where.

THE SWEET-SHOP ROUND THE CORNER

The child dreaming along a crowded street
Lost hold of his mother, who had turned to greet
Some neighbour, and mistakenly matched his tread
With a strange woman's. 'Buy me sweets,' he said,
Waving his hand, which he found warmly pressed;
So dragged her on, boisterous and self-possessed:
'The sweet-shop's round the corner!' Both went in,
And not for a long while did the child begin
To feel a dread that something had gone wrong:
Were Mother's legs so lean, or her shoes so long,
Or her skirt so patched, or her hair tousled and grey?
Why did she twitter in such a ghostly way?
'*O Mother, are you dead?*
                              What else could a child say?

DOUBLE BASS

He coils so close about his double-bass,
Serpentine and entranced,
That they form a single creature:
Which man-instrument writhes and complains,
Mouth of disaster, skeleton limbs a-twitch,
Cavernous belly booming,
Insistent fingers torturing us to love,
Its deep-gulped fumes of marihuana
Blinding our eyes with scarlet streamers. . . .

Again I turn, for your laugh-nod to lend me
Measured reassurance of sanity.

DESCENT INTO HELL

Christ harrowed Hell in pity for all damned souls
Who had perverted innocence and honour—
It was a Sabbath, the day given to rest—
But none rose with him, and his journey grieved
The hearts even of such as loved him best.

THE PARDON

Should not the white lie and the unkept promise,
    Though distant from black lie and broken vow,
Demand a kiss of pardon afterwards
    From the sworn lover? So I kiss you now,
Counting on my own pardon: who but I
    Provoked both unkept promise and white lie?

POINT OF NO RETURN

When the alcoholic passed the crucial point
Of no return, he sold his soul to priests
Who, mercifully, would not deny him drink
But remitted a thousand years of purgatory
On this condition: that he must now engage
A woman's pity, beseeching her to cure him,
Wearing her down with betterment and relapse,
Till he had won a second soul for glory,
At the point of no return.

XVIII

THE RED SHOWER

Live sparks rain from the central anvil
  In a red shower. Let all beware
Who read the event as history, frowning at
  What they may find of madness there:
  Felicity endangering despair.

ABOVE THE EDGE OF DOOM

Bats at play taunt us with 'guess how many',
And music sounds far off, tempered by sea.
Above the edge of doom sits woman
Communing with herself. 'Dear love,' says she,
As it were apostrophizing cat or dog,
'Sometimes by a delicate glance and gesture
You almost seem to understand me,
Poor honest creature of the blue eyes,
Having crept closer to my sealed bosom
With your more desperate faith in womankind
Than any other since I first flowered.

It may be best you cannot read my mind.'

WILD CYCLAMEN

'What can I do for you?' she asked gently.
I reached for pen and paper: 'Draw me flowers!'

She pursed her lips—O the smooth brown forehead
The smooth lids drooped, intent on their task—
And drew me wild Majorcan cyclamen
(Not yet in season) extravagantly petalled,
Then laughed and tossed me back the picture.

'It is nothing,' she said; yet that cyclamen odour
Hung heavy in the room for a long while;
And when she was gone, I caught myself smiling
In her own crooked way, trying to make my eyes
Sparkle like hers, though ineffectually,
Till I fell asleep; for this was my sick-bed
And her visits brief, by order.

GIFT OF SIGHT

I had long known the diverse tastes of the wood,
Each leaf, each bark, rank earth from every hollow;
Knew the smells of bird's breath and of bat's wing;
Yet sight I lacked; until you stole upon me,
Touching my eyelids with light finger-tips.
The trees blazed out, their colours whirled together,
Nor ever before had I been aware of sky.

BATXÓCA

Firm-lipped, high-bosomed, slender Queen of Beanstalk Land,
Who are more to me than any woman upon this earth
Though you live from hand to mouth, keeping no certain hours,
Disguising your wisdom with unpracticality
And your elusiveness with hugs for all and sundry,
Flaunting green, yellow and scarlet, suddenly disappearing
In a whirlwind rage and flurry of skirts, always alone
Until found, days later, asleep on a couch of broom
And incommunicable until you have breakfasted—
By what outrageous freak of dissimilarity
Were you forced, noble Batxóca, to fall so deep in love
With me as to demand marriage, despite your warning
That you and I must on no account be seen together—
A Beanstalk Queen, no less, paired with a regular man!

Did you wistfully, perhaps, expect me to say 'no'?

THE SNAP-COMB WILDERNESS

Magic is tangled in a woman's hair
For the enlightenment of male pride.
To slide a comb uxoriously
Through an even swell of tresses undisturbed
By their cascade from an exact parting
Could never hearten or enlighten me—
Not though her eyes were bluer than blue sea.
Magic rules an irreducible jungle
Dark as eclipse and scented with despair,
A stubborn snap-comb wilderness of hair,
Each strand a singular, wild, curling tree.

A SHIFT OF SCENE

To lie far off, in bed with a foul cough,
And a view of elms and roofs and six panes' worth
Of clear sky; here to watch, all the day long,
For a dove, or a black cat, or a puff of smoke
To cause a shift of scene—how could it do so?—
Or to take a pen and write—what else is there
To write but: 'I am not dead, not quite, as yet
Though I lie far off, in bed with a foul cough
And a view of elms and roofs and six panes' worth
Of clear sky'? Tell me, love, are you sick too
And plagued like me with a great hole in the mind
Where all those towers we built, and not on sand,
Have been sucked in and lost; so that it seems
No dove, and no black cat, nor puff of smoke
Can cause a shift of scene and fetch us back
To where we lie as one, in the same bed?

CHANGE

'This year she has changed greatly'—meaning you—
My sanguine friends agree,
And hope thereby to reassure me.

No, child, you never change; neither do I.
Indeed all our lives long
We are still fated to do wrong,

Too fast caught by care of humankind,
Easily vexed and grieved,
Foolishly flattered and deceived;

And yet each knows that the changeless other
Must love and pardon still,
Be the new error what it will:

Assured by that same glint of deathlessness
Which neither can surprise
In any other pair of eyes.

A COURT OF LOVE

Were you to break the vow we swore together,
The vow, I said, would break you utterly:
Despite your pleas of duty elsewhere owed,
You could no longer laugh, work, heal, do magic,
Nor in the mirror face your own eyes.

They have summoned me before their Court of Love
And warned me I must sign for your release
Pledging my word never again to draft
A similar pact, as one who has presumed
Lasting felicity still unknown in time.
What should I do? Forswear myself for you?
No man in love, plagued by his own scruples
Will ever, voluntarily, concede
That women have a spirit above vows.

BLACK

Black drinks the sun and draws all colours to it.
I am bleached white, my truant love. Come back,
And stain me with intensity of black.

BETWEEN HYSSOP AND AXE

To know our destiny is to know the horror
Of separation, dawn oppressed by night:
Is, between hyssop and axe, boldly to prove
That gifted, each, with singular need for freedom
And haunted, both, by spectres of reproach,
We may yet house together without succumbing
To the low fever of domesticity
Or to the lunatic spin of aimless flight.

SON ALTESSE

Alone, you are no more than many another
Gay-hearted, greedy, passionate noblewoman;
And I, alone, no more than a slow-witted
Passionate, credulous knight, though skilled in fight.

Then if I hail you as my Blessed Virgin
This is no flattery, nor does it endow you
With private magics which, when I am gone,
May flatter rogues or drunken renegades.

Name me your single, proud, whole-hearted champion
Whose feats no man alive will overpass;
But they must reverence you as I do; only
Conjoined in fame can we grow legendary.

Should I ride home, vainglorious after battle,
With droves of prisoners and huge heaps of spoil,
Make me dismount a half-mile from your door;
To walk barefoot in dust, as a knight must.

Yet never greet me carelessly or idly,
Nor use the teasing manners learned at Court,
Lest I be ambushed in a treacherous pass—
And you pent up in shame's black nunnery.

GOLD AND MALACHITE

After the hour of illumination, when the tottering mind
Has been by force delivered from its incubus of despair,
When all the painted, papier mâché, Mexican faces
Of demons grinning at you from hell's vaulted roof
Fade and become angelic monitors of wisdom—
Slowly the brisk intelligence wakes, to mutter questions
Of when, where, how; and which should be the first step
                                   forward. . . .

Now is the crucial moment you were forewarned against.
Stop your ears with your fingers, guard unequivocal silence
Lest you discuss wisdom in the language of unwisdom;
Roam instead through the heaped treasury of your heart:
You will find her, from whom you have been so long estranged,
Chin to knees, brooding apart on gold and malachite.
But beware again: even a shy embrace would be too explicit—
Let her learn by your gait alone that you are free at last.

AMBIENCE

The nymph of the forest, only in whose honour
These birds perform, provides an ambience
But never leads the chorus: even at dawn
When we awake to whistle, flute and pipe,
Astonished they can so extemporize
Their own parts, as it were haphazard
Each in his own time, yet avoid discordance
Or domineering, however virtuose
Or long sustained each voluntary of love.
The rare silences, too, appear like sound
Rather than pause for breath or meditation. . . .
Nor is the same piece ever given twice.

THE VOW

No vow once sworn may ever be annulled
Except by a higher law of love or mercy—
Search your heart well: is there a lie hidden
Deep in its convolutions of resolve?

For whom do you live? Can it be yourself?
For whom then? Not for this unlovely world,
Not for the rotting waters of mischance,
Nor for the tall, eventual catafalque.

You live for her who alone loves you,
Whose royal prerogative can be denied
By none observant of the awakening gasps
That greet her progress down whatever hall.

Your vow is to truth, not practicality;
To honour, not to the dead world's esteem;
To a bed of rock, not to a swan's-down pillow;
To the tears you kiss away from her black eyes.

They lament an uninstructible world of men
Who dare not listen or watch, but challenge proof
That a leap of a thousand miles is nothing
And to walk invisibly needs no artifice.

THE FROG AND THE GOLDEN BALL

She let her golden ball fall down the well
    And begged a cold frog to retrieve it;
For which she kissed his ugly, gaping mouth—
    Indeed, he could scarce believe it.

228

And seeing him transformed to his princely shape,
    Who had been by hags enchanted,
She knew she could never love another man
    Nor by any fate be daunted.

But what would her royal father and mother say?
    They had promised her in marriage
To a cousin whose wide kingdom marched with theirs,
    Who rode in a jewelled carriage.

'Our plight, dear heart, would appear past human hope
    To all except you and me: to all
Who have never swum as a frog in a dark well
    Or have lost a golden ball.'

'What then shall we do now?' she asked her lover.
    He kissed her again, and said:
'Is magic of love less powerful at your Court
    Than at this green well-head?'

THOSE WHO CAME SHORT

Those who came short of love for me or you,
Where are they now? Ill-starred and bitter-mouthed,
Cursing us for their own contrariness,
Each having fallen in turn, head over heels,
From that illusive heaven at which they flew.

Are we then poison of love-perfection
To all but our own kind? Should we beware
Of handling such intemperate shaggy creatures
As leap on us like dogs to be cosseted
And, after, claim full rights of jealousy?

At once too simple and too various
Except for ourselves, should we awhile conceal
Our studies from the world, in cool forbearance
Watching each night for another dawn to break
And the last guest to straggle home?

WHOLE LOVE

Every choice is always the wrong choice,
Every vote cast is always cast away—
How can truth hover between alternatives?

Then love me more than dearly, love me wholly,
Love me with no weighing of circumstance,
As I am pledged in honour to love you:

With no weakness, with no speculation
On what might happen should you and I prove less
Than bringers-to-be of our own certainty.
Neither was born by hazard: each foreknew
The extreme possession we are grown into.

THIS HOLY MONTH

The demon who throughout our late estrangement
Followed with malice in my footsteps, often
Making as if to stumble, so that I stumbled
And gashed my head against a live rock;
Who tore my palms on butcher's broom and thorn,
Flung me at midnight into filthy ditches
And multiplied the horrors of this house
When back I limped again to a hard bed;
Who simultaneously plagued you too
With sleeplessness, dismay and darkness,
Paralysed your hands, denied you air—
We both know well he was the same demon,
Arch-enemy of rule and calculation,
Who lives for our love, being created from it,
Astonishes us with blossom, silvers the hills
With more than moonlight, summons bees in swarms
From the Lion's mouth to fill our hives with honey,
Turns flesh into fire, and eyes into deep lakes;
And so may do once more, this holy month.

THE IMPOSSIBLE

Dear love, since the impossible proves
   Our sole recourse from this distress,
Claim it: the ebony ritual-mask of no
   Cannot outstare a living yes.

Claim it without despond or hate
   Or greed; but in your gentler tone
Say: 'This is ours, the impossible,' and silence
   Will give consent it is ours alone.

The impossible has wild-cat claws
   Which you would rather meet and die
Than commit love to time's curative venom
   And break our oath; for so would I.

THE FETTER

Concerned, against our wish, with a sick world,
Self-neglectful, tuned to knock or summons,
We make amends for follies not our own.

We have taken love through a thousand deaths;
Should either try to slip our iron fetter,
It bites yet deeper into neck and arm.

As for that act of supererogation,
The kiss in which we secretly concur,
Let laughter mitigate its quiet excess.

Could we only be a simple, bickering pair
In the tied cottage of a small estate,
With no tasks laid on us except to dig,
Hoe, fatten geese and scrape the quarter's rent,
How admirable our close interdependence;
Our insecurity how fortunate!

IRON PALACE

We stood together, side by side, rooted
At the iron heart of circumambient hills,
Parents to a new age, weeping in awe
That the lot had fallen, of all mankind, on us
Now sealed as love's exemplars.

We could not prevaricate or argue,
Citing involvement in some alien scene,
Nor plead unworthiness: none else would venture
To live detached from force of circumstance
As history neared its ending.

We told no one. These were not strange dreams
Recalled at breakfast with a yawning smile,
Nor tales for children, on the verge of sleep,
Who ask no questions. Our predicament
Remained a silent burden.

We had no token or proof, and needed none
Of what we learned that day; but laughed softly
Watching our hands engage, in co-awareness
That these red hills warned us, on pain of death,
Never to disengage them.

Woman, wild and hard as the truth may be,
Nothing can circumvent it. We stand coupled
With chains, who otherwise might live apart
Conveniently paired, each with another,
And slide securely graveward.

TRUE JOY

Whoever has drowned and awhile entered
The adamantine gates of afterwards,
Stands privileged to reject heavenly joy
(Though without disrespect for God's archangels)
With 'never again'—no moon, no herbs, no sea,
No singular love of women.

True joy, believe us, is to groan and wake
From the hallelujah choir on Fiddler's Green,
With lungs now emptied of salt water,
With gradual heat returning to clammed veins
In the first flicker of reanimation,
Repossession of now, awareness
Of her live hands and lips, her playful voice,
Her smooth and wingless shoulders.

TOMORROW'S ENVY OF TODAY

Historians may scorn the close engagement
Of Moon with Lion that we have witnessed
Here in this lair, here in this numinous grove,
May write me down as imbecile, or presume
A clot of madness festering in your heart—
Such is tomorrow's envy of today.

Today we are how we are, and how we see:
Alive, elate, untrimmed, without hazard
Of supersession: flowers that never fade,
Leaves that never shrivel, truth persistent
Not as a prophecy of bliss to fall
A thousand generations hence on lovers
More fortunately circumstanced than we,
But as a golden interlock of power
Looped about every bush and branching tree.

THE HIDDEN GARDEN

Nor can ambition make this garden theirs,
Any more than birds can fly through a window pane.
When they hint at passwords, keys and private stairs,
We are tempted often to open the front gate,
Which has no lock, and haul them bodily in,
Abashed that there they wait, disconsolate.

And yet such pity would be worse than pride:
Should we admit as love their vain self-pity,
The gate must vanish and we be left outside.

THE WEDDING

When down I went to the rust-red quarry
I was informed, by birds, of your resolve
To live with me for ever and a day—
The day being always new and antecedent.
What could we ask of Nature? Nothing more
Than to outdo herself in our behalf.

Blossoms of caper, though they smell sweet,
Have never sailed the air like butterflies
Circling in innocent dance around each other
Over the cliff and out across the bay;
Nor has broom-blossom scorched a man's finger
With golden fire, kindled by sun.

Come, maids of honour and pages chosen
To attend this wedding, charged to perform
Incomparable feats—dance, caper-blossom!
Scorch, blossom of broom, our married fingers—
Though crowds of almost-men and almost-women
Howl for their lost immediacy.

EVERYWHERE IS HERE

By this exchange of eyes, this encirclement
You of me, I of you, together we baffle
Logic no doubt, but never understanding;
And laugh instead of choking back the tears
When we say goodbye.
                              Fog gathers thick about us
Yet a single careless pair of leaves, one green, one gold,
Whirl round and round each other skippingly
As though blown by a wind; pause and subside
In a double star, the gold above the green.

Everywhere is here, once we have shattered
The iron-bound laws of contiguity,
Blazoning love as an eagle with four wings
(Their complementary tinctures counterchanged)
That scorns to roost in any terrene crag.

WHAT WILL BE, IS

Manifest reason glared at you and me
Thus ringed with love. Entire togetherness
Became for us the sole redress.

Together in heart, but our over-eager bodies
Distrained upon for debt, we shifted ground;
Which brought mistiming. Each cried out in turn,
And with a complementary delusion:
'I am free; but you? Are you still bound?'

In blood the debts were paid. Hereafter
We make no truce for manifest reason
From this side of the broad and fateful stream
Where wisdom rules from her dark cave of dream
And time is corrigible by laughter.

Moon and Sun are one. Granted, they ride
Paths uncomformable to the calendar,
And seldom does a New Moon coincide
With a New Year; yet we agree:
'What will be, is'—rejoicing at a day
Of dolphins jostling in the blue bay,
Eagles in air, and flame on every tree.

SONG: THE FAR SIDE OF YOUR MOON

The far side of your moon is black,
    And glorious grows the vine;
Ask anything of me you lack,
    But only what is mine.

Yours is the great wheel of the sun,
    And yours the unclouded sky;
Then take my stars, take every one,
    But wear them openly.

Walking in splendour through the plain
    For all the world to see,
Since none alive shall view again
    The match of you and me.

DELIVERANCE

Lying disembodied under the trees
(Their slender trunks converged above us
Like rays of a five-fold star) we heard
A sudden whinnying from the dark hill.

Our implacable demon, foaled by love,
Never knew rein or saddle; though he drank
From a stream winding by, his blue pastures
Ranged far out beyond the stellar mill.

He had seared us two so close together
That death itself might not disjoin us;
It was impossible you could love me less,
It was impossible I could love you more.

We were no calculating lovers
But gasped in awe at our deliverance
From a too familiar prison,
And vainly puzzled how it was that now
We should never need to build another,
As each, time after time, had done before.

CONJUNCTION

What happens afterwards, none need enquire:
They are poised there in conjunction, beyond time,
At an oak-tree top level with Paradise:
Its leafy tester unshaken where they stand
Palm to palm, mouth to mouth, beyond desire,
Perpetuating lark song, perfume, colour,
And the tremulous gasp of watchful winds,

Past all unbelief, we know them held
By peace and light and irrefragable love—
Twin paragons, our final selves, resistant
To the dull pull of earth dappled with shade:
Myself the forester, never known to abandon
His vigilant coursing of the greenwood's floor,
And you, dryad of dryads, never before
Yielding her whole heart to the enemy, man.

NOTHING NOW ASTONISHES

A month of vigilance draws to its close
With silence of snow and the Northern lights
In longed-for wordlessness.

This rainbow spanning our two worlds
Becomes more than a bridge between them:
They fade into geography.

Variegated with the seven colours
We twist them into skeins for hide and seek
In a lovers' labyrinth.

Can I be astonished at male trembling
Of sea-horizons as you lean towards them?
Nothing now astonishes.

You change, from a running drop of pure gold
On a silver salver, to the white doe
In nut-groves harbouring.

Let me be changed now to an eight-petalled
Scarlet anemone that will never strain
For the circling butterfly.

Rest, my loud heart. Your too exultant flight
Had raised the wing-beat to a roar
Drowning seraphic whispers.

XIX

COCK IN PULLET'S FEATHERS

Though ready enough with beak and spurs,
You go disguised, a cock in pullet's feathers,
Among those crowing, preening chanticleers.
But, dear self, learn to love your own body
In its full naked glory,
Despite all blemishes of moles and scars—
As she, for whom it shines, wholly loves hers.

DEAD HAND

Grieve for the loveless, spiritless, faceless men
Without alternative but to protract
Reason's mortmain on what their hearts deny—
Themselves—and owed small courtesy beyond
The uncovered head, as when a hearse goes by.

ARREARS OF MOONLIGHT

My heart lies wrapped in red under your pillow,
My body wanders banished among the stars;
On one terrestrial pretext or another
You still withhold the extravagant arrears
Of moonlight that you owe us,
Though the owl whoops from a far olive branch
His brief, monotonous, night-long reminder.

WHAT DID YOU SAY?

She listened to his voice urgently pleading,
So captivated by his eloquence
She saw each word in its own grace and beauty
Drift like a flower down that clear-flowing brook,
And draw a wake of multicoloured bubbles.
But when he paused, intent on her reply,
She could stammer only: 'Love, what did you say?'—
As loath as ever to hold him in her arms
Naked, under the trees, until high day.

LURE OF MURDER

A round moon suffocates the neighbouring stars
With greener light than sun through vine-leaves.
Awed by her ecstasy of solitude
I crouch among rocks, scanning the gulf, agape,
Whetting a knife on my horny sole.

Alas for the lure of murder, dear my love!
Could its employment purge two moon-vexed hearts
Of jealousy more formidable than death,
Then each would stab, stab, stab at secret parts
Of the other's beloved body where unknown
Zones of desire imperil full possession.

But never can mortal dagger serve to geld
This glory of ours, this loving beyond reason—
Death holds no remedy or alternative:
We are singled out to endure his lasting grudge
On the tall battlements of nightfall.

THE GORGE

Yonder beyond all hopes of access
Begins your queendom; here is my frontier.
Between us howl phantoms of the long dead,
But the bridge that I cross, concealed from view
Even in sunlight, and the gorge bottomless,
Swings and echoes under my strong tread
Because I have need of you.

ECSTASY OF CHAOS

When the immense drugged universe explodes
In a cascade of unendurable colour
And leaves us gasping naked,
This is no more than ecstasy of chaos:
Hold fast, with both hands, to that royal love
Which alone, as we know certainly, restores
Fragmentation into true being.

STOLEN JEWEL

You weep whole heartedly—your shining tears
Roll down for sorrow, not like mine for joy.
Dear love, should we not scorn to treat each other
With palliatives and with placebos?

Under a blinding moon you took from me
This jewel of wonder, but unaware
That it was yielded only on condition
Of whole possession; that it still denies you
Strength or desire for its restitution.

What do you fear? My hand around your throat?
What do I fear? Your dagger through my heart?
Must we not rage alone together
In lofts of singular high starriness?

THE SNAPPED THREAD

Desire, first, by a natural miracle
United bodies, united hearts, blazed beauty;
Transcended bodies, transcended hearts.

Two souls, now unalterably one
In whole love always and for ever,
Soar out of twilight, through upper air,
Let fall their sensuous burden.

Is it kind, though, is it honest even,
To consort with none but spirits—
Leaving true-wedded hearts like ours
In enforced night-long separation,
Each to its random bodily inclination,
The thread of miracle snapped?

FORTUNATE CHILD

For fear strangers might intrude upon us
You and I played at being strangers,
But lent our act such verisimilitude
That when at last, by hazard, we met alone
In a secret glen where the badger earths
We had drawn away from love: did not prepare
For melting of eyes into hearts of flowers,
For a sun-aureoled enhancement of hair,
For over-riding of death on an eagle's back—
Yet so it was: sky shuddered apart before us
Until, from a cleft of more than light, we both
Overheard the laugh of a fortunate child
Swung from those eagle talons in a gold cloth.

LOVING TRUE, FLYING BLIND

How often have I said before
That no soft 'if,' no 'either-or,'
Can keep my obdurate male mind
From loving true and flying blind?—

Which, though deranged beyond all cure
Of temporal reason, knows for sure
That timeless magic first began
When woman bared her soul to man.

Be bird, be blossom, comet, star,
Be paradisal gates ajar,
But still, as woman, bear you must
With who alone endures your trust.

THE NEAR ECLIPSE

Out shines again the glorious round sun—
After his near-eclipse when pools of light
Thrown on the turf between leaf shadows
Grew crescent-shaped like moons—dizzying us
With paraboles of colour: regal amends
To our own sun mauled barbarously
By the same wide-mouthed dragon.

DANCING FLAME

Pass now in metaphor beyond birds,
Their seasonal nesting and migration,
Their airy gambols, their repetitive song;
Beyond the puma and the ocelot
That spring in air and follow us with their eyes;
Beyond all creatures but our own selves,
Eternal genii of dancing flame
Armed with the irreproachable secret
Of love, which is: never to turn back.

BIRTH OF ANGELS

Never was so profound a shadow thrown
On earth as by your sun: a black roundel
Harbouring an unheard-of generation
Fledged by the sun ablaze above your own—
Wild beyond words, yet each of them an angel.

ON GIVING

Those who dare give nothing
Are left with less than nothing;
Dear heart, you give me everything,
Which leaves you more than everything—
Though those who dare give nothing
Might judge it left you nothing.

Giving you everything,
I too, who once had nothing,
Am left with more than everything
As gifts for those with nothing
Who need, if not our everything,
At least a loving something.

XX

THE P'ENG THAT WAS A K'UN

(Adapted from the Chinese of Lao Tse)

In Northern seas there roams a fish called K'un,
Of how many thousand leagues in length I know not,
Which changes to a bird called P'eng—its wing-span
Of how many thousand leagues in width I know not.
Every half-year this P'eng, that was a K'un,
Fans out its glorious feathers to the whirlwind
And soars to the most Southerly pool of Heaven.

The Finch and Sparrow, thus informed, debated:
'We by our utmost efforts may fly only
To yonder elm. How can the P'eng outdo us?'
Though, indeed, neither started as a fish.

LIKE OWLS

The blind are their own brothers; we
Form an obscure fraternity
Who, though not destitute of sight
Know ourselves doomed from birth to see,
Like owls, most clearly in half light.

IN PERSPECTIVE

What, keep love in *perspective?*—that old lie
Forced on the Imagination by the Eye
Which, mechanistically controlled, will tell
How rarely table-sides run parallel;
How distance shortens us; how wheels are found
Oval in shape far oftener than round;
How every ceiling-corner's out of joint;
How the broad highway tapers to a point—
Can all this fool us lovers? Not for long:
Even the blind will sense that something's wrong.

THE UTTER RIM

But if that Cerberus, my mind, should be
Flung to earth by the very opiate
That frees my senses for undared adventure,
Waving them wide-eyed past me to explore
Limitless hells of disintegrity,
Endless, undifferentiatable fate
Scrolled out beyond the utter rim of nowhere,
Scrolled out . . . . . .
                    who on return fail to surrender
Their memory trophies, random wisps of horror
Trailed from my shins or tangled in my hair?

UNICORN AND THE WHITE DOE

Unicorn with burning heart
Breath of love has drawn
On his desolate peak apart
At rumour of dawn,

Has trumpeted his pride
These long years mute,
Tossed his horn from side to side,
Lunged with his foot.

Like a storm of sand has run
Breaking his own boundaries,
Gone in hiding from the sun
Under camphor trees.

Straight was the course he took
Across the plain, but here with briar
And mire the tangled alleys crook,
Baulking desire.

A shoulder glistened white—
The bough still shakes—
A white doe darted out of sight
Through the forest brakes.

Tall and close the camphors grow
The grass grows thick—
Where you are I do not know,
You fly so quick.

Where have you fled from me?
I pursue, you fade,
I hunt, you hide from me
In the chequered glade.

Often from my hot lair
I would watch you drink,
A mirage of tremulous air,
At the pool's brink.

Vultures, rocking high in air
By the western gate,
Warned me with discordant cry
You are even such as I;
You have no mate.

(1920—recast 1966)

BOWER-BIRD

The Bower-bird improvised a cool retreat
For the hen he honoured, doing his poor best
With parrot-plumage, orchids, bones and corals,
To engage her fancy.
                    But this was no nest . . .
So, though the Penguin dropped at his hen's feet
An oval stone to signal: 'be my bride',
And though the Jackdaw's nest was glorified
With diamond rings and brooches massed inside,
It was the Bower-bird who contented me
By not equating love with matrimony.

MIST

Fire and Deluge, rival pretenders
To ruling the world's end; these cannot daunt us
Whom flames will never singe, nor floods drown,
While we stand guard against their murderous child
Mist, that slily catches at love's throat,
Shrouding the clear sun and clean waters
Of all green gardens everywhere—
The twitching mouths likewise and furtive eyes
Of those who speak us fair.

THE WORD

The Word is unspoken
Between honest lovers:
They substitute a silence
Or wave at a wild flower,
Sighing inaudibly.

That it exists indeed
Will scarcely be disputed:
The wildest of conceptions
Can be reduced to speech—
Or so the Schoolmen teach.

You and I, thronged by angels,
Learned it in the same dream
Which startled us by moon-light,
And that we still revere it
Keeps our souls aflame.

'God' is a standing question
That still negates an answer.
The Word is not a question
But simple affirmation,
The antonym of 'God'.

Who would believe this Word
Could have so long been hidden
Behind a candid smile,
A sweet but hasty kiss
And always dancing feet?

PERFECTIONISTS

Interalienation of their hearts
It was not, though both played resentful parts
In proud unwillingness to share
One house, one pillow, the same fare.
It was perfectionism, they confess,
To know the truth and ask for nothing less.

Their fire-eyed guardians watched from overhead:
'These two alone have learned to love,' they said,
'But neither can forget
They are not worthy of each other yet.'

PRISON WALLS

Love, this is not the way
To treat a glorious day:
To cloud it over with conjectured fears,
Wiping my eyes before they brim with tears
And, long before we part,
Mourning the torments of my jealous heart.

That you have tried me more
Than who else did before,
Is no good reason to prognosticate
My last ordeal: when I must greet with hate
Your phantom fairy prince
Conjured in childhood, lost so often since.

Nor can a true heart rest
Resigned to second best—
Why did you need to temper me so true
That I became your sword of swords, if you
Must nail me on your wall
And choose a painted lath when the blows fall?

Because I stay heart-whole,
Because you bound your soul
To mine, with curses should it wander free,
I charge you now to keep full faith with me
Nor can I ask for less
Than your unswerving honest-heartedness.

Then grieve no more, but while
Your flowers are scented, smile
And never sacrifice, as others may,
So clear a dawn to dread of Judgement Day—
Lest prison walls should see
Fresh tears of longing you let fall for me.

A DREAM OF HELL

You reject the rainbow
Of our Sun castle
As hyperbolic;

You enjoin the Moon
Of our pure trysts
To condone deceit;

Lured to violence
By a lying spirit,
You break our troth.

Seven wide, enchanted
Wards of horror
Lie stretched before you,

To brand your naked breast
With impious colours,
To band your thighs.

How can I discharge
Your confused spirit
From its chosen hell?

You who once dragged me
From the bubbling slime
Of a tidal reach,

Who washed me, fed me,
Laid me in white sheets,
Warmed me in brown arms,

Would you have me cede
Our single sovereignty
To your tall demon?

OUR SELF

When first we came together
It was no chance foreshadowing
Of a chance happy ending.
The case grows always clearer
By its own worse disorder:
However reasonably we oppose
That unquiet integer, our self, we lose.

Robert Graves, 1960.

A bracelet invisible
~~for~~ for your busy wrist
Twisted from silver
Of ~~the~~ a chill night:
From silver of the Moon,
~~from~~ her sheer halo —
Here the scheming demons
Pale ~~in~~ their flight.

A Bracelet

A bracelet invisible for your busy wrist,
Twisted from silver of a chill night,
From silver of the full Moon, from her sheer halo:
Here the scheming demons pale in their flight .

Worksheets for *A Bracelet*. (*The Malahat Review*)

A BRACELET

A bracelet invisible
For your busy wrist,
Twisted from silver ~~Of a chill night:~~
From silver of the Moon,
From her sheer halo
~~Here the scheming demons~~
~~Pale in their flight.~~
Of a falling star

Spilt afar

clear

A BRACELET

A bracelet invisible
For your busy wrist,
Twisted from silver
Spilt afar,
From silver of the Moon,
From her sheer halo,
From the ~~cheate~~ beauty
Of a shooting star.

Robert Graves, 1961. (New York *Times*)

BITES AND KISSES

Heather and holly,
Bites and kisses,
A courtship-royal
On the hill's red cusp.
Look up, look down,
Gaze all about you—
A livelier world
By ourselves contrived:

Swan in full course
Up the Milky Way,
Moon in her wildness,
Sun ascendant
In Crab or Lion,
Beyond the bay
A pride of dolphins
Curving and tumbling
With bites and kisses . . .

Or dog-rose petals
Well-starred by dew,
Or jewelled pebbles,
Or waterlilies open
For the dragon-flies
In their silver and blue.

SUN-FACE AND MOON-FACE

We twin cherubs above the Mercy Seat,
Sun-face and Moon-face,
Locked in the irrevocable embrace
That guards our children from defeat,
Are fire not flesh; as none will dare deny
Lest his own soul should die.

FREEHOLD

Though love expels the ugly past
Restoring you this house at last—
This generous-hearted mind and soul
Reserved from alien control—
How can you count on living free
From sudden jolts of history,
From interceptive sigh or stare
That heaves you back to how-things-were
And makes you answerable for
The casualties of bygone war?
Yet smile your vaguest: make it clear
That then was then, but now is here.

THE NECKLACE

Variegated flowers, nuts, cockle-shells
And pebbles, chosen lovingly and strung
On golden spider-webs with a gold clasp
For your neck, naturally: and each bead touched
By a child's lips as he stoops over them:
Wear these for the new miracle they announce—
All four cross-quarter-days beseech you—
Your safe return from shipwreck, drought and war,
Beautiful as before, to what you are.

A BRACELET

A bracelet invisible
For your busy wrist,
Twisted from silver
Spilt afar,
From silver of the clear Moon,
From her sheer halo,
From the male beauty
Of a shooting star.

BLACKENING SKY

Lightning enclosed by a vast ring of mirrors,
Instant thunder extravagantly bandied
Between red cliffs no hawk may nest upon,
Triumphant jetting, passion of deluge: ours—
With spray that stuns, dams that lurch and are gone. . . .

But against this insensate hubbub of subsidence
Our voices, always true to a fireside tone,
Meditate on the secret marriage of flowers
Or the bees' paradise, with much else more;
And while the sky blackens anew for rain,
On why we love as none ever loved before.

BLESSED SUN

Honest morning blesses the Sun's beauty;
Noon, his endurance; dusk, his majesty;
Sweetheart, our own twin worlds bask in the glory
And searching wisdom of that single eye—
Why must the Queen of Night on her moon throne
Tear up their contract and still reign alone?

LION-GENTLE

Love, never disavow our vow
Nor wound your lion-gentle:
Take what you will, dote on it, keep it,
But pay your debts with a grave, wilful smile
Like a woman of the sword.

SPITE OF MIRRORS

O what astonishment if you
Could see yourself as others do,
Foiling the mirror's wilful spite
That shows your left cheek as the right
And shifts your lovely crooked smile
To the wrong corner! But meanwhile
Lakes, pools and puddles all agree
(Bound in a vast conspiracy)
To reflect only your stern look
Designed for peering in a book—
No easy laugh, no glint of rage,
No thoughts in cheerful pilgrimage,
No start of guilt, no rising fear,
No premonition of a tear.

How, with a mirror, can you keep
Watch on your eyelids closed in sleep?
How judge which profile to bestow
On a new coin or cameo?
How, from two steps behind you, stare
At your firm nape discovered bare
Of ringlets as you bend and reach
Transparent pebbles from the beach?
Love, if you long for a surprise
Of self-discernment, hold my eyes
And plunge deep down in them to see
Sights never long withheld from me.

PRIDE OF LOVE

I face impossible feats at your command,
Resentful at the tears of love you shed
For the faint-hearted sick who flock to you;
But since all love lies wholly in the giving,
Weep on: your tears are true,
Nor can despair provoke me to self-pity
Where pride alone is due.

HOODED FLAME

Love, though I sorrow, I shall never grieve:
Grief is to mourn a flame extinguished;
Sorrow, to find it hooded for the hour
When planetary influences deceive
And hope, like wine, turns sour.

INJURIES

Injure yourself, you injure me:
Is that not true as true can be?
Nor can you give me cause to doubt
It works the other way about;
So what precautions must I take
Not to be injured for love's sake?

HER BRIEF WITHDRAWAL

'Forgive me, love, if I withdraw awhile:
It is only that you ask such bitter questions,
Always another beyond the extreme last.
And the answers astound: you have entangled me
In my own mystery. Grant me a respite:
I was happier far, not asking, nor much caring,
Choosing by appetite only: self-deposed,
Self-reinstated, no one observing.
When I belittled this vibrancy of touch
And the active vengeance of these folded arms
No one could certify my powers for me
Or my saining virtue, or know that I compressed
Knots of destiny in a careless fist,
I who had passed for a foundling from the hills
Of innocent and flower-like phantasies,
Though minting silver by my mere tread. . . .
Did I not dote on you, I well might strike you
For implicating me in your true dream.'

THE CRANE

The Crane lounes loudly in his need,
    And so for love I loune:
Son to the sovereign Sun indeed,
    Courier of the Moon.

STRANGENESS

You love me strangely, and in strangeness
I love you wholly, with no parallel
To this long miracle; for each example
Of love coincidence levels a finger
At strangeness undesigned as unforeseen.

And this long miracle is to discover
The inmost you and never leave her;
To show no curiosity for another;
To forge the soul and its desire together
Gently, openly and for ever.

Seated in silence, clothed in silence
And face to face—the room is small
But thronged with visitants—
We ask for nothing: we have all.

XXI

SONG: HOW CAN I CARE?

How can I care whether you sigh for me
    While still I sleep alone swallowing back
The spittle of desire, unmanned, a tree
    Pollarded of its crown, a dusty sack
    Tossed on the stable rack?

How can I care what coloured frocks you wear,
    What humming-birds you watch on jungle hills,
What phosphorescence wavers in your hair,
    Or with what water-music the night fills—
    Dear love, how can I care?

SONG: THOUGH ONCE TRUE LOVERS

Though once true lovers,
    We are less than friends.
What woman ever
    So ill-used her man?
That I played false
    Not even she pretends:
May God forgive her,
    For, alas, I can.

SONG: CHERRIES OR LILIES

Death can have no alternative but Love,
Or Love but Death.
Acquaintance dallying on the path of Love,
Sickness on that of Death,
Pause at a bed-side, doing what they can
With fruit and flowers bought from the barrow man.

Death can have no alternative but Love,
Or Love but Death.
Then shower me cherries from your orchard, Love,
Or strew me lilies, Death:
For she and I were never of that breed
Who vacillate or trifle with true need.

SONG: CROWN OF STARS

Lion-heart, you prowl alone
True to Virgin, Bride and Crone;
None so black of brow as they
Now, tomorrow, yesterday.
Yet the night you shall not see
Must illuminate all three
As the tears of love you shed
Blaze about their single head
And a sword shall pierce the side
Of true Virgin, Crone and Bride
Among mansions of the dead.

SONG: THE PALM TREE

Palm-tree, single and apart
        In your serpent-haunted land,
Like the fountain of a heart
        Soaring into air from sand—
None can count it as a fault
That your roots are fed with salt.

Panniers-full of dates you yield,
        Thorny branches laced with light,
Wistful for no pasture-field
        Fed by torrents from a height,
Short of politics to share
With the damson or the pear.

Never-failing phoenix tree
        In your serpent-haunted land,
Fount of magic soaring free
        From a desert of salt sand;
Tears of joy are salty too—
Mine shall flow in praise of you.

SONG: FIG TREE IN LEAF

One day in early Spring
Upon bare branches perching
        Great companies of birds are seen
        Clad all at once in pilgrim green
Their news of love to bring:

Their fig tree parable,
For which the world is watchful,
        Retold with shining wings displayed:
        Her secret flower, her milk, her shade,
Her scarlet, blue and purple.

264

SONG: DEW-DROP AND DIAMOND

The difference between you and her
(Whom I to you did once prefer)
Is clear enough to settle:
She like a diamond shone, but you
Shine like an early drop of dew
Poised on a red rose-petal.

The dew-drop carries in its eye
Mountain and forest, sea and sky,
With every change of weather;
Contrariwise, a diamond splits
The prospect into idle bits
That none can piece together.

SONG: SULLEN MOODS

Love, never count your labour lost
        Though I turn sullen or retired
Even at your side; my thought is crossed
        With fancies by no evil fired.

And when I answer you, some days,
        Vaguely and wildly, never fear
That my love walks forbidden ways,
        Snapping the ties that hold it here.

If I speak gruffly, this mood is
        Mere indignation at my own
Shortcomings, plagues, uncertainties:
        I forget the gentler tone.

You, now that you have come to be
        My one beginning, prime and end,
I count at last as wholly me,
        Lover no longer nor yet friend.

Help me to see you as before
    When overwhelmed and dead, almost,
I stumbled on that secret door
    Which saves the live man from the ghost.

Be once again the distant light,
    Promise of glory, not yet known
In full perfection—wasted quite
    When on my imperfection thrown.

SONG: JUST FRIENDS

Just friend, you are my only friend—
You think the same of me
And swear our love must never end
Though lapped in secrecy,
As all true love should be.
They ask us: 'What about you two?'
I answer 'Only friends' and you:
'Just friends' gently agree.

SONG: OF COURSE

No, of course we were never
    Off course in our love,
Being nourished by manna
    That dripped from above,

And our secret of loving
    Was taught us, it seems,
By ravens and owlets
    And fast-flowing streams.

We had sealed it with kisses,
    It blazed from our eyes,
Yet all was unspoken
    And proof against lies.

For to publish a secret
    Once learned in the rain
Would have meant to lose course
    And not find it again.

So this parting, of course,
    Is illusion, not fate,
And the love in your letters
    Comes charged overweight.

SONG: THREE RINGS FOR HER

Flowers remind of jewels;
Jewels, of flowers;
Flowers, of innocent morning;
Jewels, of honest evening—
Emerald, moonstone, opal—
For so I mean, and meant.
Jewels are longer lasting—
Emerald, moonstone, opal;
Opal, emerald, moonstone:
Moonstone, opal, emerald—
And wear a livelier scent.

SINCÈREMENT

J'étais confus à cet instant.
Quelle honte d'avoir écrit
L'adverbe aveugle 'sincèrement'—
'Je t'aime' m'aurait suffi
Sans point et sans souci.

DANS UN SEUL LIT

Entre deux belles femmes dans un seul lit
Cet homme, se sentant interdit,
Des convenances n'ose pas faire foin
Mais opte pour elle qu'il aime le moins.

Entre deux beaux hommes en pareil cas,
Une dame sans moeurs si délicats
Mais sans s'exprimer en termes crus,
Se penche vers lui qu'elle aime le plus.

POSSIBLY

Possibly is not a monosyllable;
    Then answer me
At once if possible
    Monosyllabically,
No will be good, *Yes* even better
Though longer by one letter.

Possibly is not a monosyllable,
    And my heart flies shut
At the warning rumble
    Of a suspended *But* . . .
O love, be brief and exact
In confession of simple fact.

IS NOW THE TIME?

If he asks, 'Is now the time?', it is not the time.
She turns her head from his concern with time
As a signal not to haste it;
And every time he asks: 'Is now the time?'
A hundred nights are wasted.

268

TWINS

Siamese twins: one, maddened by
The other's moral bigotry,
Resolved at length to misbehave
And drink them both into the grave.

SAIL AND OAR

Woman sails, man must row:
Each, disdainful of a tow,
Cuts across the other's bows
Shame or fury to arouse—
And evermore it shall be so,
Lest man sail, or woman row.

GOOSEFLESH ABBEY

Nuns are allowed fully liberty of conscience.
Yet might this young witch, when she took the veil,
Count on an aged Abbess's connivance
At keeping toad-familiars in her cell?
Some called it liberty; but others, licence—
And how was she to tell?

THE HOME-COMING

At the tangled heart of a wood I fell asleep,
Bewildered by her silence and her absence—
As though such potent lulls in love were not
Ordained by the demands of pure music.

269

A bird sang: 'Close your eyes, it is not for long—
Dream of what gold and crimson she will wear
In honour of your oak-brown.'

It was her hoopoe. Yet, when the spread heavens
Of my feast night glistened with the shooting stars
And she walked unheralded up through the dim light
Of the home lane, I did not recognise her—
So lost a man can be
Who feeds on hopes and fears and memory.

WITH THE GIFT OF A LION'S CLAW

Queen of the Crabs, accept this claw
Plucked from a Lion's patient paw;
It shall propel her forward who
Ran sideways always hitherto.

WIGS AND BEARDS

In the bad old days a bewigged country Squire
Would never pay his debts, unless at cards,
Shot, angled, urged his pack through standing grain,
Horsewhipped his tenantry, snorted at the arts,
Toped himself under the table every night,
Blasphemed God with a cropful of God-damns,
Aired whorehouse French or lame Italian,
Set fashions of pluperfect slovenliness
And claimed siegneurial rights over all women
Who slept, imprudently, under the same roof.

Taxes and wars long ago ploughed them under—
'And serve the bastards right' the Beards agree,
Hurling their empties through the café window
And belching loud as they proceed downstairs.
Latter-day bastards of that famous stock,
They never rode a nag, nor gaffed a trout,
Nor winged a pheasant, nor went soldiering,
But remain true to the same hell-fire code
In all available particulars
And scorn to pay their debts even at cards.
Moreunder (which is to subtract, not add),
Their ancestors called themselves gentlemen
As they, in the same sense, call themselves artists.

PERSONAL PACKAGING, INC.

Folks, we have zero'd in to a big break-thru:
Our boys are learning how to package *people*
By a new impermeable-grading process
In cartons of mixed twenties—all three sexes!

Process involves molecular adjustment
To micro-regulated temperatures,
Making them unexpendable time-wise
Thru a whole century . . . Some clients opt for
Five thousand years, or six, in real deep freeze—
A chance what sensible guy would kick against
To pile up dollars at compound interest?
Nor do we even propose that they quit smoking
Or, necessarily, be parted from their wives.

WORK ROOM

Camp-stool for chair once more and packing case for table;
All histories of doubt extruded from this room
With its menacing, promising, delusive, toppling bookshelves;
Nothing now astir but you in my fresh imagination,
And no letters but yours ever demanding answers.
To start all over again; indeed, why should I not?—
With a new pen, clean paper, full inkpot.

THE ARK

Beasts of the field, fowls likewise of the air,
Came trooping, seven by seven or pair by pair;
And though from Hell the arch-fiend Samael
Bawled out 'Escapist!' Noah did not care.

ALL EXCEPT HANNIBAL

Trapped in a dismal marsh, he told his troops:
'No lying down, lads! Form your own mess-groups
And sit in circles, each man on the knees
Of the man behind; then nobody will freeze.'

They obeyed his orders, as the cold sun set,
Drowsing all night in one another's debt,
All except Hannibal himself, who chose
His private tree-stump—he was one of those!

THE BEGGAR MAID AND KING COPHETUA

To be adored by a proud Paladin
Whom the wide world adored,
To queen it over countless noblewomen:
What fame was hers at last,
What lure and envy!

Yet, being still a daughter of the mandrake
She sighed for more than fame;
Not all the gold with which Cophetua crowned her
Could check this beggar-maid's
Concupiscence.

Sworn to become proverbially known
As martyred by true love,
She took revenge on his victorious name
That blotted her own fame
For woman's magic.

True to her kind, she slipped away one dawn
With a poor stable lad,
Gaunt, spotted, drunken, scrawny, desperate,
Mean of intelligence
As bare of honour.

So pitiable indeed that when the guards
Who caught them saw the green
Stain on her finger from his plain brass ring
They gaped at it, too moved
Not to applaud her.

FOR EVER

Sweetheart, I beg you to renew and seal
With a not supererogatory kiss
Our contract of 'For Ever'.
                          Learned judges
Deplore the household sense 'interminable':
True love, they rule, never acknowledges
Future or past, only a perfect now. . . .
But let it read 'For Ever,' anyhow!

JUGUM IMPROBUM

Pyrrha, jugo tandem vitulum junges-ne leoni?
Sit tibi dilectus, num stricto verbere debet
Compelli pavitans medium moriturus in ignem.

DE ARTE POETICA

De minimis curat non Lex, utcumque poeta.

SIT MIHI TERRA LEVIS

Ante mortem qui defletus
    Solis lucem repperit
Ante Mortem perquietus,
    Erato, domum redit.

XXII

ASTYMELUSA*

'Astymelusa!'
              Knees at your approach
Suddenly give, more than in sleep or death—
As well they may; such love compels them.
'Astymelusa!'
              But no answer comes.
Crowned with a leafy crown, the girl passes
Like a star afloat through glittering sky,
Or a golden flower, or drifted thistledown.

* A fragment by the Dorian Greek poet Alcman, seventh century B.C., found among the Oxyrhynchus papyri.

TOUSLED PILLOW

She appeared in Triad—Youth, Truth, Beauty—
Full face and profiles whispering together
All night at my bed-foot.
                          And when dawn came
At last, from a tousled pillow resolutely
I made my full surrender:
'So be it, Goddess, claim me without shame
And tent me in your hair.'
                          Since when she holds me
As close as candlewick to candleflame
And from all hazards free,
My soul drawn back to its virginity.

TO BE IN LOVE

To spring impetuously in air and remain
Treading on air for three heart-beats or four,
Then to descend at leisure; or else to scale
The forward-tilted crag with no hand-holds;
Or, disembodied, to carry roses home
From a Queen's garden—this is being in love,
Graced with *agilitas* and *subtilitas*
At which few famous lovers ever guessed
Though children may foreknow it, deep in dream,
And ghosts may mourn it, haunting their own tombs,
And peacocks cry it, in default of speech.

FACT OF THE ACT

On the other side of the world's narrow lane
You lie in bed, your young breasts tingling
With imagined kisses, your lips puckered,
Your fists tight.

Dreaming yourself naked in my arms,
Free from discovery, under some holm oak;
The high sun peering through thick branches,
All winds mute.

Endlessly you prolong the moment
Of your delirium: a first engagement,
Silent, inevitable, fearful,
Honey-sweet.

Will it be so in fact? Will fact mirror
Your virginal ecstasies:
True love, uncircumstantial,
No blame, no shame?

It is for you, now, to say 'come';
It is for you, now, to prepare the bed;
It is for you as the sole hostess
Of your white dreams—

It is for you to open the locked gate,
It is for you to shake red apples down,
It is for you to halve them with your hands
That both may eat.

Yet expectation lies as far from fact
As fact's own after-glow in memory;
Fact is a dark return to man's beginnings,
Test of our hardihood, test of a wilful
And blind acceptance of each other
As also flesh.

TO OGMIAN HERCULES

Your Labours are performed, your Bye-works too;
Your ashes gently drift from Oeta's peak.
Here is escape then, Hercules, from empire.

Lithe Hebë, youngest of all Goddesses,
Who circles on the Moon's broad threshing floor
Harboured no jealousy for Megara,
Augë, Hippolytë, Deianeira,
But grieved for each in turn. You broke all hearts,
Burning too Sun-like for a Grecian bride.

Rest your immortal head on Hebë's lap,
What wars you started let your sons conclude,
Meditate a new Alphabet, heal wounds,
Draw poets to you with long golden chains
But still go armed with club and lion's pelt.

ARROW SHOTS

Only a madman could mistake,
    When shot at from behind a tree,
The whizz and thud that arrows make—
    Yours, for example, fired at me.

Some bows are drawn to blind or maim,
    I have known others drawn to kill,
But truth in love is your sole aim
    And proves your vulnerary skill.

Though often, drowsing at mid-day,
    I wince to find myself your mark,
Let me concede the hit, but say:
    'Your hand is steadiest after dark.'

SHE TO HIM

To have it, sweetheart, is to know you have it
Rather than think you have it;
To think you have it is a wish to take it,
Though afterwards you would not have it—
And thus a fear to take it.
Yet if you know you have it, you may take it
And know that still you have it.

WITHIN REASON

You have wandered widely through your own mind
And your own perfect body;
Thus learning, within reason, gentle one,
Everything that can prove worth the knowing.

278

A concise wisdom never attained by those
Bodiless nobodies
Who travel pen in hand through others' minds,
But without reason,
Feeding on manifold contradiction.

To stand perplexed by love's inconsequences
Like fire-flies in your hair
Or distant flashes of a summer storm:
Such are the stabs of joy you deal me
Who also wander widely through my mind
And still imperfect body.

THE YET UNSAYABLE

It was always fiercer, brighter, gentler than could be told
Even in words quickened by Truth's dark eye:
Its absence, whirlpool; its presence, deluge;
Its time, astonishment; its magnitude,
A murderous dagger-point.
                              So we surrender
Our voices to the dried and scurrying leaves
And choose our own long-predetermined path
From the unsaid to the yet unsayable
In silence of love and love's temerity.

NONE THE WISER

They would be none the wiser, even could they overhear
My slurred ecstatic mumbling or grow somehow aware
Of eyes ablaze behind shut lids in the attic gloom.

Even if they adjured me on pain of death to disclose
All that I see and am when I so absent myself,
What would they make of steady, somnolent light-rings
Converging, violet-blue or green hypnotic gold,
Upon a warded peep-hole, as it were a rift in Space,
Through which I peer, as it might be into your eyes,
And pass disembodied, a spiral wisp or whorl
Tall, slanted, russet-red, crowned with a lunar nimbus?—
To you the central flow, the glow, the ease, the hush
Of music drawn through irrecoverable modes.
And then such after-glory, meteors across the heart
When I awake, astonished, in the bed where once you dreamed.

'Metaphysical' they would comment lamely, 'metaphysical';
But you would smile at me for leaving so much out.

THE NARROW SEA

With you for mast and sail and flag,
And anchor never known to drag,
Death's narrow but oppressive sea
Looks not unnavigable to me.

THE OLIVE-YARD

Now by a sudden shift of eye
The hitherto exemplary world
Takes on immediate wildness
And birds, trees, winds, the very letters
Of our childhood's alphabet, alter
Into rainbowed mysteries.

Flesh is no longer flesh, but power;
Numbers, no longer arithmetical,
Dance like lambs, fly like doves;
And silence falls at last, though silken branches
Gently heave in the near olive-yard
And vague cloud labours on.

Whose was the stroke of summer genius
Flung from a mountain fastness
Where the griffon-vulture soars
That let us read our shrouded future
As easily as a book of prayer
Spread open on the knee?

XXIII

SONG: DREAM WARNING

A lion in the path, a lion;
A jewelled serpent by the sun
Hatched in a desert silence
And stumbled on by chance;
A peacock crested with green fire,
His legs befouled in mire;
Not less, an enlacement of seven dreams
On a rainbow scale returning
To the drum that throbs against their melodies
Its dark insistent warning.

SONG: BEYOND GIVING

There is a giving beyond giving:
    Yours to me
Who awoke last night, hours before the dawn,
    Set free
By one intolerable lightning stroke
    That ripped the sky
To understand what love withholds in love,
    And why.

SONG: THE SIGIL

Stumbling up an unfamiliar stairway
   Between my past and future
And overtaken by the shadowy mind
   Of a girl dancing for love,
   I glanced over my shoulder.

She had read my secret name, that was no doubt,
   For which how could I blame her?
Her future paired so gently with my own,
   Her past so innocently,
   It flung me in a fever.

Thereupon, as on every strange occasion,
   The past relived its future
With what outdid all hopes and fantasies—
   How could I not concede
   My sigil in its favour?

SONG: BASKET OF BLOSSOM

Jewels here lie heaped for you
Under jasmine, under lilac—
Leave them undisclosed awhile;
If the blossoms be short-lasting
Smile, but with your secret smile.

I have always from the first
Made my vow in honour's name
Only thus to fetch you jewels,
Never vaunting of the same.

SONG: YESTERDAY ONLY

Not today, not tomorrow,
Yesterday only:
A long-lasting yesterday
Devised by us to swallow
Today with tomorrow.

When was your poem hidden
Underneath my pillow,
When was your rose-bush planted
Underneath my window—
Yesterday only?

Green leaves, red roses,
Blazoned upon snow,
A long-lasting yesterday,
Today with tomorrow,
Always and only.

SONG: TWINNED HEART

Challenged once more to reunite,
    Perfect in every limb
But screened against the intrusive light
    By ghosts and cherubim,

I call your beauty to my bed,
    My pride you call to yours
Though clouds run maniac overhead
    And cruel rain down pours,

With both of us prepared to wake
    Each in a bed apart,
True to a spell no power can break:
    The beat of a twinned heart.

SONG: OLIVE TREE

Call down a blessing
On that green sapling,
A sudden blessing
For true love's sake
On that green sapling
Framed by our window
With her leaves twinkling
As we lie awake.
Two birds flew from her
In the eye of morning
Their folded feathers
In the sun to shake.

Augury recorded,
Vision rewarded
With an arrow flying
With a sudden sting,
With a sure blessing,
With a double dart,
With a starry ring,
With music from the mountains
In the air, in the heart
This bright May morning
Re-echoing.

SONG: ONCE MORE

These quiet months of watching for
An endless moment of once more
May not be shortened,

But while we share them at a distance,
In irreproachable persistence,
Are strangely brightened.

And these long hours of perfect sleep
When company in love we keep,
By time unstraitened,

Yield us a third of the whole year
In which to embrace each other here,
Sleeping together, watching for
An endless moment of once more
By dreams enlightened.

SONG: THE PROMISE

While you were promised to me
But still were not yet given,
There was this to be said:
Though wishes might be wishes,
A promise was a promise—
Like the shadow of a cedar,
Or the moon overhead,
Or the firmness of your fingers,
Or the print of your kisses,
Or your lightness of tread,
With not a doubt between us
Once bats began their circling
Among the palms and cedars
And it was time for bed.

SONG: VICTIMS OF CALUMNY

Equally innocent,
Confused by evil,
Pondering the event,
Aloof and penitent,
With hearts left sore
By a cruel calumny,
With eyes half-open now
To its warped history,
But undeceivably
Both in love once more.

SONG: TO A ROSE

Queen of Sharon in the valley,
Clasp my head your breasts between:
Darkly blind me to your beauty—
Rose renowned for blood-red berries
Ages earlier than for fragrant
Blossom and sweet hidden honey,
Save by studious bees.

SONG: THE CLOCKS OF TIME

The clocks of time divide us:
You sleep while I wake—
No need to think it monstrous
Though I remain uneasy,
Watchful, albeit drowsy,
Communing over wastes of sea
With you, my other me.

Too strict a concentration,
Each on an absent self,
Distracts our prosecution
Of what this love implies:
Genius, with its complexities
Of working backwards from the answer
To bring a problem near.

But when your image shortens
(My eyes thrown out of focus)
And fades in the far distance—
Your features indistinguishable,
Your gait and form unstable—
Time's heart revives our closeness
Hand in hand, lip to lip.

SONG: WHEREVER WE MAY BE

Wherever we may be
There is mindlessness and mind,
There is lovelessness and love,
There is self, there is unself,
Within and without;
There is plus, there is minus;
There is empty, there is full;
There is God, the busy question
In denial of doubt.

There is mindlessness and mind,
There is deathlessness and death,
There is waking, there is sleeping,
There is false, there is true,
There is going, there is coming,
But upon the stroke of midnight
Wherever we may be,
There am I, there are you.

XXIV

GOLD CLOUD

Your gold cloud, towering far above me,
Through which I climb from darkness into sleep
Has the warmth of sun, rain's morning freshness
And a scent either of wood-smoke or of jasmine;
Nor is the ascent steep.

Our creature, Time, bends readily as willow:
We plan our own births, that at least we know,
Whether in the lovely moment of death
Or when we first meet, here in Paradise,
As now, so years ago.

COMPACT

My love for you, though true, wears the
    extravagance of centuries;
Your love for me is fragrant, simple and millennial.
Smiling without a word, you watch my extravagances
    pass;
To check them would be presumptuous and
    unmaidenly—
As it were using me like an ill-bred schoolboy.

Dear Live-apart, when I sit confused by the active
    spites
Tormenting me with too close sympathy for fools,
Too dark a rage against hidden plotters of evil,
Too sour a mind, or soused with sodden wool-bales—
I turn my eyes to the light smoke drifting from
    your fire.

Our settled plan has been: never to make plans—
The future, present and past being already settled
Beyond review or interpretative conjecture
By the first decision of truth that we clasped hands
    upon:
To conserve a purity of soul each for the other.

TRIAL OF INNOCENCE

Urged by your needs and my desire,
I first made you a woman; nor was either
Troubled by fear of hidden evil
Or of temporal circumstance;
For circumstances never alter cases
When lovers, hand in hand, face trial
Pleading uncircumstantial innocence.

LOVE GIFTS

Though love be gained only by truth in love
Never by gifts, yet there are gifts of love
That match or enhance beauty, that indeed
Fetch beauty with them. Always the man gives,
Never the woman—unless flowers or berries
Or pebbles from the shore.
                              She welcomes jewels
To ponder and pore over tremblingly
By candlelight. 'Why does he love me so,
Divining my concealed necessities?'
And afterwards (there is no afterwards
In perfect love, nor further call for gifts)
Writes: 'How you spoil me!', meaning: 'You are
    mine',
But sends him cornflowers, pinks and columbine.

MANKIND AND OCEAN

You celebrate with kisses the good fortune
Of a new and cloudless moon
(Also the tide's good fortune),
Content with July fancies
To brown your naked bodies
On the slopes of a sea-dune.

Mankind and Ocean, Ocean and mankind:
Those fatal tricks of temper,
Those crooked acts of murder
Provoked by the wind—
I am no Ocean lover,
Nor can I love mankind.

To love the Ocean is to taste salt,
To drink the blood of sailors,
To watch the waves assault
Mast-high a cliff that shudders
Under their heartless hammers. . . .
Is wind alone at fault?

POISONED DAY

The clouds dripped poisonous dew to spite
A day for weeks looked forward to. True love
Sickened that evening without remedy:
We neither quarrelled, kissed, nor said good-night
But fell asleep, our arms around each other,
And awoke to the gentle hiss of rain on grass
And thrushes calling that the worst was over.

VIRGIN MIRROR

Souls in virginity joined together
    Rest unassailable:
Ours is no undulant fierce rutting fever
    But clear unbroken lunar magic able
    To mirror loves illimitable.

When first we chose this power of being
    I never paused to warn you
What ruinous charms the world was weaving;
    I knew you for a child fostered in virtue
    And swore no hand could hurt you.

Then should I suffer nightmares now
    Lest you, grown somewhat older,
Be lured to accept a worldly where and how,
    Carelessly breathing on the virgin mirror,
    Clouding love's face for ever?

WHAT IS LOVE?

But what is love? Tell me, dear heart, I beg you.
Is it a reattainment of our centre,
A core of trustful innocence come home to?

Is it, perhaps, a first wild bout of being,
The taking of our own extreme measure
And for a few hours knowing everything?

Or what is love? Is it primeval vision
That stars our course with oracles of danger
And looks to death for timely intervention?

SECRET THEATRE

When from your sleepy mind the day's burden
Falls like a bushel sack on a barn floor,
Be prepared for music, for natural mirages
And for night's incomparable parade of colour.

Neither of us daring to assume direction
Of an unforeseen and fiery entertainment,
We clutch hands in the seventh row of the stalls
And watch together, quivering, astonished, silent.

It is hours past midnight now; a flute signals
Far off; we mount the stage as though at random,
Boldly ring down the curtain, then dance out our love:
Lost to the outraged, humming auditorium.

HOW IT STARTED

It started, unexpectedly of course,
At a wild midnight dance, in my own garden,
To which indeed I was not invited:
I read: 'Teen-agers only.'

In the circumstances I stayed away
Until you fetched me out on the tiled floor
Where, acting as an honorary teen-ager,
I kicked off both my shoes.

Since girls like you must set the stage always,
With lonely men for choreographers,
I chose the step, I even called the tune;
And we both danced entranced.

Here the narrator pauses circumspectly,
Knowing me not unpassionate by nature
And the situation far from normal:
Two apple-seeds had sprouted. . . .

Recordable history began again
With you no longer in your late teens
And me socially (once more) my age—
Yet that was where it started.

BRIEF REUNION

Our one foreboding was: we might forget
How strangely close absence had drawn us,
How close once more we must be drawn by parting—
Absence, dark twin of presence!

Nor could such closeness be attained by practice
Of even the most heroic self-deceit:
Only by inbred faculties far wiser
Than any carnal sense—

Progress in which had disciplined us both
To the same doting pride: a stoicism
Which might confuse, at every brief reunion,
Presence with pangs of absence.

And if this pride should overshoot its mark,
Forcing on us a raw indifference
To what might happen when our hearts were fired
By renewed hours of presence?

Could we forget what carnal pangs had seized us
Three summers past in a burst of moonlight,
Making us more possessive of each other
Than either dared concede?—a prescience
Of the vast grief that each sublunary pair
Transmits at last to its chance children
With tears of violence.

THE JUDGES

Crouched on wet shingle at the cove
In day-long search for treasure-trove—
Meaning the loveliest-patterned pebble,
Of any colour imaginable,
Ground and smoothed by a gentle sea—
How seldom, Julia, we agree
On our day's find: the perfect one
To fetch back home when day is done,
Splendid enough to stupefy
The fiercest, most fastidious eye—
Tossing which back we tell the sea:
'Work on it one more century!'

LOVE AND NIGHT

Though your professions, ages and conditions
Might seem to any sober person
Irreconcilable,

Yet still you claim the inalienable right
To kiss in corners and exchange long letters
Patterned with well-pierced hearts.

When judges, dazzled by your blazing eyes,
Mistake you both for Seventh Day Adventists
(Heaven rest their innocent souls!)

You smile impassively and say no word—
The why and how of magic being tabu
Even in courts of Law.

Who could have guessed that your unearthly glow
Conceals a power no judgement can subdue,
Nor act of God, nor death?

Your love is not desire but certainty,
Perfect simultaneity,
Inheritance not conquest;

Long silences divide its delicate phases
With simple absence, almost with unbeing,
Before each new resurgence.

Such love has clues to a riddling of the maze:
Should you let fall the thread, grope for it,
Unawed by the thick gloom.

Such love illuminates the far house
Where difficult questions meet their answers
And lies get scoured away.

Your powers to love were forged by Mother Night—
Her perfect discipline of thought and breath—
Sleep is their sustenance.

You prophesy without accessories:
Her words run splashed in light across your walls
For reading as you wake.

But Night, no doubt, has deathless other secrets
Guarded by her unblinking owls against
All clumsy stumbling on them.

CHILD WITH VETERAN

You were a child and I your veteran;
An age of violence lay between us,
Yet both claimed citizenship of the same land
Conversing in our own soft, hidden language,
Often by signs alone.

Our eyelids closed, little by little,
And we fell chained in an enchantment
Heavier than any known or dreamed before,
Groping in darkness for each other's fingers
Lifting them to our lips.

Here brooded power beyond comparison,
Tremendous as a thousand bee-stings
Or a great volley of steel-tipped arrows
With which to take possession of a province
That no one could deny us,
For the swift regeneration of dead souls
And the pride of those undead.

SUPERSTITION

Forget the foolishness with which I vexed you:
Mine was a gun-shy superstition
Surviving from defeat in former loves
And banished when you stood staring aghast
At the replacement of your sturdy lover
By a disconsolate waif.

Blame the foul weather for my aching wounds,
Blame ugly history for my wild fears,
Nor ever turn from your own path; for still
Despite your fancies, your white silences,
Your disappearances, you remain bound
By this unshakeable trust I rest in you.

Go, because inner strength ordains your journey,
Making a necessary occasion seem
No more incidental. Love go with you
In distillation of all past and future—
You, a clear torrent flooding the mill-race,
Forcing its mill to grind
A coarse grain into flour for angels' bread.

PURIFICATION

'He numbed my heart, he stole away my truth,
He laid hands on my body.
Never had I known ecstasy like that:
I could have flown with him to the world's end
And thought of you no more.'

'Wake, dearest love, here in my own warm arms,
That was a nightmare only.
You kept the wall-side, leaving me the outer,
No demon slid between us to molest you.
This is a narrow bed.'

I would have brought her breakfast on a tray
But she seemed haunted still
By terror that in nine short months, maybe,
A demon's litter, twitching scaly tails,
Would hang from either breast.

And still she shuddered inconsolably
All day; our true love-magic
Dwindled and failed. 'He swore to take me
The round of Paris, on his midnight tours,
Fiddling for me to dance.'

Thus to have murdered love even in dream
Called for purification;
And (as the Great Queen yearly did at Paphos)
Down to the sea she trod and in salt water
Renewed virginity.

POWERS UNCONFESSED

Diffidently when asked who might I be,
I agreed that, yes, I ruled a small kingdom
Though, like yourself, free to wander abroad
Hatless, barefooted and incognito.

Abruptly we embraced—a strange event,
The casual passers-by taking less notice
Than had this been a chance meeting of cousins—
Nor did we argue over protocol.

You, from your queendom, answerable only
To royal virtue, not to a male code,
Knew me for supernatural, like yourself,
And fell at once head over heels in love;
As I also with you—but lamentably
Never confessed what wrathful powers attest
The Roman jealousy of my male genius.

PANDORA

But our escape: to what god did we owe it,
Pandora, my one love?
White-faced we lay, apart and all but dead.

In place of magic had you offered fancy
(Being still a girl and over-credulous)
To honour my poor genius?—
And with your careless innocence of death
Concealed the mischief and those unseen Spites
For long months haunting you and me, your Titan,
Chasing away the honey-bees of love?

Though my acute dream-senses, apprehending,
Warned me with fevers, chills and violences
That the postern gate was forced
And the keep in instant peril,
Why did my eyes stay blind and my ears deaf?

And this escape: to what god did we owe it,
Or to what unborn child?

SOLOMON'S SEAL

Peace is at last confirmed for us:
A double blessing, heavily priced,
Won back as we renew our maiden hearts
In a magic known to ourselves only,
Proof against furious tides of error
And bitter ironies of the self-damned:

Perfect in love now, though not sharing
The customary pillow—and our reasons
Appear shrouded in dark Egyptian dreams
That recreate us as a single being
Wholly in love with love.

Under each pyramid lies inverted
Its twin, the sister-bride to Pharaoh,
And so Solomon's seal bears witness.

Therefore we neither plead nor threaten
As lovers do who have lost faith—
Lovers not riven together by an oath
Sworn on the very brink of birth,
Nor by the penetrative ray of need
Piercing our doubled pyramid to its bed.

All time lies knotted here in Time's caress,
And so Solomon's seal bears witness.

TO PUT IT SIMPLY

Perfect reliance on the impossible
   By strict avoidance of all such conjecture
As underlies the so-called possible:
   That is true love's adventure.

Put it more simply: all the truth we need
   Is ours by curious preknowledge of it—
On love's impossibility agreed,
   Constrained neither by horoscope nor prophet.

Or put it still more simply: all we know
Is that love is and always must be so.

IN THE NAME OF VIRTUE

In the name of Virtue, girl,
Why must you try so hard
In the hard name of Virtue?
Is not such trying, questioning?
Such questioning, doubting?
Such doubting, guessing?
Such guessing, not-knowing?
Such not-knowing, not-being?
Such not-being, death?
Can death be Virtue?

Virtue is from listening
To a private angel,
An angel overheard
When the little-finger twitches—
The bold little-finger
That refused education:
When the rest went to college
And philosophized on Virtue,
It neither went, nor tried.

Knowing becomes doing
When all we need to know
Is how to check our pendulum
And move the hands around
For a needed golden instant
Of the future or past—
Then start time up again
With a bold little-finger
In Virtue's easy name.

TO TELL AND BE TOLD

What is it I most want in all the world?
To be with you at last, alone in the world,
And as I kiss with you to tell and be told.

A child you no more are, yet as a child
You foresaw miracles when no more a child—
So spread a bed for us, to tell and be told.

You wear my promises on rings of gold,
I wear your promise on a chain of gold:
For ever and once more to tell and be told.

THE THEME OF DEATH

Since love is an astonished always
Challenging the long lies of history,
Yesterday when I chose the theme of death
You shook a passionate finger at me:
'Wake from your nightmare! Would you murder love?
Wake from your nightmare!'

No, sweetheart! Death is nightmare when conceived
As God's Last Judgement, or the curse of Time—
Its intransgressible bounds of destiny;
But love is an astonished always
With death as affidavit for its birth
And timeless progress.

What if these tombs and catafalques conspire,
Menacing us with gross ancestral fears,
To dissipate my living truth, and yours,
To induct us into ritual weeping?
Our love remains a still astonished always,
Pure death its witness.

AT THE WELL

To work it out even a thought better
Than ever before—yet a thought rare enough
To raise a sigh of wonder—
That is your art (he said) but mine also
Since first I fell upon the secret
And sighed for wonder that our dry mouths
After a world of travel
Were drawn together by the same spell
To drink at the same well.

Coincidence (she said) continues with us,
Secret by secret,
Love's magic being no more than obstinacy
In love's perfection—
Like the red apple, highest on the tree
Reserved for you by me.

XXV

LOGIC

Clear knowledge having come
Of an algebraic queendom,
Compulsive touch and tread
By a public voice dictated
Proclaims renewed loyalty
To a defunct geometry:
Blue-prints of logic—

Logic, tricking the tongue
With its fool's learning,
Prescribed excess,
Devoted emptiness,
With dull heart-burning
For a forgotten peace
For work beyond employment,
For trust beyond allegiance,
For love beyond enjoyment,
For life beyond existence,
For death beyond decease.

ROBBERS' DEN

They have taken Sun from Woman
And consoled her with Moon;
They have taken Moon from Woman
And consoled her with Seas;
They have taken Seas from Woman
And consoled her with Stars;
They have taken Stars from Woman
And consoled her with Trees;
They have taken Trees from Woman
And consoled her with Tilth;
They have taken Tilth from Woman
And consoled her with Hearth;
They have taken Hearth from Woman
And consoled her with Praise—
Goddess, the robbers' den that men inherit
They soon must quit, going their ways,
Restoring you your Sun, your Moon, your Seas,
Your Stars, your Trees, your Tilth, your Hearth—
But sparing you the indignity of Praise.

THE ACCOMPLICE

Mercury, god of larceny
And banking and diplomacy,
Marks you as his accomplice.

No coins hang from his watch-chain
Where once he used to wear them:
He has done with toys like these.

Would you prove your independence
By entering some Order
Or taking your own life?

He will, be sure, divinely
Revenge the moral fervour
Of your disloyalties.

For his fistful of signed contracts
And million-dollar bank-notes
Bear witness to his credit
With your colleagues, friends, assistants
And your own faithful wife.

FIRST LOVE

Darling, if ever on some night of fever
But with your own full knowledge . . .
Darling, confess how it will be if ever
You violate your true-love pledge
Once offered me unprompted,
Which I reciprocated
Freely, fully and without restraint
Nor ever have abjured since first we kissed?
Will that prove you a liar and me a saint,
Or me a fool and you a realist?

THROUGH A DARK WOOD

Together, trustfully, through a dark wood—
But headed where, unless to the ancient, cruel,
Inescapable, marital pitfall
With its thorny couch for the procreation
Of love's usurpers or interlopers?
Or worse by far, should each be trapped singly
But for true-love's sake gulp down a jealousy
And grief at not having suffered jointly. . . .

Together, through a dark wood, trustfully.

IN THE VESTRY

It is over now, with no more need
For whispers, for brief messages posted
In the chestnut-tree, for blank avoidance
Of each other's eyes at festivals,
For hoarded letters, for blossom-tokens,
For go-betweens or confidants.

Well, are you glad that all is over now?
Be as truthful as you dare.
Posted at last as would-be man and wife
Behaving as the Lord Himself enjoined,
Repudiating your lascivious past,
Each alike swearing never to retrieve it,
Particularly (God knows) with someone else—
Marriage being for procreation only—
Are you both glad and sure that all is over?

WHEN LOVE IS NOT

'Where is love when love is not?'
    Asked the logician.
'We term it Omega Minus,'
    Said the mathematician.

'Does that mean marriage or plain Hell?'
    Asked the logician.
'I was never at the altar,'
    Said the mathematician.

'Is it love makes the world go round?'
    Asked the logician.
'Or you might reverse the question,'
    Said the mathematician.

THE REITERATION

The death of love comes from reiteration:
A single line sung over and over again—
No prelude and no end.

The word is not, perhaps, 'reiteration'—
Nature herself repunctuates her seasons
With the same stars, flowers, fruits—
Though love's foolish reluctance to survive
Springs always from the same mechanical fault:
The needle jumps its groove.

SEMI-DETACHED

Her inevitable complaint or accusation
Whatever the Major does or leaves undone,
Though, being a good wife, never before strangers,
Nor, being a good mother, ever before their child . . .
With no endearments except for cats and kittens
Or an occasional bird rescued from cats . . .
Well, as semi-detached neighbours, with party-walls
Not altogether sound-proof, we overhear
The rare explosion when he retaliates
In a sudden burst of anger, although perhaps
(We are pretty sure) apologizing later
And getting no forgiveness or reply.

He has his own resources—bees and gardening—
And, we conclude, is on the whole happy.
They never sleep together, as they once did
Five or six years ago, when they first arrived,
Or so we judge from washing on their line—
Those double sheets are now for guests only—
But welcome streams of visitors. How many
Suspect that the show put on by both of them,
Of perfect marital love, is apology
In sincere make-believe, for what still lacks?

If ever she falls ill, which seldom happens,
We know he nurses her indefatigably,
But this she greets, we know, with sour resentment,
Hating to catch herself at a disadvantage,
And crawls groaning downstairs to sink and oven.
If he falls ill she treats it as affront—

Except at the time of that car-accident
When he nearly died, and unmistakable grief
Shone from her eyes for almost a whole fortnight,
But then faded . . .
      He receives regular airmail
In the same handwriting, with Austrian stamps.
Whoever sends it, obviously a woman,
Never appears. Those are his brightest moments.
Somehow they take no holidays whatsoever
But are good neighbours, always ready to lend
And seldom borrowing. Our child plays with theirs;
Yet we exchange no visits or confidences.
Only once I penetrated past their hall—
Which was when I fetched him in from the wrecked
      car
And alone knew who had caused the accident.

IAGO

Iago learned from that old witch, his mother,
How to do double murder
On man and woman fallen deep in love;
Lie first to her, then lie again to him,
Make each mistrustful of the honest other.
Guilt and suspicion wear the same sick face—
Two deaths will follow in a short space.

AGAINST WITCHCRAFT

No smile so innocent or angelic
As when she nestled to his wounded heart,
Where the slow poison worked within
And eggs of insane fever incubated . . .

Out, witch, out! Here are nine cloves of garlic
That grew repellent to the Moon's pull;
Here too is every gift you ever gave him,
Wrapped in a silken cloth.
Your four-snake chariot awaits your parting
And here I plant my besom upside down.

MAN OF EVIL

But should I not pity that poor devil,
Such a load of guilt he carries?
He debauched the daughter of his benefactor—
A girl of seventeen—her brother too,
At the same drunken picnic.

Pushes hard drugs, abstains from them himself;
His first wife ended in a mad-house,
The second was found drowned in a forest pool—
The Coroner, observing his distress,
Called for an open verdict.

And so on, oh and so on—why continue?
He complains always of his luckless childhood
And fills commiserating eyes with tears,
The truth is: he was evil from the womb
And both his parents knew it.

He cowers and sponges when his guilt is plain
And his bank-account runs dry.
O, that unalterable black self-pity,
Void of repentance or amendment,
Clouding his Universe!

But who can cast out evil? We can only
Learn to diagnose that natal sickness,
The one known cure for which, so far, is death.
Evil is here to stay unendingly;
But so also is Love.

THE RAFT

Asleep on the raft and forced far out to sea
By an irresistible current:
No good, no good!

O for a sister island! Ships were scarce
In that unhomely latitude,
And he lacked food.

No canoes would row out to his rescue;
No native ever called him brother—
What was brotherhood?

He asked another question: which to choose?
A drowning vision of damnation
Or slow starvation?

Even savages, hungry for his flesh,
Would offer him a happier exit;
And he need not fight.

Yet, having always drifted on the raft
Each night, always without provision,
Loathing each night,

So now again he quaked with sudden terror
Lest the same current, irresistibly
Reversed, should toss him back
Once more on the same shore—
As it did every night.

TOLLING BELL

'But why so solemn when the bell tolled?'
'Did you expect me to stand up and caper?'
'Confess, what are you trying to hide from me?
Horror of death?'
                        'That seventeenth-century
Skeletal effigy in the Church crypt?'
'Or is it fear, perhaps, of a second childhood?
Of incurable sickness? Or of a strange someone
Seated in your own chair at your own table?
Or worse, of that chair gone?'
                            'Why saddle me
With your own nightmares?'
                            'Fear of the other world?'
'Be your own age! What world exists but ours?'
'Distaste for funerals?'

'Isn't it easier
To play the unweeping corpse than the pall-bearer?'
'Why so mysterious?'
                  'Why so persistent?'
'I only asked why you had looked solemn
When the bell tolled.'
                    'Angered, not solemn, angered
By all parochially enforced grief.
Death is a private, ungainsayable act.'
'Privately, then, what does Death mean to you?'
'Only love's gentle sigh of consummation,
Which I have little fear of drawing too soon.'

THE HERO

Slowly with bleeding nose and aching wrists
After tremendous use of feet and fists
He rises from the dusty schoolroom floor
And limps for solace to the girl next door,
Boasting of kicks and punches, cheers and noise,
And far worse damage done to bigger boys.

BLANKET CHARGE

This fever doubtless comes in punishment
For crimes discovered by your own conscience:
You lie detained here on a blanket charge
    And between blankets lodged.

So many tedious hours of light and dark
To weigh the incriminatory evidence—
With your head somewhat clearer by midday
    Than at its midnight worst.

Ignorance of the Law is no defence
In any Court; but can you plead 'not guilty
Of criminal intent' without a lawyer
 To rise on your behalf?

However long the sentence passed on you,
The term served here will, you assume, be taken
Into consideration; you have proved,
 Surely, a model prisoner?

The worst is finding where your fault lay
In all its pettiness; do you regret
It was not some cardinal, outrageous sin
 That drew crowds to the gibbet?

THE UNCUT DIAMOND

This is ours by natural, not by civil, right:
An uncut diamond, found while picnicking
Beside blue clay here on the open veldt!
It should carve up to a walnut-sized brilliant
And a score of lesser gems.

What shall we do? To be caught smuggling stones
Assures us each a dozen years in gaol;
And who can trust a cutting-agency?
So, do you love me?
 Or must I toss it back?

THE STRAYED MESSAGE

Characteristic, nevertheless strange:
Something went badly wrong at the Exchange,
And my private message to you, in full detail,
Got broadcast over eleven frequencies
With the usual, though disquieting, consequences
Of a torrential amatory fan-mail.

THE RISK

Though there are always doctors who advise
Fools on the care of their own foolish bodies,
And surgeons ready to rush up and set
Well-fractured arms or thighs, never forget
That you are your own body and alone
Can give it a true medical opinion
Drawn not from catalogued analogies
But from a sense of where your danger lies,
And how it obstinately defies the danger.

Your body, though yourself, can play the stranger
As when it falls in love, presuming on
Another's truth and perfect comprehension,
And fails to ask you: dare it run the risk
Of a mild cardiac lesion or slipped disk?

SOMETHING TO SAY

(Dialogue between Thomas Carlyle and Lewis Caroll)

T.C.   'Would you care to explain
Why they fight for your books
With already too many
Tight-packed on their shelves
(Many hundreds of thousands
Or hundreds of millions)
As though you had written
Those few for themselves?'

L.C.   'In reply to your query:
I wrote for one reason
And only one reason
(That being my way):
Not for fame, not for glory,
Nor yet for distraction,
But oddly enough
I had something to say.'

T.C.   'So you wrote for one reason?
Be damned to that reason!
It may sound pretty fine
But relinquish it, pray!
There are preachers in pulpits
And urchins in playgrounds
And fools in asylums
And beggars in corners
And drunkards in gutters
And bandits in prisons
With all the right reasons
For something to say.'

TROUBLESOME FAME

To be born famous, as your father's son,
  Is a fate troublesome enough, unless
Like Philip's Alexander of Macedon
  You can out-do him by superb excess
Of greed and profligacy and wantonness.

To become famous as a wonder-child
  Brings no less trouble, with whatever art
You toyed precociously, for Fame had smiled
  Malevolence at your birth . . . Only Mozart
Played on, still smiling from his placid heart.

To become famous while a raw young man
  And lead Fame by the nose, to a bitter end,
As Caesar's nephew did, Octavian
  Styling himself Augustus, is to pretend
Peace in the torments that such laurels lend.

To become famous in your middle years
  For merit not unblessed by accident—
Encountering cat-calls, missiles, jeers and sneers
  From half your uncontrollable parliament—
Is no bad fate, to a good sportsman sent. . . .

But Fame attendant on extreme old age
  Falls best. What envious youth cares to compete
With a lean sage hauled painfully upstage,
  Bowing, gasping, shuffling his frozen feet—
A ribboned hearse parked plainly down the street?

OCCASIONALIA

THE IMMINENT SEVENTIES

Man's life is threescore years and ten,*
　　Which God will surely bless;
Still, we are warned what follows then—
　　Labour and heaviness—

And understand old David's grouch
　　Though he (or so we're told)
Bespoke a virgin for his couch
　　To shield him from the cold. . . .†

Are not all centuries, like men,
　　Born hopeful too and gay,
And good for seventy years, but then
　　Hope slowly seeps away?

True, a new geriatric art
　　Prolongs our last adventures
When eyes grow dim, when teeth depart:
　　For glasses come, and dentures—

Helps which these last three decades need
　　If true to Freedom's cause:
Glasses (detecting crimes of greed)
　　Teeth (implementing laws).

* *Psalms* XC, 10.
† *1 Kings* I, 1–15.

CAROL OF PATIENCE

Shepherds armed with staff and sling,
   Ranged along a steep hillside,
Watch for their anointed King
   By all prophets prophesied—
Sing patience, patience,
Only still have patience!

Hour by hour they scrutinize
   Comet, planet, planet, star,
Till the oldest shepherd sighs:
   'I am frail and he is far.'
Sing patience etc.

'Born, they say, a happy child;
   Grown, a man of grief to be,
From all careless joys exiled,
   Rooted in eternity.'
Sing patience etc.

Then another shepherd said:
   'Yonder lights are Bethlehem;
There young David raised his head
   Destined for the diadem.'
Sing patience etc.

Cried the youngest shepherd: 'There
   Our Redeemer comes tonight,
Comes with starlight on his hair,
   With his brow exceeding bright.'
Sing patience etc.

'Sacrifice no lamb nor kid,
   Let such foolish fashions pass;
In a manger find him hid,
   Breathed upon by ox and ass.'
Sing patience etc.

Dance for him and laugh and sing,
   Watch him mercifully smile,
Dance although tomorrow bring
   Every plague that plagued the Nile!
Sing patience, patience,
Only still have patience!

H

H may be N for those who speak
Russian, although long E in Greek;
And cockneys, like the French, agree
That H is neither N nor E
Nor Hate's harsh aspirate, but meek
And mute as in *Humanity*.

INVITATION TO BRISTOL

'Come as my doctor,
Come as my lawyer,
Or come as my agent
(First practise your lies)
For Bristol is a small town
Full of silly gossip
And a girl gets abashed by
Ten thousand staring eyes.'

'Yes, I'll come as your lawyer
Or as your god-father,
Or even as Father Christmas?—
Not half a bad disguise—
With a jingle of sleigh bells,
A sack full of crackers
And a big bunch of mistletoe
For you to recognize.'

POEM: A REMINDER

Capital letters prompting every line,
Lines printed down the centre of each page,
Clear spaces between groups of these, combine
In a convention of respectable age
To mean: 'Read carefully. Each word we chose
Has rhythm and sound and sense. This is not prose.'

poem: a reminder

capitallet

    -ers prompting ev

        -eryline lines printed down the
cen
        -tre of each page clear

spaces between

groups of these combine in a con

v
  e
    n
      t
        i
          o
            n

of respectable age to mean read

care

    -fully each word we chose has

rhythm and
sound and
sense this is

notprose

THE STRANGLING IN MERRION SQUARE

None ever loved as Molly loved me then,
    With her whole soul, and yet
How might the patientest of Irishmen
    Forgive, far less forget
Her long unpaid and now unpayable debt?
There's scarce a liveried footman in the Square
But can detail you how and when and where.

SONG: THE SUNDIAL'S LAMENT

(*Air: The Groves of Blarney*)

Since much at home on
My face and gnomon,
The sun refuses
Daylight to increase;
Yet certain powers dare
Miscount my hours there
Though sun and shadow still collogue in peace.

These rogues aspire
To act Hezekiah
For whom Isaiah
In a day of trial,
All for delaying
His end by praying
Turned back the shadow
On my honest dial.

Nay, Sirs, though willing
To abase the shilling
From noble twelvepence
To the half of ten,
Pray go no further
On this path of murther:
If hours be Dismalised,
Sure, I'm finished then.

ANTORCHA Y CORONA, 1968

Píndaro no soy, sino cabellero
De San Patricio; y nuestro santo
Siglos atrás se hizo mejicano.

Todos aquí alaban las mujeres
Y con razón, como divinos seres—
Por eso entrará en mis deberes

A vuestra Olimpiada mejicana
El origen explicar de la corona:
En su principio fué femenina. . . .

Antes que Hercules con paso largo
Metros midiera para el estadio
Miles de esfuerzos así alentado—

Ya antes, digo, allí existia
Otra carrera mas apasionada
La cual presidia la diosa Hera.

La virgen que, a su fraternidad
Supero con maxima velocidad
Ganaba el premio de la santidad:

La corona de olivo. . . . Me perdonará
El respetable, si de Atalanta
Sueño, la corredora engañada

Con tres manzanas, pero de oro fino. . . .
Y si los mitos griegos hoy resumo
Es que parecen de acuerdo pleno,

A la inventora primeval del juego,
A la Santa Madre, más honores dando
Que no a su portero deportivo.

En tres cientas trece Olimpiadas
Este nego la entrada a las damas
Amenazandolas, ai, con espadas!

Aquí, por fin, brindemos por la linda
Enriqueta de Basilio: la primera
Que nos honra con antorcha y corona.*

* This poem, with its English translation, was read at the Mexican Cul-
tural Olympiads and awarded the Gold Medal for Poetry.

TORCH AND CROWN, 1968

(*English translation of the foregoing*)

No Pindar, I, but a poor gentleman
Of Irish race. Patrick, our learned saint,
Centuries past made himself Mexican.

All true-bred Mexicans idolize women
And with sound reason, as divine beings,
I therefore owe it you as my clear duty

At your Olympics, here in Mexico,
To explain the origin of the olive crown:
In the Golden Age women alone could wear it.

Long before Hercules with his huge stride
Paced out the circuit of a stadium,
Provoking men to incalculable efforts,

Long, long before, in Argos, had been run
Even more passionately, a girls' foot race
Under the watchful eye of Mother Hera.

The inspired runner who outstripped all rivals
Of her sorority and finished first
Bore off that coveted and holy prize—

The olive crown. Ladies and gentlemen,
Forgive me if I brood on Atalanta,
A champion quarter-miler tricked one day

By three gold apples tumbled on her track;
And if I plague you with these ancient myths
That is because none of them disagrees

In paying higher honours to the foundress
Of all competitive sport—the Holy Mother—
Than to her sportive janitor, Hercules.

Three hundred and thirteen Olympic Games
Hercules held, though warning off all ladies,
Even as audience, with the naked sword!

So homage to Enriqueta de Basilio
Of Mexico, the first girl who has ever
Honoured these Games with torch and olive crown!

THE AWAKENING

Just why should it invariably happen
That when the Christian wakes at last in Heaven
He finds two harassed surgeons watching by
In white angelic smocks and gloves, and why
Looking so cross and (as three junior nurses
Trundle the trolley off with stifled curses)
Why joking that the X-ray photograph
Must have been someone else's—what a laugh!—?

Now they may smoke. . . . A message from downstairs
Says: 'Matron says, God's due soon after Prayers.'

ARMISTICE DAY, 1918

What's all this hubbub and yelling,
    Commotion and scamper of feet,
With ear-splitting clatter of kettles and cans,
    Wild laughter down Mafeking Street?

O, those are the kids whom we fought for
    (You might think they'd been scoffing our rum)
With flags that they waved when we marched off to
        war
    In the rapture of bugle and drum.

Now they'll hang Kaiser Bill from a lamp-post,
    Von Tirpitz they'll hang from a tree. . . .
We've been promised a 'Land Fit for Heroes'—
    What heroes we heroes must be!

And the guns that we took from the Fritzes,
    That we paid for with rivers of blood,
Look, they're hauling them down to Old Battersea
        Bridge
    Where they'll topple them, souse, in the mud!

But there's old men and women in corners
  With tears falling fast on their cheeks,
There's the armless and legless and sightless—
  It's seldom that one of them speaks.

And there's flappers gone drunk and indecent
  Their skirts kilted up to the thigh,
The constables lifting no hand in reproof
  And the chaplain averting his eye. . . .

When the days of rejoicing are over,
  When the flags are stowed safely away,
They will dream of another wild 'War to End Wars'
  And another wild Armistice day.

But the boys who were killed in the trenches,
  Who fought with no rage and no rant,
We left them stretched out on their pallets of mud
  Low down with the worm and the ant.

THE PRIMROSE BED

The eunuch and the unicorn
  Walked by the primrose bed;
The month was May, the time was morn,
  Their hearts were dull as lead.

'Ah, unicorn', the eunuch cried,
  'How tragic is our Spring,
With stir of love on every side,
  And loud the sweet birds sing.'

Then, arm and foreleg intertwined,
  Both mourned their cruel fate—
The one was single of his kind,
  The other could not mate.

XXVI

THE HOOPOE TELLS US HOW

Recklessly you offered me your all,
Recklessly I accepted,
Laying my large world at your childish feet
Beyond all bounds of honourable recall:
Wild, wilful, incomplete.

Absence reintegrates our pact of pacts—
The hoopoe tells us how:
With bold love-magic, Moon in *Leo*,
Sun in *Pisces*, blossom upon bough.

THE WAND

These tears flooding my eyes, are they of pain
Or of relief: to have done with other loves,
To abstain from childish folly?

It has fallen on us to become exemplars
Of a love so far removed from gallantry
That we now meet seldom in a room apart
Or kiss goodnight, or even dine together
Unless in casual company.

For while we walk the same green paradise
And confidently ply the same green wand
That still restores the wilting hopes of others
Far more distressed than we,
How can we dread the broad and bottomless mere
Of utter infamy sunk below us
Where the eggs of hatred hatch?

FIVE

Five beringed fingers of Creation,
Five candles blazing at a shrine,
Five points of her continuous pentagram,
Five letters in her name—as five in mine.
I love, therefore I am.

QUINQUE

Quinque tibi luces vibrant in nomine: quinque
   Isidis in stella cornua sacra deae.
Nonne etiam digitos anuli quinque Isidis ornant?
   Ornant te totidem, Julia. . . . Sum, quod amo.

ARROW ON THE VANE

Suddenly, at last, the bitter wind veers round
From North-East to South-West. It is at your orders;
And the arrow on our vane swings and stays true
To your direction. Nothing parts us now.
What can I say? Nothing I have not said,
However the wind blew. I more than love,
As when you drew me bodily from the dead.

GORGON MASK

When the great ship ran madly towards the rocks
An unseen current slewed her into safety,
A dying man ashore took heart and lived,
And the moon soared overhead, ringed with three
    rainbows,
To announce the birth of a miraculous child.
Yet you preserved your silence, secretly
Nodding at me across the crowded hall.

The ship carried no cargo destined for us,
Nor were her crew or master known to us,
Nor was that sick man under our surveillance,
Nor would the child ever be born to you,
Or by me fathered on another woman—
Nevertheless our magic power ordained
These three concurrent prodigies.

Stranger things bear upon us. We are poets
Age-old in love: a full reach of desire
Would burn us both to an invisible ash. . . .
Then hide from me, if hide from me you must,
In bleak refuge among nonentities,
But wear your Gorgon mask of divine warning
That, as we first began, so must we stay.

TO BE POETS

We are two lovers of no careless breed,
Nor is our love a curiosity
(Like honey-suckle shoots from an oak tree
Or a child with two left hands) but a proud need
For royal thought and irreproachable deed;
What others write about us makes poor sense,
Theirs being a no-man's land of negligence.

To be poets confers Death on us:
Death, paradisal fiery conspectus
For those who bear themselves always as poets,
Who cannot fall beneath the ignoble curse
(Whether by love of self, whether by scorn
Of truth) never to die, never to have been born.

WITH A GIFT OF RINGS

It was no costume jewellery I sent:
True stones cool to the tongue, their settings ancient,
Their magic evident.
Conceal your pride, accept them negligently
But, naked on your couch, wear them for me.

CASSE-NOISETTE

As a scurrying snow-flake
Or a wild-rose petal
Carried by the breeze,
Dance your nightly ballet
On the set stage.

And although each scurrying
Snow-flake or rose-petal
Resembles any other—
Her established smile,
Her well-schooled carriage—

Dance to Rule, ballet-child;
Yet never laugh to Rule,
Never love to Rule!
Keep your genius hidden
By a slow rage.

So let it be your triumph
In this nightly ballet
Of snow-flakes and petals,
To present love-magic
In your single image—
With a low, final curtsey
From the set stage.

THE GARDEN

Enhanced in a tower, asleep, dreaming about him,
The twin buds of her breasts opening like flowers,
Her fingers leafed and wandering . . .

                                        Past the well
Blossoms an apple-tree, and a horde of birds
Nested in the close thickets of her hair
Grumble in dreamy dissonance,
Calling him to the garden, if he dare.

THE GREEN-SAILED VESSEL

We are like doves, well-paired,
Veering across a meadow—
Children's voices below,
Their song and echo;

Like raven, wren or crow
That cry and prophesy,
What do we not foreknown,
Whether deep or shallow?

Like the tiller and prow
Of a green-sailed vessel
Voyaging, none knows how,
Between moon and shadow;

Like the restless, endless
Blossoming of a bough
Like tansy, violet, mallow,
Like the sun's afterglow.

Of sharp resemblances
What further must I show
Until your black eyes narrow,
Furrowing your clear brow?

DREAMING CHILDREN

They have space enough, however cramped their
    quarters,
  And time enough, however short their day,
In sleep to chase each other through dream orchards
  Or bounce from rafters into buoyant hay.

But midnight thunder rolls, with frequent flashes,
  Wild hail peppers the farm-house roof and walls,
Wild wind sweeps from the North, flattening the
    bushes
  As with a crash of doom chain-lightning falls.

Split to its tap-roots, their own favourite oak-tree
  Glows like a torch across the narrow heath.
She shudders: 'Take me home again! It scares me!
  Put your arms round me, we have seen death!'

THE PROHIBITION

You were by my side, though I could not see you,
Your beauty being sucked up by the moon
In whose broad light, streaming across the valley,
We could match colours or read the finest print,
While swart tree shadows rose from living roots
Like a stockade planted against intrusion.

But since dawn spread, birds everywhere wakeful
And the sun risen masterly from the East,
Where are you now? Not standing at my side
But gone with the moon, sucked away into daylight,
All magic vanished, save for the rare instant
When a sudden arrow-shot transfixes me.

Marry into your tribe, bear noble sons
Never to call me father—which is forbidden
To poets by the laws of moon magic,
The Goddess being forever a fierce virgin
And chastening all love with prohibition
Of what her untranslatable truth transcends.

SERPENT'S TAIL

When you are old as I now am
I shall be young as you, my lamb;
For lest love's timely force should fail
The Serpent swallows his own tail.

UNTIL WE BOTH...

Until we both . . .
                    Strolling across Great Park
With a child and a dog, greeting the guardian lions
At the royal entrance, slowly rounding the mere
Where boats are sailed all day, this perfect Sunday,
Counting our blessings peacefully enough . . .

Until we both, at the same horrid signal,
The twelfth stroke of a clock booming behind us,
Sink through these nonchalant, broad, close-cut lawns
To a swirling no-man's land shrouded in smoke
That feeds our kisses with bright furnace embers,
And we beg anguished mercy of each other,
Exchanging vow for vow, our lips blistered . . .

Until we both . . .
                    Until we both at once . . .
Have you more courage, love, even than I
Under this final torment?
Shall we ever again greet our guardian lions
And the boats on the Great Mere?

THE ROSE

When was it that we swore to love for ever?
When did this Universe come at last to be?
The two questions are one.

Fetch me a rose from your rose-arbour
To bless this night and grant me honest sleep:
Sleep, not oblivion.

TESTAMENT

Pure melody, love without alteration,
Flame without smoke, cresses from a clean brook,
The sun and moon as it were casting dice
With ample falls of rain,
Then comes the peaceful moment of appraisal,
The first and last lines of our testament,
With you ensconced high in the castle turret,
Combing your dark hair at a silver mirror,
And me below, sharpening my quill again.

This body is now yours; therefore I own it.
Your body is now mine; therefore you own it.
As for our single heart, let it stay ours
Since neither may disown it
While still it flowers in the same dream of flowers.

THE CRAB-TREE

Because of love's infallibility,
Because of love's insistence—
And none can call us liars—
Spring heaps your lap with summer buds and flowers
And lights my mountain peaks with Beltane fires.

The sea spreads far below; its blue whale's-back
Forcing no limit on us;
We watch the boats go by
Beyond rain-laden ranks of olive trees
And, rising, sail in convoy through clear sky.

Never, yet always. Having at last perfected
Utter togetherness
We meet nightly in dream
Where no voice interrupts our confidences
Under the crab-tree by the pebbled stream.

THREE LOCKED HOOPS

Yourself, myself and our togetherness
Lock like three hoops, exempt from time and space.
Let preachers preach of sovereign trinities,
Yet can such ancient parallels concern us
Unless they too spelt He and She and Oneness?

CLIFF AND WAVE

Since first you drew my irresistible wave
To break in foam on your immovable cliff,
We occupy the same station of being—
Not as in wedlock harboured close together,
But beyond reason, co-identical.
Now when our bodies hazard an encounter,
They dread to engage the fury of their senses,
And only in the brief dismay of parting
Will your cliff shiver or my wave falter.

HER BEAUTY

Let me put on record for posterity
The uniqueness of her beauty:
Her black eyes fixed unblinking on my own,
Cascading hair, high breasts, firm nose,
Soft mouth and dancer's toes.

Which is, I grant, cautious concealment
Of a new Muse by the Immortals sent
For me to honour worthily—
Her eyes brimming with tears of more than love,
Her lips gentle, moving secretly—

And she is also the dark hidden bride
Whose beauty I invoke for lost sleep:
To last the whole night through without dreaming—
Even when waking is to wake in pain
And summon her to grant me sleep again.

ALWAYS

Slowly stroking your fingers where they lie,
Slowly parting your hair to kiss your brow—
For this will last for always (as you sigh),
Whatever follows now.

Always and always—who dares disagree
That certainty hangs upon certainty?
Yet who ever encountered anywhere
So unendurably circumstanced a pair
Clasped heart to heart under a blossoming tree
With such untamable magic of despair,
Such childlike certainty?

DESERT FRINGE

When a live flower, a single name of names,
Thrusts with firm roots into your secret heart
Let it continue ineradicably
To scent the breeze not only on her name-day
But on your own: a hedge of roses fringing
Absolute desert strewn with ancient flints
And broken shards and shells of ostrich eggs—
Where no water is found, but only sand,
And yet one day, we swear, recoverable.

THE TITLE OF POET

Poets are guardians
Of a shadowy island
With granges and forests
Warmed by the Moon.

Come back, child, come back!
You have been far away,
Housed among phantoms,
Reserving silence.

Whoever loves a poet
Continues whole-hearted,
Her other loves or loyalties
Distinct and clear.

She is young, he is old
And endures for her sake
Such fears of unease
A distance provokes.

Yet how can he warn her
What natural disasters
Will plague one who dares
To neglect her poet? . . .
For the title of poet
Comes only with death.

DEPTH OF LOVE

Since depth of love is never gauged
By proof of appetites assuaged,
Nor dare you set your body free
To take its passionate toll of me—
And with good reason—
What now remains for me to do
In proof of perfect love for you
But as I am continue,
The ecstatic bonds of monk or nun
Made odious by comparison?

BREAKFAST TABLE

Breakfast peremptorily closes
The reign of Night, her dream extravagances
Recalled for laughter only.

Yet here we sit at our own table,
Brooding apart on spells of midnight love
Long irreversible:

Spells that have locked our hearts together,
Never to falter, never again to stray
Into the fierce dichotomy of Day;
Night has a gentler laughter.

THE HALF-FINISHED LETTER

One day when I am written off as dead—
My works widely collected, rarely read
Unless as Literature (examiners
Asking each student which one he prefers
And how to classify it), my grey head
Slumped on the work-desk—they will find your name
On a half-finished letter, still the same
And in my characteristic characters:
That's one thing will have obdurately lasted.

THE HAZEL GROVE

To be well loved,
Is it not to dare all,
Is it not to do all,
Is it not to know all?
To be deep in love?

A tall red sally
Had stood for seventy
Years by the pool
(And that was plenty)
Before I could shape
My harp from her poll.

Now seven hundred
Years will be numbered
In our hazel grove
Before this vibrant
Harp falls silent—
For lack of strings,
Not for lack of love.

PITY

Sickness may seem a falling out of love,
With pleas for pity—love's lean deputy.
If so, refuse me pity, wait, love on:
Never outlaw me while I yet live.
The day may come when you too, falling sick,
Implore my pity. Let me, too, refuse it
Offering you, instead, my pitiless love.

SILENT VISIT

I was walking my garden
Judiciously, calmly,
Curved mattock in hand
Heavy basket on shoulder,
When all of a sudden

You kissed me most kindly
From forehead to chin,
Though arriving unseen
As a pledge of love-magic
And wordlessly even.

Had you come, long-announced,
Wearing velvets and silk
After travels of grandeur
From Greece to the Yemen,
Socotra and Aden.

With no rapture of silence
Nor rapture of absence—
No poem to greet you,
No burst of green glory
From trees in my garden. . . .

But you came, a grown woman,
No longer the child
Whom I loved well enough
When your age was just seven—
Who would enter alone
The close thickets of Eden
And there would run wild.

CORONET OF MOONLIGHT

Such was the circumstance of our first love:
Sea, silence, a full moon.
Nevertheless, even the same silence
Amended by a distant nightingale
From the same past, and gently heaving surf,
Brings me no sure revival of our dream—
For to be surely with you is to sleep,
Having well earned my coronet of moonlight
By no mere counting of processional sheep.

SONG: TO BECOME EACH OTHER

To love you truly
    I must become you,
And so to love you
    I must leave behind
All that was not you:
    All jewelled phantoms,
All fabrications
    Of a jealous mind.

For man and woman
    To become each other
Is far less hard
    Than would seem to be:
An eternal serpent
    With eyes of emerald
Stands curled around
    This blossoming tree.

Though I seem old
    As a castle turret
And you as young
    As the grass beneath
It is no great task
    To become each other
Where nothing honest
    Goes in fear of death.

HEAVEN

Laugh still, write always lovingly, for still
You neither will nor can deny your heart,
Which always was a poet's,
Even while our ways are cruelly swept apart.
But though the rose I gave you in your childhood
Has never crumbled yellowing into dust
Neither as yet have needles pricked your conscience,
Which also is a poet's,
To attempt the miracles which one day you must.

Meanwhile reject their Heaven, but guard our own
Here on this needle-point, immediately
Accessible, not sprawled like theirs across
Limitless outer space. If to those angels
We seem a million light-years yet unborn,
And cannot more concern them than they us,
Let our own Heaven, with neither choir nor throne
Nor janitor, rest inexpugnable
And private for our gentler love alone.

GROWING PAINS

My earliest love, that stabbed and lacerated,
Must I accept it as it seemed then—
Although still closely documented, dated
And even irreversibly annotated
By your own honest pen?

Love never lies, even when it most enlarges
Dimensions, griefs, or charges,
But, come what must, remains
Irrevocably true to its worst growing pains.

FRIDAY NIGHT

On the brink of sleep, stretched in a wide bed,
  Rain pattering at the windows
And proud waves booming against granite rocks:
  Such was our night of glory.

Thursday had brought us dreams only of evil,
  As the muezzin warned us:
'Forget all nightmare once the dawn breaks,
  Prepare for holy Friday!'

Friday brings dreams only of inward love
    So overpassing passion
That no lips reach to kiss, nor hands to clasp,
    Nor does foot press on foot.

We wait until the lamp has flickered out
    Leaving us in full darkness,
Each still observant of the other's lively
    Sighs of pure content.

Truth is prolonged until the grey dawn:
    Her face floating above me,
Her black hair falling cloudlike to her breasts,
    Her lovely eyes half-open.

THE PACT

The identity of opposites had linked us
In our impossible pact of only love
Which, being a man, I honoured to excess
But you, being woman, quietly disregarded—
Though loving me no less—
And, when I would have left you, envied me
My unassuageable positivity.

POOR OTHERS

Hope, not Love, twangles her single string
Monotonously and in broken rhythms.
Can Hope deserve praise?

I fell in love with you, as you with me.
Hope envies us for being otherwise
Than honest Hope should be.

No charm avails against the evil eye
Of envy but to spit into our bosoms
And so dissemble

That we are we and not such luckless others
As hope and tremble.
Shifting the blame to fathers or to mothers
For being themselves, not others:
Alas, poor others!

A TOAST TO DEATH

This is, indeed, neither the time nor the place
For victory celebrations. Victory over what?
Over Death, his grinning image and manifesto
Of which, as children, we have been forewarned
And offered a corpse's frigid hand to kiss.

Contrariwise, let me raise this unsteady glass
In a toast to Death, the sole deviser of life,
Our antenatal witness when each determined
Sex, colour, humour, religion, limit of years,
Parents, place, date of birth—
A full conspectus, with ourselves recognized
As viable capsules lodged in the fifth dimension,
Never to perish, time being irrelevant,
And the reason for which, and sole excuse, is love—
Tripled togetherness of you with me.

THE YOUNG SIBYL

The swing has its bold rhythm,
Yet a breeze in the trees
Varies the music for her
As down the apples drop
In a row on her lap.

Though still only a child
She must become our Sibyl,
A holder of the apple
Prophesying wild
Histories for her people.

Five apples in a row,
Each with ruddy cheeks,
So too her own cheeks glow
As the long swing creaks,
Pulsing to and fro.

RECORDS

Accept these records of pure love
With no end or beginning, written for
Yourself alone, not the abashed world,
Timeless therefore—

Whose exaltations clearly tell
Of a past pilgrimage through hell,
Which in the name of love I spare you.
Hell is my loneliness, not ours,
Else we should harrow it together.

Love, have you walked worse hells even than I,
Through echoing silence where no midge or fly
Buzzes—hells boundless, without change of weather?

Robert Graves.

above: Left to right–Laszlo Kery, Robert and Beryl Graves in Budapest, 1974. (*The Malahat Review*)

opposite: Graves in Crakow, 1974. (*The Malahat Review*)

In Majorca. (Douglas Glass Photo/*The Malahat Review*)

THE FLOWERING ALOE

The century-plant has flowered, its golden blossom
Showering honey from seven times our height:
Now the stock withers fast and wonder ends.
Yet from its roots eventually will soar
Another stock to enchant your great-grandchildren
But vex my jealous, uninvited ghost,
These being no blood of mine.

CIRCUS RING

How may a lover draw two bows at once
Or ride two steeds at once,
Firm in the saddle?
Yet these are master-feats you ask of me
Who loves you crazily
When in the circus ring you rock astraddle
Your well-matched bay and grey—
Firing sharp kisses at me.

AGELESS REASON

We laugh, we frown, our fingers twitch
Nor can we yet prognosticate
How we shall learn our fate—
The occasion when, the country which—
Determined only that this season
Of royal tremulous possession
Shall find its deathless reason.

AS WHEN THE MYSTIC

To be lost for good to the gay self-esteem
That carried him through difficult years of childhood,
To be well stripped of all tattered ambitions
By his own judgement, now scorning himself
As past redemption—
                           this is anticipation
Of true felicity, as when the mystic
Starved, frightened, purged, assaulted and ignobled
Drinks Eleusinian ambrosia
From a gold cup and walks in Paradise.

UNPOSTED LETTER
(1963)

Can you still love, having once shared love's secret
With a man born to it?
Then sleep no more in graceless beds, untrue
To love, where jealousy of the secret
Will scorch away your childlike sheen of virtue—
Did he not confer crown, orb and sceptre
On a single-hearted, single-fated you?

XXVII

BIRTH OF A GODDESS

It was John the Baptist, son to Zechariah,
Who assumed the cloak of God's honest Archangel
And mouthpiece born on Monday, Gabriel,
And coming where his cousin Mary span
Her purple thread or stitched a golden tassel
For the curtain of the Temple Sanctuary,
Hailed her as imminent mother, not as bride—
Leaving the honest virgin mystified.

Nor would it be a man-child she must bear:
Foreseen by John as a Messiah sentenced
To ransom all mankind from endless shame—
But a Virgin Goddess cast in her own image
And bearing the same name.

BEATRICE AND DANTE

He, a grave poet, fell in love with her.
She, a mere child, fell deep in love with love
And, being a child, illumined his whole heart.

From her clear conspect rose a whispering
With no hard words in innocency held back—
Until the day that she became woman,

Frowning to find her love imposed upon:
A new world beaten out in her own image—
For his own deathless glory.

THE DILEMMA

Tom Noddy's body speaks, not so his mind;
  Or his mind speaks, not so Tom Noddy's body.
Undualistic truth is hard to find
  For the distressed Tom Noddy.

Mind wanders blindly, body misbehaves;
  Body sickens, mind at last repents,
Each calling on the heart, the heart that saves,
  Disposes, glows, relents.

Which of these two must poor Tom's heart obey:
  The mind seduced by logical excess
To misbehaviour, or its lonely prey—
  The unthinking body sunk in lovelessness?

THE GENTLEMAN

That he knows more of love than you, by far,
And suffers more, has long been his illusion.
His faults, he hopes, are few—maybe they are
With a life barred against common confusion;
But that he knows far less and suffers less,
Protected by his age, his reputation,
His gentlemanly sanctimoniousness,
Has blinded him to the dumb grief that lies
Warring with love of love in your young eyes.

THE WALL

A towering wall divides your house from mine.
You alone hold the key to the hidden door
That gives you secret passage, north to south,
Changing unrecognizably as you go.
The south side borders on my cherry orchard
Which, when you see, you smile upon and bless.
The north side I am never allowed to visit;
Your northern self I must not even greet,
Nor would you welcome me if I stole through.

I have a single self, which never alters
And which you love more than the whole world
Though you fetch nothing for me from the north
And can bring nothing back. To be a poet
Is to have no wall parting his domain,
Never to change. Whenever you stand by me
You are the Queen of poets, and my judge.
Yet you return to play the Mameluke
Speaking a language alien to our own.

WOMEN AND MASKS

Translated from Gabor Devesceri's Hungarian

Women and masks: an old familiar story.
Life slowly drains away and we are left
As masks of what we were. The living past
Rightly respects all countenances offered
As visible sacrifices to the gods
And clamps them fast even upon live faces.
Let face be mask then, or let mask be face—
Mankind can take its ease, may assume godhead.
Thus God from time to time descends in power
Graciously, not to a theologian's hell
But to our human hell enlaced with heaven.

Let us wear masks once worn in the swift circlings
And constant clamour of a holy dance
Performed always in prayer, in the ecstasy
Of love-hate murder—today's children always
Feeling, recording, never understanding.

Yet this old woman understands, it seems,
At least the unimportance of half-knowledge,
Her face already become mask, her teeth
Wide-gapped as though to scare us, her calm face
Patterned with wrinkles in unchanging grooves
That outlive years, decades and centuries.
Hers is a mask remains exemplary
For countless generations. Who may wear it?
She only, having fashioned it herself.
So long as memory lasts us, it was hers.

Behind it she assembles her rapt goodness,
Her gentle worth already overflooding
The mask, her prison, shaming its fierce, holy
Terror: for through its gaping sockets always
Peer out a pair of young and lovely eyes.

TILTH

('Robert Graves, the British veteran, is no longer in the poetic swim.
He still resorts to traditional metres and rhyme, and to such out-
dated words as *tilth*; withholding his 100% approbation also from
contemporary poems that favour sexual freedom.'

From a New York critical weekly)

Gone are the drab monosyllabic days
When 'agricultural labour' still was *tilth*;
And '100% approbation', *praise*;
And 'pornographic modernism', *filth*—
Yet still I stand by *tilth* and *filth* and *praise*.

THE LAST FISTFUL

He won her Classic races, at the start,
With a sound wind, strong legs and gallant heart;
Yet she reduced his fodder day by day
Till she had sneaked the last fistful away—
When, not unnaturally, the old nag died
Leaving her four worn horseshoes and his hide.

THE TRADITIONALIST

Respect his obstinacy of undefeat,
His hoarding of tradition,
Those hands hung loosely at his side
Always prepared for hardening into fists
Should any fool waylay him,
His feet prepared for the conquest of crags
Or a week's march to the sea.

If miracles are recorded in his presence
As in your own, remember
These are no more than time's obliquities
Gifted to men who still fall deep in love
With real women like you.

THE PREPARED STATEMENT

The Prepared Statement is a sure stand-by
For business men and Ministers. A lie
Blurted by thieves caught in the very act
Shows less regard, no doubt, for the act's fact
But more for truth; and all good thieves know why.

357

ST ANTONY OF PADUA

Love, when you lost your keepsake,
The green-eyed silver serpent,
And called upon St Antony
  To fetch it back again,
The fact was that such keepsakes
Must never become idols
And meddle with the magic
  That chains us with its chain:
Indeed the tears it cost you
By sliding from your finger
Was Antony's admonishment
  That magic must remain
Dependent on no silver ring
Nor serpent's emerald eyes
But equally unalterable,
  Acceptable and plain . . .
Yet none the less St Antony
(A blessing on his honesty!)
Proved merciful to you and me
  And found that ring again.

BROKEN COMPACT

It was not he who broke their compact;
But neither had he dared to warn her
How dangerous was the act.
It might have seemed cruel blackmail,
Not mere foreknowledge, to confess
What powers protected and supported him
In his mute call for singleheartedness.

It was she indeed who planted the first kiss,
Pleading with him for true togetherness—
Therefore her faults might well be charged against
    him.
She dared to act as he had never dared.
Nor could he change: his heart remaining full,
Commanded by her, yet unconquerable,
Blinding her with its truth.
                    So, worse than blind,
He suffered more than she in body and mind.

A DREAM OF FRANCES SPEEDWELL

I fell in love at my first evening party.
You were tall and fair, just seventeen perhaps,
Talking to my two sisters. I kept silent
And never since have loved a tall fair girl,
Until last night in the small windy hours
When, floating up an unfamiliar staircase
And into someone's bedroom, there I found her
Posted beside the window in half-light
Wearing that same white dress with lacy sleeves.
She beckoned. I came closer. We embraced
Inseparably until the dream faded.
Her eyes shone clear and blue. . . .

Who was it, though, impersonated you?

THE ENCOUNTER

Von Masoch met the Count de Sade
  In Hell as he strode by.
'Pray thrash me soundly, Count!' he begged.
  His lordship made reply:

'What? Strike a lacquey who *enjoys*
    Great blows that bruise and scar?'
'I love you, Count,' von Masoch sighed,
    'So cruel to me you are.'

AGE GAP

My grandfather, who blessed me as a child
Shortly before the Diamond Jubilee,
Was born close to the date of Badajoz
And I have grandchildren well past your age—
One married, with a child, expecting more.

How prudently you chose to be a girl
And I to be a boy! Contrary options
Would have denied us this idyllic friendship—
Boys never fall in love with great-grandmothers.

NIGHTMARE OF SENILITY

Then must I punish you with trustfulness
Since you can trust yourself no more and dread
Fresh promptings to deceive me? Or instead
Must I reward you by deceiving you,
By heaping coals of fire on my own head?
Are truth and friendship dead?

And why must I, turning in nightmare on you,
Bawl out my lies as though to make them true?
O if this Now were once, when pitifully
You dressed my wounds, kissed and made much of me,
Though warned how things must be!

Very well, then: my head across the block,
A smile on your pursed lips, and the axe poised
For a merciful descent. Ministering to you
Even in my torment, praising your firm wrists,
Your resolute stance. . . . How else can I protect you
From the curse my death must carry, except only
By begging you not to prolong my pain
Beyond these trivial years?

                              I am young again.
I watch you shrinking to a wrinkled hag.
Your kisses grow repulsive, your feet shuffle
And drag. Now I forget your name and forget mine . . .
No matter, they were always equally 'darling'.
Nor were my poems lies; you made them so
To mystify our friends and our friends' friends.
We were the loveliest pair: all-powerful too,
Until you came to loathe me for the hush
That our archaic legend forced on you.

RESEARCH AND DEVELOPMENT: CLASSIFIED

We reckon Cooke our best chemist alive
And therefore the least certain to survive
Even by crediting his way-out findings
To our Department boss, Sir Bonehead Clive.

Those Goblins, guessing which of us is what
(And, but for Cooke, we're far from a bright lot),
Must either pinch his know-how or else wipe him.
He boasts himself quite safe. By God, he's not!

In fact, we all conclude that Cooke's one hope
Is neither loud heroics nor soft soap:
Cooke must defect, we warn him, to the Goblins,
Though even they may grudge him enough rope.

FOOLS

There is no fool like an old fool,
  Yet fools of middling age
Can seldom teach themselves to reach
  True folly's final stage.

Their course of love mounts not above
  Some five-and-forty years,
Though God gave men threescore and ten
  To scald with foolish tears.

THOSE BLIND FROM BIRTH

Those blind from birth ignore the false perspective
Of those who see. Their inward-gazing eyes
Broaden or narrow no right-angle;
Nor does a far-off mansion fade for them
To match-box size.

Those blind from birth live by their four sound senses.
Only a fool disguises voice and face
When visiting the blind. Smell, tread and hand-clasp
Announce just why, and in what mood, he visits
That all-observant place.

THE GATEWAY

After three years of constant courtship
Each owes the other more than can be paid
Short of a single bankruptcy.
                         Both falter
At the gateway of the garden; each advances
One foot across it, hating to forgo
The pangs of womanhood and manhood;
Both turn about, breathing love's honest name,
Too strictly tied by bonds of miracle
And lasting magic to be easily lured
Into acceptance of concubinage:
Its deep defraudment of their regal selves.

ADVICE FROM A MOTHER

Be advised by me, darling:
If you hope to keep my love,
Do not marry that man!

I cannot be mistaken:
There is murder on his conscience
And fear in his heart.

I knew his grandparents:
The stock is good enough,
Clear of criminal taint.

And I find no vice in him,
Only a broken spirit
Which the years cannot heal;

And gather that, when younger,
He volunteered for service
With a secret police;

That one day he had orders
From a number and a letter
Which had to be obeyed,

And still cannot confess,
In fear for his own life,
Nor make reparation.

The dead in their bunkers
Call to him every night:
'Come breakfast with us!'

No gentleness, no love,
Can cure a broken spirit;
I forbid you to try.

A REDUCED SENTENCE

They were confused at first, being well warned
That the Governor forbade, by a strict rule,
All conversation between long-term prisoners—
Except cell-mates (who were his own choice);
Also, in that mixed prison, the two sexes
Might catch no glimpse whatever of each other
Even at fire-drill, even at Church Service.

Yet soon—a most unusual case—this pair
Defied the spirit, although not the letter,
Of his harsh rules, using the fourth dimension
For passage through stone walls and cast-iron doors
As coolly as one strolls across Hyde Park:
Bringing each other presents, kisses, news.

By good behaviour they reduced their sentence
From life to a few years, then out they went
Through three-dimensional gates, gently embraced . . .
And walked away together, arm in arm. . . .
But, home at last, halted abashed and shaking
Where the stairs mounted to a double bed.

ABSENT CRUSADER

An ancient rule prescribed for true knights
Was: 'Never share your couch with a true lady
Whom you would not care in honour to acknowledge
As closest to your heart, on whose pure body
You most would glory to beget children
And acknowledge them your own.'

The converse to which rule, for fine ladies,
No knight could preach with firm authority;
Nor could he venture to condemn any
Who broke the rule even while still sharing
Oaths of love-magic with her absent knight,
Telling herself: 'This is not love, but medicine
For my starved animal body; and my right.
Such peccadilloes all crusades afford—
As when I yield to my own wedded Lord.'

COMPLAINT AND REPLY

I

After our death, when scholars try
To arrange our letters in due sequence,
No one will envy them their task,
You sign your name so lovingly
So sweetly and so neatly
That all must be confounded by
Your curious reluctance,
Throughout this correspondence,
To answer anything I ask
Though phrased with perfect prudence . . .
Why do you wear so blank a mask,
Why always baulk at a reply
Both in and out of sequence,
Yet sign your name so lovingly,
So sweetly and so neatly?

II

Oh, the dark future! I confess
Compassion for your scholars—yes.
Not being myself incorrigible,
Trying most gallantly, indeed,
To answer what I cannot read,
With half your words illegible
Or, at least, any scholar's guess.

MY GHOST

I held a poor opinion of myself
When young, but never bettered my opinion
(Even by comparison)
Of all my fellow-fools at school or college.

Passage of years induced a tolerance,
Even a near-affection, for myself—
Which, when you fell in love with me, amounted
(Though with my tongue kept resolutely tied)
To little short of pride.

Pride brought its punishment: thus to be haunted
By my own ghost whom, much to my disquiet,
All would-be friends and open enemies
Boldly identified and certified
As me, including him in anecdotal
Autobiographies.

Love, should you meet him in the newspapers
In planes, on trains, or at large get-togethers,
I charge you, disregard his foolish capers;
Silence him with a cold unwinking stare
Where he sits opposite you at table
And let all present watch amazed, remarking
On how little you care.

SONG: RECONCILIATION

The storm is done, the sun shines out,
    The blackbird calls again
With bushes, trees and long hedgerows
    Still twinkling bright with rain.

Sweet, since you now can trust your heart
    As surely as I can,
Be still the sole woman I love
    With me for your sole man.

For though we hurt each other once
    In youthful blindness, yet
A man must learn how to forgive
    What women soon forget.

367

KNOBS AND LEVERS

Before God died, shot while running away,
He left mankind His massive hoards of gold:
Which the Devil presently appropriated
With the approval of all major trusts
As credit for inhumanizable
Master-machines and adequate spare-parts.

Men, born no longer in God's holy image,
Were graded as ancillary knobs or levers
With no Law to revere nor faith to cherish.
'You are free, Citizens,' old Satan crowed;
And all felicitated one another
As quit of patriarchal interference.

This page turns slowly: its last paragraph
Hints at a full-scale break-down implemented
By famine and disease. Nevertheless
The book itself runs on for five more chapters.
God died; clearly the Devil must have followed.
But was there not a Goddess too, God's mother?

THE VIRUS

We can do little for these living dead
Unless to help them bury one another
By an escalation of intense noise
And the logic of computers.
They are, we recognize, past praying for—
Only among the moribund or dying
Is treatment practical.

Faithfully we experiment, assuming
That death is a still undetected virus
And most contagious where
Men eat, smoke, drink and sleep money:
Its monstrous and unconscionable source.

DRUID LOVE

No Druid can control a woman's longing
Even while dismally foreboding
Death for her lover, anguish for herself
Because of bribes accepted, pledges broken,
Breaches hidden.
                    More than this, the Druid
May use no comminatory incantations
Against either the woman or her lover,
Nor ask what punishment she herself elects.

But if the woman be herself a Druid?
The case worsens: he must flee the land.
Hers is a violence unassessable
Save by herself—ultimate proof and fury
Of magic power, dispelling all restraint
That princely laws impose on those who love.

PROBLEMS OF GENDER

Circling the Sun, at a respectful distance,
Earth remains warmed, not roasted; but the Moon
Circling the Earth, at a disdainful distance,
Will drive men lunatic (should they defy her)
With seeds of wintry love, not sown for spite.

Mankind, so far, continues undecided
On the Sun's gender—grammars disagree—
As on the Moon's. Should Moon be god, or goddess:
Drawing the tide, shepherding flocks of stars
That never show themselves by broad daylight?

Thus curious problems of propriety
Challenge all ardent lovers of each sex:
Which circles which at a respectful distance,
Or which, instead, at a disdainful distance?
And who controls the regal powers of night?

JUS PRIMAE NOCTIS

Love is a game for only two to play at,
Nor could she banish him from her soft bed
Even on her bridal night, *jus primae noctis*
Being irreversibly his. He took the wall-side
Long ago granted him. Her first-born son
Would claim his name, likeness and character.
Nor did we ask her why. The case was clear:
Even though that lover had been nine years dead
She could not banish him from her soft bed.

CONFESS, MARPESSA

Confess, Marpessa, who is your new lover?
Could he be, perhaps, that skilful rough-sea diver
Plunging deep in the waves, curving far under
Yet surfacing at last with controlled breath?

Confess, Marpessa, who is your new lover?
Is he some ghoul, with naked greed of plunder
Urging his steed across the gulf of death,
A brood of dragons tangled close beneath?

Or could he be the fabulous Salamander,
Courting you with soft flame and gentle ember?
Confess, Marpessa, who is your new lover?

DREAM RECALLED ON WAKING

The monstrous and three-headed cur
Rose hugely when she stroked his fur,
Using his metapontine tail
To lift her high across the pale.

Ranging those ridges far and near
Brought blushes to her cheek, I fear,
Yet who but she, the last and first
Could dare what lions never durst?

Proud Queen, continue as you are,
More steadfast than the Polar Star,
Yet still pretend a child to be
Gathering sea-wrack by the sea.

WORK DRAFTS

I am working at a poem, pray excuse me,
Which may take twenty drafts or more to write
Before tomorrow night,
But since no poem should be classed with prose,
I must not call it 'work', God knows—
Again, excuse me!

My poem (or non-poem) will come out
In the *New Statesman* first, no doubt,
And in hard covers gradually become
A handsome source of supplementary income,
Selected for *Great Poems*—watch the lists—
And by all subsequent anthologists.

Poems are not, we know, composed for money
And yet my work (or play)-drafts carefully
Hatched and cross-hatched by puzzling layers of ink
Are not the detritus that you might think:
They fetch from ten to fifty bucks apiece
In sale to Old Gold College Library
Where swans, however black, are never geese—
Excuse me and excuse me, pray excuse me!

COLOPHON

Dutifully I close this book. . . .
Its final pages, with the proud look
Of timelessness that your love lends it,
Call only for a simple Colophon
(Rose, key or shepherd's crook)
To announce it as your own
Whose coming made it and whose kiss ends it.

XXVIII

THE PROMISED BALLAD

This augurs well; both in their soft beds
Asleep, unwakably far removed,
Nevertheless as near as makes no odds—
Proud fingers twitching, all but touching.

What most engages him are his own eyes
Beautified by dreaming how one day
He will cast this long love-story as a ballad
For her to sing likewise—
How endless lovers will accept its marvels
As true, which they must be indeed:
Freed of dark witches and tall singing devils.

THE IMPOSSIBLE DAY

A day which never could be yesterday
Nor ever can become tomorrow,
Which framed eternity in a great lawn
Beside the appletrees, there in your garden—
We never shall dismiss it.

Threats of poverty, or of long absence,
Foreknowledge of ten thousand strokes
Threatened against our love by a blank world—
How suddenly they vanished and were gone;
We had fallen in love for ever.

Our proof of which, impossibility,
Was a test of such true magic
As no one but ourselves could answer for.
Both of us might be dead, but we were not,
Our light being still most needed.

And if some unannounced oppression breaks
To chase the governing stars from a clear sky,
Thunder rolling at once from west and east
What should we lovers fear from such a scene
Being incontestably a single heart?

Then say no more about eternity
That might compel us into fantasy:
One day remains our sure centre of being,
Substance of curious impossibility
At which we stand amazed.

THE POET'S CURSE

Restore my truth, love, or have done for good—
Ours being a simple compact of the heart
Guiding each obstinate body
And slow mind regularly—
Each always with a proud faith in the other's
Proud faith in love, though often wrenched apart
By the irresistible Nightmare that half-smothers—
But bound for ever by the poet's curse
Intolerably guarding ill from worse.

SEVEN YEARS

Where is the truth to indulge my heart,
These long years promised—
Truth set apart,
Not wholly vanished.
I still have eyes for watching,
Hands for holding fast,
Legs for far-striding
Mouth for truth-telling—
Can the time yet have passed,
For loving and for listening?

LOVE AS LOVELESSNESS

What she refused him—in the name of love
And the hidden tears he shed—
She granted only to such soulless blades
As might accept her casual invitation
To a loveless bed.

Each year of the long seven gnawed at her heart,
Yet never would she lay
Tokens of his pure love under her pillow
Nor let him meet, by chance, her new bedfellow;
Thus suffering more than he.

Seven years had ended, the fierce truth was known.
Which of these two had suffered most?
Neither enquired and neither cared to boast:
'Not you, but I. It was myself alone.'
In loneliness true love burns to excess.

THE SCARED CHILD

It is seven years now that we first loved—
Since you were still a scared and difficult child
Confessing less than love prompted,
Yet one night coaxed me into bed
With a gentle kiss
And there blew out the candle.
Had you then given what your tongue promised,
Making no fresh excuses
And never again punished your true self
With the acceptance of my heart only,
Not of my body, nor offered your caresses
To brisk and casual strangers—
How would you stand now? Now in love's full glory
That jewels your fingers immemorially
And brines your eyes with bright prophetic tears.

AS ALL MUST END

All ends as all must end,
And yet cannot end
The way that all pretend,
Nor will it have been I
Who forged the obtrusive lie
But found sufficient wit
To contradict it.

Never was there a man
Not since this world began
Who could outlie a woman:
Nor can it have been you
Who tore our pact in two
And shaking your wild head
Laid a curse on my bed.

I hid in the deep wood,
Weeping where I stood,
Berries my sole food,
But could have no least doubt
That you would search me out,
Forcing from me a kiss
In its dark recesses.

TOUCH MY SHUT LIPS

Touch my shut lips with your soft forefinger,
Not for silence, but speech—
Though we guard secret words of close exchange,
Whispering each with each,
Yet when these cloudy autumn nights grow longer
There falls a silence stronger yet, we know,
Than speech: a silence from which tears flow.

THE MOON'S LAST QUARTER

So daylight dies.
The moon's in full decline,
Nor can those misted early stars outshine her.
But what of love, counted on to discount
Recurrent terror of the moon's last quarter?

Child, take my hand, kiss it finger by finger!
Can true love fade? I do not fear death
But only pity, with forgetfulness
Of love's timeless vocabulary

And an end to poetry
With death's mad aircraft rocketing from the sky.
Child, take my hand!

TRUE EVIL

All bodies have their yearnings for true evil,
A pall of darkness blotting out the heart,
Nor can remorse cancel luckless events
That rotted our engagements with Heaven's truth;
These are now history. Therefore once more
We swear perpetual love at love's own altar
And reassign our bodies, in good faith,
To faith in their reanimated souls.

But on our death beds shall our flaming passions
Revert in memory to their infantile
Delight of mocking the stark laws of love?
Rather let death concede a warning record
Of hells anticipated but foregone.

WHEN AND WHY

When and why we two need never ask—
It is not, we know, our task
Though both stand bound still to accept
The close faith we have always kept
With contradictions and the impossible:
To work indeed as one for ever
In rapt acknowledgment of love's low fever.

THE WINDOW PANE

To bed, to bed: a storm is brewing.
Three natural wonders—thunder, lightning, rain—
Test our togetherness. The window pane,
Regaling us with vistas of forked lightning,
Grants our mortality fair warning;
And every stroke reminds us once again
How soon true love curves round to its beginning.

PRIDE OF PROGENY

While deep in love with one another,
Those seven long earlier years, we two
Would often kiss, lying entranced together
Yet never do what simpler lovers do
In generous pride of generous progeny;
Counting ourselves as poets only,
We judged it false to number more than two.

THAT WAS THE NIGHT

That was the night you came to say goodnight,
Where from the roof hung gargoyles of protection
And our eyes ached, but not intolerably,
The scene for once being well:
We had no now that did not spell forever
Though traffic growled and wild cascades of rain
Rattled against each streaming window pane.

They had gone at last, we reassured each other,
Even those morbid untranslatable visions
Whose ancient terrors we were pledged to accept,
Whose broken past lay resolutely elsewhere.
Hell, the true worldly Hell, proved otherwise:
Dry demons having drunk our marshes dry.

SONG: THE QUEEN OF TIME

Two generations bridge or part us.
The case, we grant, is rare—
Yet while you dare, I dare:
Our curious love being age-long pledged to last,
Posterity, even while it ridicules,
Cannot disprove the past.

Neither of us would think to hedge or lie—
Too well we know the cost:
Should the least canon of love's law be crossed,
Both would be wholly lost—
You, queen of time, and I.

SHOULD I CARE?

'Should I care' she asked, 'his heart being mine,
If his body be another's?—
Should I long for children and a full clothes-line?
Children, indeed, need mothers,
But do they still need fathers?
And now that money governs everything
Should a country need a king?'

TIMELESS MEETING

To have attained an endless, timeless meeting
By faith in the stroke which first engaged us,
Driving two hearts improbably together
Against all faults of history
And bodily disposition—

What does this mean? Prescience of new birth?
But one suffices, having paired us off
For the powers of creation—
Lest more remain unsaid.

Nor need we make demands or deal awards
Even for a thousand years:
Who we still are we know.

Exchange of love-looks came to us unsought
And inexpressible:

To which we stand resigned.

ENVOI

There is no now for us but always,
Nor any I but we—
Who have loved only and love only
From the hilltops to the sea
In our long turbulence of nights and days:
A calendar from which no lover strays
In proud perversity.

XXIX

OURS IS NO WEDLOCK

Ours is no wedlock, nor could ever be:
We are more, dear heart, than free.
Evil surrounds us—love be our eye-witness—
Yet while a first childish togetherness
Still links this magic, all terror of lies
Fades from our still indomitable eyes:
We love, and none dares gibe at our excess.

THE CRYSTAL

Incalculably old,
True gift from true king—
Crystal with streaks of gold
For mounting in a ring—
Be sure this gem bespeaks
A sunrise love-making:
To kiss, to have, to hold.

THE DISCARDED LOVE POEM

Should I treat it as my own
Though loth to recall
The occasion, the reason,
The scorn of a woman
Who let no tears fall?

It seems no mere exercise
But grief from a wound
For lovers to recognise:
A scar below the shoulder,
White, of royal size.

How did she treat the occasion?
In disdainful mood?
Or as death to her womanhood?
As the Devil's long tooth?
As the end of all truth?

A CHARM FOR SOUND SLEEPING

A charm for sound sleeping,
A charm against nightmares,
A charm against death—
Without rhyme, without music,
Yet short of deceit?

How to master such magic
How acquire such deep knowledge,
How secure such full power?
Would you shrink from her answer?
Would you dare face defeat?

For to work out of time,
To endure out of space,
To live within her truth—
That alone is full triumph
And honour complete.

EARLIER LOVERS

First came fine words softening our souls for magic,
Next came fine magic, sweetening hope with sex;
Lastly came love, training both hearts for grief—
Magical grief that no honour could vex.

Was it ever granted earlier true lovers—
Whether equally bruised need not concern us—
To anticipate such hand-in-hand conformity?
If so, how were they named? And was their glory
Fixed by an oath you never dared deny me?

FAST BOUND TOGETHER

Fast bound together by the impossible,
The everlasting, the contempt for change,
We meet seldom, we kiss seldom, seldom converse,
Sharing no pillow in no dark bed,
Knowing ourselves twin poets, man with woman,
A millennial coincidence past all argument,
All laughter and all wonder.

THE NEW ETERNITY

We still remain we;
The how and where now being stationary
Need not henceforth concern us;
Nor this new eternity
Of love prove dangerous
Even though it still may seem
Posted and hidden past all dream.

HISTORY OF THE FALL

But did not Adam, Eve's appointed playmate,
Honour her as his goddess and his guide,
Finding her ten times hardier than himself:
Resistant to more sickness and worse weather?
Did he not try his muscles in Eve's service—
Fell trees, shoulder vast boulders, run long errands?

Hers was a pure age, until humankind
Ate flesh like the wild beasts. Fruits, roots, and herbs
Had been their diet before world-wide drought
Forced famine on them: before witless Adam
Disobeyed orders, tossing sacred apples
From Eve's green tree, driving and butchering deer,
Teaching his sons to eat as now he ate.

Eve forced the family from their chosen Eden . . .
And Cain killed Abel, battening on the corpse.

£ s. d.

When *Libra, Solidus, Denarius*
Ruled our metallic currency,
They satisfied and steadied us:—
Pounds, shillings, pence, all honest British money.

True, the gold *libra* weighed twelve ounces once.
The *solidus*, gold equally,
Worth twenty-five *denarii*—
Money that did not burn,
Money which in its turn . . .

'What happened to the *solidus*?' you ask me.
Reduced at last to an unsilvered shilling
Of twelve *denarii*—'pence', or bronze money—
It faded pitifully into the blue . . .
As for the *libra,* having done with gold,
It languished among paper promises
Based on hopes, lies and shrewd financial guesses.
But mourn for the French *sou,* as is most proper:
Three hundred ounces, once, all of pure copper.

THREE WORDS ONLY

Tears from our eyes
Start out suddenly
Until wiped away
By the gentle whisper
Of three words only.

And how should we stifle
Grief and jealousy
That would jerk us apart
Were it not for an oracle
Of three words only?

Three words only,
Full seven years waiting
With prolonged cruelty
Night by night endured
For three words only.

Sweetheart, I love you
Here in the world's eye
And always shall do
With a perfect faith
In three words only.

Let us boast ourselves
Still to be poets
Whose power and whose faith
Hang at this tall altar
Of three words only.

TRUE MAGIC

Love, there have necessarily been others
When we are forced apart
Into far-off continents and islands
Either to sleep alone with an aching heart
Or admit casual lovers . . .

Is the choice murderous? Seven years have passed
Yet each remains the other's perfect love
And must continue suffering to the last . . .
Can continence claim virtue in preserving
An oath hurtful and gruelling?

Patience! No firm alternative can be found
To absolute love; we therefore plead for none
And are poets, thriving all hours upon true magic
Distilled from poetry—such love being sacred
And its breach wholly beyond absolution.

THE TOWER OF LOVE

What demon lurked among those olive-trees,
Blackening your name, questioning my faith,
Raising sudden great flaws of desperate wind,
Making a liar of me?
Confess: was it the demon Jealousy?

Has there been any gift in these eight years
That ever you refused when gently asked?
Or that I ever chose to refuse you—
For fear of loving you too dearly—
However much I had failed to demand?

Forgive, and teach me to forgive myself.
This much we know: lifting our faith above
All argument and idle contradiction,
We have won eternity of togetherness
Here in this tall tower blessed for us alone.

THE LOVE LETTER

It came at last, a letter of true love,
Not asking for an answer,
Being itself the answer
To such perversities of absence
As day by day distress us—
Spring, summer, autumn, winter—
With due unhappiness and unease.

What may I say? What must I not say?
Ours is an evil age, afflicting us
With acts of unexampled cruelty
Even in this fast circle of friends,
Offering no choice between disease and death—
With love balanced above profound deeps . . .
Yet here is your love letter.

Why must we never sleep in the same bed
Nor view each other naked
Though our hearts and minds require it
In proof of honest love?
Can it be because poetic magic
Must mount beyond all sensual choosing
To a hidden future and forgotten past?

SONG: SEVEN FRESH YEARS

Two full generations
Had parted our births
Yet still I could love you
Beyond all concealment,
All fear, all reproach,
Until seven fresh years
Ruling distance and time
Had established our truth.

Love brooded undimmed
For a threatening new age,
So we travelled together
Through torment and error
Beyond jealousy's eras
Of midnight and dawn,
Until seven fresh years
Ruling distance and time
Had established our truth.

LOVE CHARMS

How closely these long years have bound us
Stands proved by constant imminence of death—
On land, on water, and in the sky—
As by our love-charms worn on the same finger
Against a broken neck or sudden drowning—
Should we debate them?

To have done with quarrels and misunderstandings
Seems of small import even though emphasising
The impossibility of a fatal breach.
And yet how strange such charms may seem,
    how wanton,
And forced on us by what? Not by the present
Nor the past either, nor the random future:
Here we lie caught in love's close net of truth.

ELSEWHERE

Either we lodge diurnally here together
Both in heart and in mind,
Or awhile you lodge elsewhere—
And where, dear heart, is *Elsewhere?*

Elsewhere may be your casual breach of promise—
Unpunishable since unbound by oath—
Yet still awhile *Elsewhere.*

As a veteran I must never break my step,
As a poet I must never break my word,
Lest one day I should suddenly cease to love you
And remain unloved elsewhere.
Come, call on me tonight—
Not marching, love, but walking.

AS A LESS THAN ROBBER

You can scarcely grant me now
What was already granted
In bland self-deprivation
Only to other debtors
To whom you owed nothing.

And had I cause for complaint
After my honest absence
That for seven long years
I never dared insist
That you should keep faith?

Now in reward for waiting,
Being still a mere nobody,
Let me plead without reproach
As a less than robber
That I am owed nothing.

WHAT CAN WE NOT ASK?

What can we not ask you?
                    Being a woman
You still alert the world and, still being men,
We never dare gainsay you, nor yet venture
To descend the mountain when your bells chime
The midday feast and nature gives assent.

Whatever hours they strike, you are found true
To your lovely self and to yourself only:
Silent yet still uncontradictable.
Did we ever see you stumble, taking thought?

What rights have men in such divinity,
Widely though they may move within its shade,
Abstaining still from prayers.

TWO CRUCIAL GENERATIONS

Two crucial generations parted them,
Though neither chargeable as an offence—
Nor could she dare dismiss an honest lover
For no worse crime than mere senility,
Nor could he dare to blame her, being himself
Capable of a passionate end to love
Should she show signs of mocking at old age?
Then why debate the near impossible
Even in fitful bouts of honest rage.

TO COME OF AGE

At last we could keep quiet, each on his own,
Signalling silently though memorably
His news or latest unnews.

When younger we had spent those wintry evenings
In shoutings and wild laughter—
We dared not come of age.

Unless obsessed by love none of us changed.
How could we change? Has true love ever changed?
Not in our day, but only in another's.

Tell me, my heart of hearts, I still beseech you:
When dare we reasonably come of age?

XXX

SINGLENESS IN LOVE

And the magic law long governing our lives
As poets, how should it be rightly phrased?
Not as injunction, not as interdiction,
But as true power of singleness in love
(The self-same power guarding the fifth dimension
In which we live and move
Perfect in time gone by and time foreknown)
Our endless glory to be bound in love,
Nor ever lost by cheating circumstance.

SEPTEMBER LANDSCAPE

Olive-green, sky-blue, gravel-brown,
With a floor of tumbled locusts,
And along the country lane
Isabel dances dressed in red
Erect, thinking aloud,
Framed against sudden cloud
And its bold promise of much-needed rain.

CRUCIBLES OF LOVE

From where do poems come?
From workshops of the mind,
As do destructive armaments,
Philosophic calculations,
Schemes for man's betterment?

Or are poems born simply
From crucibles of love?
May not you and I together
Engrossed with each other
Assess their longevity?

For who else can judge merits
Or define demerits—
This remains a task for lovers
Held fast in love together
And for no others.

AT THE GATE

Where are poems? Why do I now write none?
This can mean no lack of pens, nor lack of love,
But need perhaps of an increased magic—
Where have my ancient powers suddenly gone?

Tonight I caught a glimpse of her at the gate
Grappling a monster never found before,
And jerking back its head. Had I come too late?
Her eyes blazed fire and I could look no more.

What could she hold against me? Never yet
Had I lied to her or thwarted her desire,
Rejecting prayers that I could never forget,
Stealing green leaves to light an alien fire.

WOMAN POET AND MAN POET

Woman poet and man poet
Fell in love each with the other.
It was unsafe for either
To count on sunny weather,
The body being no poet.

Yet it had been the woman
Who drew herself apart,
Cushioned on her divan,
And lent some bolder man
Her body, not her heart.

When seven long years were over
How would their story end?
No change of heart for either,
Mere changes in the weather,
A lover being no friend.

THE FIELD-POSTCARD

475 *Graves* (*Robert*) AUTOGRAPH POSTCARD signed (written in
pencil), 1.R.W. Fus. B.E.F. Nov 27, '15 to Edward Marsh, autograph
address panel on verso signed, Post Office and Censor's postmarks   £30
"In the last few days I've been made a captain and shifted here. I won't
get any leave till January at the earliest . . ."

Back in '15, when life was harsh
And blood was hourly shed,
I reassured Sir Edward Marsh
So far I was not dead.

My field-postcard duly arrived,
It seems, at Gray's Inn Square
Where Eddie, glad I still survived,
Ruffled his thinning hair . . .

A full half century out of sight
It lay securely hid
Till Francis Edwards with delight
Sold it for thirty quid.
But who retained the copyright,
The invaluable copyright?
In common law *I* did.

IF NO CUCKOO SINGS

And if no cuckoo sings,
What can I care, or you?
Each heart will yet beat true
While outward happenings
Kaleidoscopically continue.

Year in, year out, we lie
Each in a lonely bed
With vows of true love read
Like prayers, though silently,
To a well-starred and open sky.

Fierce poems of our past—
How can they ever die,
Condemned by love to last
Word for word and exactly
Under a wide and changeful sky?

THE MOON'S TEAR

Each time it happened recklessly:
No poet's magic could release her
From those feckless unfathomable demands
Of anger and imprudence,
Those pleas of cruelly injured innocence.

Why should he keep so strange a woman
Close at his elbow fitfully observing
The end of a world that was?
Must he fetch a moon's black tear to tame her
For ever and a day?

SONG:
FROM OTHERWHERE OR NOWHERE

Should unknown messengers appear
From otherwhere or nowhere,
Treat them with courtesy,
Listen most carefully
Never presume to argue.
Though the sense be unintelligible,
Accept it as true.

Otherwhere is a lonely past,
Nowhere a far future
To which love must have access
In time of loneliness.
Listen most carefully:
Though the sense be unintelligible,
Accept it as true.

A distant flower-garden,
A forgotten forest,
Islands on a lake
Teeming with salmon,
Its waters dark blue—
Though the sense be unintelligible
Accept it as true.

NAME

Caught by the lure of marriage,
Casting yourself in prospect
As perfect wife and mother
Through endless years of joy,
Be warned by one who loves you
Never to name your first-born
Until you know the father
And: is it girl or boy?

Nine months in mortal darkness
Let it debate the future,
Reviewing its inheritance
Through three-score generations,
From both sides of the family,
A most exacting game;
Then, just before delivery,
Prepare for a soft whisper
As it reveals its name.

TWO DISCIPLINES

Fierce bodily control, constant routine,
Precision and a closely smothered rage
Alike at ballet-school and the manége:
These harden muscles, these bolster the heart
For glorious records of achievement
To glow in public memory apart.
Which disciplines (ballet and horsemanship)
Have proved no less reciprocally exclusive—
Note their strange differences in gait and carriage—
Than permissivity and Christian marriage.

THE UGLY SECRET

Grow angry, sweetheart, if you must, with me
Rather than with yourself. This honest shoulder
Will surely shrug your heaviest blow away,
So you can sleep the sounder.

As for the ugly secret gnawing at you
Which you still hide for fear of hurting me,
Here is my blank pledge of forgiveness—
Nor need you ever name the enemy,
Nor need I ever guess.

MOUNTAIN LOVERS

We wandered diligently and widely
On mountains by the sea,
Greeting no *now* that was not *always*,
Nor any *I* but *we*,
And braved a turbulence of nights and days
From which no honest lover strays,
However stark the adversity.

THREE TIMES IN LOVE

You have now fallen three times in love
With the same woman, first indeed blindly
And at her blind insistence;

Next with your heart alive to the danger
Of what hers might conceal, although such passion
Strikes nobly and for ever;

Now at last, deep in dream, transported
To her rose garden on the high ridge,
Assured that there she can deny you
No deserved privilege,
However controvertible or new.

THREE YEARS WAITING

Have we now not spent three years waiting
For these preposterous longings to make sense—
Mine and what I divine to be your secret
Since gently you tighten your lips on its conclusion
Though never registering a copyright?

Since these are poems in their first making,
Let us refrain from secret consideration
Of their bewildered presence.
                         What is a poem
Unless a shot in the night with a blind arrow
From a well-magicked bowstring?

THE SENTENCE

Is this a sentence passed upon us both
For too ambitious love in separation:
Not as an alien intervention or intrusion
But as heaviness and silence,
As a death in absence?

We have lived these seven years beyond recourse,
Each other's single love in separation:
A whispered name before sleep overtakes us
And before morning wakes us
At some far-distant station.

Let us not hold that either drew apart
In weariness or anger or adventure,
Or the resolve to nurse a single heart. . . .
Call it an irresistible thunderbolt.
It was not my fault, love, nor was it your fault.

SPRING 1974

None yet have been good jocund days,
Clear dawning days,
Days of leisure and truth
Reflecting love's sharp gaze,
Being born, alas, in an evil month
By fetid marsh or by fouled river
Maligned in Hell, accursed in Heaven,
Always by love unshriven,
Void still of honest praise.

ADVENT OF SUMMER

You have lived long but over-lonely,
My grey-haired fellow-poet
Sighing for new melodies
In face of sullen grief,
With wanings of old friendship,
With sullen repetition—
For who can thrive in loneliness,
Accepting its cold needs?

Let love dawn with the advent
Of a cool, showery summer
With no firm, fallen apricots
Nor pods on any beanstalk,
Nor strawberries in blossom,
Nor cherries on the boughs.

Let us deny the absurdities
Of every true summer:
Let us never live ill-used
Or derided by new strangers;
Let us praise the vagrant thrushes
And listen to their songs.

THE UNPENNED POEM

Should I wander with no frown, these idle days,
My dark hair trespassing on its pale brow—
If so, without companionship or praise,
Must I revisit marshes where frogs croak
Like me, mimicking penitential ways?

Are you still anchored to my slow, warm heart
After long years of drawing nightly nearer
And visiting our haunted room, timely
Ruffling its corners with love's hidden mop?
And still must we not part?

What is a poem if as yet unpenned
Though truthful and emancipated still
From what may never yet appear,
From the flowery riches of still silent song
From golden hours of a wakeful Spring?

Approach me, Rhyme; advise me, Reason!
The wind blows gently from the mountain top.
Let me display three penetrative wounds
White and smooth in this wrinkled skin of mine,
Still unacknowledged by the flesh beneath.

A poem may be trapped here suddenly,
Thrusting its adder's head among the leaves,
Without reason or rhyme, dumb—
Or if not dumb, then with a single voice
Robbed of its chorus.

Here looms November. When last did I approach
Paper with ink, pen, and the half truth?
Advise me, Reason!

THE GREEN WOODS OF UNREST

Let the weeks end as well they must
Not with clouds of scattered dust
But in pure certainty of sun—
And with gentle winds outrun
By the love that we contest
In these green woods of unrest.
You, love, are beauty's self indeed,
Never the harsh pride of need.

INDEX OF TITLES

INDEX TO FIRST LINES OF POEMS

433

438

439

441